Engaging Minds

Learning and Teaching
in a Complex World

Engaging Minds

Learning and Teaching
in a Complex World

Brent Davis
Dennis Sumara
York University

Rebecca Luce-Kapler
Queen's University

 LAWRENCE ERLBAUM ASSOCIATES, PUBLISHERS
2000   Mahwah, New Jersey   London

Lawrence Erlbaum Associates, Inc., Publishers
10 Industrial Avenue
Mahwah, NJ 07430

Cover design by Kathryn Houghtaling Lacey

Library of Congress Cataloging-in-Publication Data

Davis, Brent.
Engaging minds : learning and teaching in a complex world /
  Brent Davis, Dennis Sumara, Rebecca Luce-Kapler.
        p.   cm.
    Includes bibliographical references and index.
ISBN 0-8058-3785-X (pbk : alk. paper)
1. Learning. 2. Teaching.   I. Sumara, Dennis J., 1958
    II. Luce-Kapler, Rebecca.   III. Title.
LB1060 .D38   2000
370.15 23 dc21   00-027199
                                                               CIP

Books published by Lawrence Erlbaum Associates are printed on
acid-free paper, and their bindings are chosen for strength and
durability.

Printed in the United States of America
10 9 8 7 6 5 4 3 2 1

Contents

Acknowledgments

We would like to acknowledge the support and advice given us by our teachers and colleagues in the Department of Secondary Education at the University of Alberta. In particular, we want to thank Tom Kieren for his many contributions to our thinking.

More globally, we would like to recognize those teachers, researchers, and scholars who have labored to interrupt the assumptions and traditions which frame popular understandings of learning and teaching. Many, but certainly not all of these persons are mentioned in our "Reading Possibilities" section.

And, more locally, we are indebted to our undergraduate students (in EDUC 3030 at York University and in PROF 191 at Queen's University) whose engagements with and responses to earlier drafts of the book proved invaluable in the production of this version. We are also grateful to the students in the Fall 1999 doctoral seminar at York University for their very close and critical readings of an earlier version.

0   Opening Words

The selection of an image for the cover of a new book is usually among the final tasks for authors, undertaken near the end of the production process.

For us, the idea of using the picture of an apple tree was one of our first points of agreement as we began the project that has become this text. Our intention in writing was to assemble an introduction to recent developments in discussions of learning, pedagogy, and schooling, one that could be used to prompt examinations of the complexities of teaching while refusing simplistic notions or unresolvable tensions that sometimes infuse popular debates.

So conceived, it's no surprise that we settled on an image involving an apple: Newton's apple has become a symbol of sudden insight, Eden's apple has become a symbol of the perils of knowing, and the apple on the corner of a desk has become a symbol of the relationship between learner and teacher. Nor would a tree be unexpected, given the pervasiveness of this image in discussions of schooling — including, for example, trees and branches of knowledge, roots and growth of understanding, seeds and fruits of learning.

But the image has deeper meanings for us: To begin, apples and apple trees aren't autonomous forms, but aspects of more complex systems. They are embedded in larger ecologies of relationships. To understand why an apple tree produces such an abundance of fruit, for example, we must consider the life of the tree in relation to the life of the forest of which it is a part. An apple tree is caught up in webs of exchange, providing shelter and sustenance for insects and birds and mammals. They, in turn, pollinate its blossoms, distribute its seeds, and fertilize its roots. The interdependencies extend even further, as these living forms participate with others in the interchange of oxygen and carbon dioxide and in the movement of water around the planet — aspects of seasonal patterns and annual cycles that unite ground and sky, organic and inorganic, life and death, past and present.

In social terms, the modern apple tree is, in many ways,

Fig. 0.1. Classic icon of the relationship between teacher and student, one of the more prominent and long-standing emblems of education is the apple.

It is also a symbol that can be used to point to some emerging sensibilities in discussions of learning, teaching, and learning to teach.

a living record of recent human history. Most of the apples that we find in our supermarkets are hybrids of Asian and European species, reflecting cross fertilization of not just plant varieties, but of civilizations over past centuries. Moreover, in its engineered flavor and texture, as well as in its size and unmarked surface, each apple bears a trace of intertwined historical events and social movements, including industrialization, urbanization, capitalism, and modern science.

More subtly, the very form of a tree is a record of its flow through time. Its precise pattern of branches on branches on branches is simultaneously unpredictable and familiar. It is similar to the branching patterns that we see in other trees, in their roots, in the veins of their leaves, in river deltas, in lightning bolts, and in brain neurons. Yet it is utterly unique, a still-forming product of the interlocked and complex dynamics of climate, other living forms, and information once contained in a tiny seed. For us, then, the form of a tree is a reminder of the patterns that connect living forms to one another. More important, the image reminds us of the complexity of every moment.

Awarenesses of these complex webs of interdependence, emergence, and form reach deeply into the history of human understanding, evident in the myths and the folklore of virtually every society. But it is only recently that such appreciations have returned to the fore in discussions of academic matters, having been eclipsed for centuries by habits of precise definition, unambiguous classification, and linear logic. Such has certainly been the case in discussions of what it means to educate. In university bookstores and professional libraries, the shelves set aside for texts on teaching are often dominated by thick tomes that speak authoritatively to such well delineated concerns as lesson planning, classroom management, evaluation procedures, and questioning strategies. Such categories are often fragmented even further into specific technical proficiencies which are then presented as the foundations of practice. These points project a conception of "good teaching" as they find their ways onto the checklists that have so often been used to assess beginning teachers.

We have had a great deal of experience with these checklists in our careers as public school teachers and, more recently, in our work with pre-service teachers. Most disconcerting to us have been those moments of working with

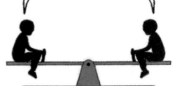

What really matters is one's **theory**. It's important to have a coherent and logically defensible system of beliefs in order to determine the best actions in a particular situation.

When you're teaching, you don't have time to sort through the logical implications of every decision. Rather, good teaching is all about sound, rehearsed, mastered **practice**.

SHAKY COMMON GROUND

Knowing and doing are two different things — that is, theory (what one believes about the world) can be separated from practice (how one behaves in the world).

Fig. 0.2. This image can be found in several places in this book. It is used to serve two interrelated purposes: First, it points to some of the more prominent debates in popular discussions of learning and teaching. Second, it is used to

teacher candidates who seem to do everything "by the book" — that is, who offer clear learning objectives, who pace lessons well, who distribute questions evenly, and so on — but who are plainly ineffective in their roles. Impeccable lessons are created and implemented, but often only by ignoring the contingencies of the classroom. It has been especially disturbing for us to realize how checklists and "How to Teach" manuals have contributed to this deflection of attention away from children's learning and onto teachers' performances.

highlight how the conflicting opinions represented in many of these debates often rest on the same sorts of (troublesome) assumptions.

In this case, for instance, an all too common worry in teacher education is an emphasis on *theory* at the expense of *practice* (or, sometimes, vice versa). Such a concern relies on the belief that the two can be separated.

We reject such an assumption in this text. Instead, we work from the premises that all practice is theorized (that is, all actions derive from particular ways, explicit and tacit, of seeing the world) and that all theory influences practice (that is, how we think influences how we act, although not always in obvious or conscious ways).

Hence, to wonder if this is a book about *theory*, a book about *practice*, or a book about bringing the two together, is to miss the whole point. Theory and practice should never have been pried apart.

Recent discussions of the nature and processes of learning have presented a challenge to the reductive, fragmenting mentality underlying checklists, lesson plan formats, evaluation rubrics, and similar artifacts. Emerging from such seemingly disparate domains as anthropology, neurology, sociology, psychology, mathematics, computer science, cultural studies, ecology, and biology, there has been a confluence of ideas around the embedded nature and adaptive dynamics of that complex process that is called *learning*. This confluence of thought has helped to uncover some of the self-perpetuating and uncritical "common sense" about learning and teaching that is used to structure and defend schooling practices.

Linked to these emergent notions, new webs of interpretation about what schooling does, what learning is, and who teachers are have come to the fore over the past few decades. Across these influences and perspectives, new ways of talking about learning and teaching have arisen, ones that locate formal education in a complex ecology of unfolding events. Such discourses have revealed the poverty of management-oriented and skills-based conceptions of instruction as they have offered more engaged, participatory, and organic senses of teaching.

It was our aim in creating this text to develop these ideas into a wide-ranging but coherent discussion of what it means to teach. Our tack has been to focus not on teaching, but on learning: What is learning? What is its relationship to teaching? What theories and beliefs are in circulation, and how do these notions enable or constrain one's teaching?

Our principal strategy in this project is to focus on the language used to frame educational worries. Specifically, we attempt to interrupt the reductive certainty that is implied in more instrumental accounts of schooling. Rather than presenting a facade of confident assurance around questions of what it means to educate, in fact, we approach tentatively the complex phenomena of learning and teaching — an attitude that we have attempted to foreground in some playful use of language. Such terms as "Engaging Minds" and "Opening Words" are intended to highlight the necessary ambiguity of language. Interpretable both as noun phrases (objects) and as verb phrases (actions), such headings reflect the necessary conditions for movement and growth — that is, the coupled capacities to fix and unfix, to anchor one's step in order to push into the next. "Opening Words," for instance, is more than an "Introduction" to the book. It is also intended to flag our emphasis on interrogating the habits of thinking that are implicit in the language used to describe learning and teaching.

That is, "Opening Words" and our other titles point to the conviction that a change in how we teach must be accompanied by a change in vocabulary: We must be atten-

---

Troubling Habits

A main focus of this text is language. As authors, we work from the conviction that the words and images that are used to describe learning and teaching compel particular ways of acting — ways that are not always sound.

Consider, for example, the metaphor that is embedded in the increasingly common phrase, "the business of schooling." In this figurative frame, learners are cast as consumers or clients, education is a product, teachers are labor resources, and knowledge is a commodity.

This cascade of metaphors could be easily extended. In fact, it often is, although not always consciously. For instance, if one accepts that schooling is a business, then it suddenly seems appropriate to expect that there be some system of "quality control" in place — and, indeed, that very phrase is often heard in reference to all-too-common batteries of formal examinations. Going further, the overarching metaphor of "school as business" could be used to argue for cost effectiveness and resource use efficiency. Not surprisingly, these phrases have come to be used in justifications of cutbacks in educational funding, increases in class sizes, reductions in preparation time, and so on.

In the process, many of the major concerns of schooling are eclipsed. For instance, the roles of the school in the making of culture and in the formation of learners' identities are ignored. Moreover, knowledge is frozen into a *thing* and teaching is reduced to transmission — moves which, as we develop in this book, are not simply inadequate descriptions, but often patently wrong.

Unfortunately, many of these notions are tightly woven through our language. Hence, the process of investigating habits of mind is more involved that simply offering new metaphors for such matters as learning, mind, identity, teaching, and so on. Rather, it also demands an engagement in the very difficult task of interrogating habits of thought that are deeply inscribed.

tive to the webs of meaning that are knitted into habits of description. We thus write from the premise that new words and different ways of speaking are needed in order to open up new possibilities.

That means that we are unable to offer this text as a definitive work on teaching. Quite the contrary, it is presented as a contribution to an unfolding conversation about what it means to educate and to be educated. That being said, the book is intended to be helpful to teachers. We do give specific advice on matters of preparing for teaching, working with learners, and so on. But such advice is not in the form of rules and guidelines aimed at controlling learning. Rather, it is about complexity and indeterminacy — about creating the conditions that are necessary for engaging minds.

The Book's Structure

The book is organized into a weave of five parallel chapters, each of which is comprised of three sections. Section A of each chapter, our "Working Ideas," is used to present and develop conceptual matters. The foci of these sections include perception, cognition, ability, identity, and language, as such topics relate to questions of learning and teaching.

Each of these opening discussions is followed by a Section B, "Telling Experiences." These are accounts of learning and teaching drawn from our own experiences as educators and educational researchers. The occasions described are not, in our opinion, especially exceptional. They are, rather, events during which particular sensibilities were enacted, ones that we feel are consistent with each chapter's particular focus.

Sections C of the chapters, "Interpreting Events," are attempts to develop some fairly specific suggestions for teaching. These discussions are used to elaborate some of the principles presented in the opening sections and to translate some of the specificities of the second sections into recommendations that we believe are informed, defensible, and practical. With them, we aim to offer rather specific advice to teachers with regard to such matters as preparing for teaching, interpreting student responses, and so on. At the same time, however, we refuse to reduce these principles to recipes and procedures. As such, there are no

Fig. 0.3. The term *lock-in* has recently been used to name a quality that is typical of any dynamic collective — whether a collective of neurons, organs, people, species, or whatever.

For these complex forms, some patterns of acting come to be so habitual or ritualized that they can refuse alteration, even if the viability of the system is at stake. For humans, the notion applies on several levels — and, in particular to the tendency for belief and interpretive systems to become so familiar that they're not just imagined to be correct, but the only structures possible.

The book might be described as an attempt to highlight some instances of lock-in in modern schooling practices.

templates to help plan lessons, there are no procedures for managing classrooms, there are no taxonomies for classifying questions. Instead, there is advice that we feel renders such technocratic formulations problematic.

Lest we be misinterpreted here, our suggestion is not that lesson plans and management strategies are bad things. Quite the contrary, none of us has ever entered a classroom without some specific preparation and some well-honed abilities to organize learning. Rather, our point is that such worries are often born of and sustained by particular, fragmented beliefs about what it means to teach. A more complex, ecologically minded attitude toward teaching, we suggest, prompts different emphases, ones that elaborate without denying concerns for technical competency.

Our point, then, is that lesson planning, classroom management, and so on cannot be considered as isolated topics. By way of illustration, a classroom activity that permits learners to adapt the task to their specific levels of understanding would mitigate the needs to remediate slow learners and to otherwise occupy advanced learners — which is to say, many *management* problems derive from planning strategies that are too rigid for the diversity that is present among any group of learners. Similarly, *lesson planning* is an immense worry if teaching is understood to be a performance, rather than a matter of enabling learning. Our refusal to treat such intertwined matters as

---

Weaves and Texts

The word *text* derives from the Latin *textura* (web) which, in turn, comes from the Latin verb, *texere* (to weave).

There is a certain irony in this etymology that has to do with one of the major criticisms of conventional academic work. Understood as reliant on the printed text — which is sometimes seen as a unified, relentlessly linear, straightforward, uncompromising genre — such writings are often condemned as limited and limiting.

We agree and we disagree. On the one hand, we do see a problem with the rigidly linear rational argument that was so powerfully enabled by the written word. On the

other hand, we understand language to be an evolving form and texts to be woven into the complex lives of individuals and cultures. In spite of appearances, then, the written word is never really static, never completely linear.

In this text, we use a number of strategies to underscore these points. For instance, our five chapters are each divided into three parallel sections in a manner that might be interpreted in terms of horizontal and vertical strands of a weave. As well, we have inserted side notes and inset boxes to highlight points, to elaborate, and to otherwise prevent the illusion of a linear read.

isolatable is thus not a denial of their importance, but an attempt to highlight the complexities of learning and teaching.

The book ends with a section entitled "Reading Possibilities." In this list of references, we acknowledge some of the important influences on our thinking. In effect, this section represents our attempt to shift the focus onto the broader web of thought in which various ideas have come to form while providing direction to those readers interested in more fully developed discussions of the issues at hand.

The book is not intended to be read from start to finish. Chapters can be considered in any order, as can their sections. We have, in fact, inserted deliberate interruptions to the flow of the text, in the forms of margin notes and inset boxes. These moments are intended as much to interrupt the linearity of the writing as they are to highlight and elaborate particular points in the text. That is, to the extent possible, we have attempted to present a resource that, true to the origin of the word *text*, is a weave, a web of relationships.

Chapter 1

Learning and Teaching Frames

Frame shares a history with the word *from*. The original sense of both terms had to do with movement or advancement.

Those senses are lost in many conventional uses of the word. Such phrases as "building frame" or the "picture frame," for example, suggest rigidity, not motion.

The senses intended here are more toward the original meaning. First, as hinted by its relationship to *from*, *frame* is used to refer to the ways our perceptions and interpretations are caught up in personal and collective histories. We are *framed* by where we are *from*. And, because we are never still, our frames are constantly evolving. This sense is suggested by the phrase "frames of reference."

Second, as suggested by the phrase "frames of mind," *frame* is used here to convey senses of *being oriented to* or *advancing toward* some goal. "Teaching and learning frames," then, is a reminder of the ways that complex histories are knitted into intentions and expectations — notions that are often somewhat flattened by popular references to *lesson outcomes* or *curriculum objectives*.

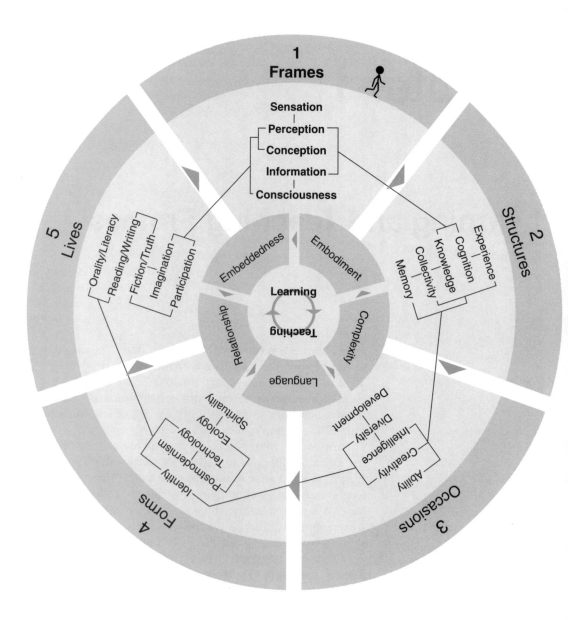

Why educate?

As straightforward as this question might seem, discussions of the issue inevitably get caught up in arguments about what should be learned and how it might best be taught. In particular, "Why educate?" often serves as a lightning rod for varied opinions about the purposes of education, the place of schools, and the role of teachers.

Across opinions, though, there seems to be one point of agreement: that formal efforts to educate have to do with prompting learners to notice certain aspects of their worlds and to interpret those elements in particular ways. Or, in other words, formal education has to do with one group's desires — conscious and not conscious — to have another group *see* things in the same way. Parents' efforts to educate their children, governments' efforts to educate the general public, and teachers' efforts to educate their students all share this goal.

A question that is not often asked, though, is: What is the nature of this *seeing* — that is, of perception? That is the question that frames this chapter. The premise of this opening discussion is that commonsense assumptions about perception, though often problematic, have profound shaping influences on educational philosophies and teaching practices.

▼

To help get at these matters, this chapter is developed around a series of "experiments" in perception. The first of these involves the image to the left.

With the book about 30 cm (12 inches) from your face, cover your right eye and place a fingertip on the gray dot. Stare at that fingertip with your left eye and maintain that focus as you slide your finger to the triangle. Without shifting your gaze from your moving fingertip, try to attend to what happens to the dot.

That dot should disappear from view. (If it persists, try sliding your finger a bit more to the right. It might also help to turn the book a few degrees counterclockwise. Be sure to concentrate your vision only on your fingertip.)

Fig. 1.1. A "Blind Spot" experiment. (The instructions begin just beneath the triangle, to the right.)

Why does this happen? The physiological explanation is simple: The optic nerve passes through the back of your eye, leaving an area where there are no light-sensitive cells. But this is not the really interesting part.

Try the experiment again, this time attending to what happens with the black line when the dot falls into your blind spot. For most people, the "missing" part of the line seems to be filled in — that is, consciousness is deceived into thinking there is no gap in the visual field. Such self-deception is constant. Every functioning human eye has a blind spot, yet few humans are aware of the holes these spots should leave in visual perception.

The intriguing aspect of such "blind spot" demonstrations, then, is not that there is a gap, but that the visual field seems to be seamless and uninterrupted. In other words, it is not so much that the hole is not seen, but that we don't see that we don't see it.

This sort of demonstration points to an important realization: Perception is not about channeling information into the brain; rather, perception is more a matter of expectation and past experience. In this case, experience has "taught" that there are no holes in the universe, and so nonconscious processes fill in the blind spot with what should probably be there.

The upshot is that eyes are not cameras onto the world, ears are not microphones, and so on. The actual situation is far more complex. For instance, nerve cells run in *both* directions between the brain and sense organs — and there is more communication *from the brain to the sense organ* than *from the organ to the brain*. That means that perception isn't a passive event or a "taking things in." Quite the contrary, sense organs actively fish for sensation, making perception more a matter of imposing expectation on experience.

For the educator, these assertions raise a critical issue. In a phrase, perception and conception are inseparable. Hence, everything one learns plays a role in how one perceives — and vice versa. There are immediate implications for the what's, how's, and why's of teaching.

Such are the issues explored in this chapter. The aims here are to examine habits of perception and to look at the ways that one's knowledge and actions are entwined with such habits. It is oriented by the question, what do *teaching* and *learning* mean when perception is perceived as something more complex than "taking things in."

Fig. 1.2. A popular technique in drawing classes is to contrast the results of sketching a familiar figure that is first presented right-side-up and the same figure presented upside-down. (Apparently, it is a popular technique among forgers as well.)

Most of the time, people find that the second approach — sketching the inverted object — is easier and more accurate.

Why?

Part of the answer is that perception has to do with relationships — or, more precisely, with expected relationships. We can't help but notice (or think we're noticing) what we're used to noticing. Turning something upside down disrupts that expectation and, hence, makes it easier to attend to the relationships among curves and angles.

What is "information"?

One of the many phenomena that intrigued researchers and theorists in the early days of modern science was the nature of heat. An idea that rose to prominence in the 1700s was that it was an invisible, massless material. The flow of this substance, dubbed *caloric*, was thought to correspond to the transfer or movement of heat.

The idea has long since been discarded as naïve and fanciful.

It is interesting to note, though, that similar sorts of notions persist today — in particular, with regard to popular conceptions of *information*. For the most part, information is uncritically discussed as though it were some invisible, massless substance that flows among people and that is lying "out there" in vast pools waiting to be absorbed through the senses.

Conventional electronic technologies have bolstered this notion, deriving in large part from the current habit of thinking of the mind in terms of a computer. There genuinely seem to be flows of something (usually identified as electrons) within computers, along phone lines, and through input devices. It follows that the same notions could be applied to human perception. However, the senses are not input devices, nerve fibres are not wires, neurons are not computer chips, the brain is not a central processing unit. Rather, each of these is a complex form — dynamic, adaptive, participatory.

In other words, these agents are not conduits for some mysterious fluid. Rather, it seems to make more sense to think of information in terms of events that affect the activities of these agents. In terms of the individual's perceptions, information might best be described as detectable differences or changes. That is, *information consists of variations, irregularities, and so on that are significant enough to impinge on the senses.*

That is how the term "information" is used in this text. To elaborate, the assertion that the human eye is capable of registering up to 10 million bits of information each second is neither a reference to an intangible fluid nor an analogy to computer input. Rather, it is a statement about the number of perceptual possibilities that are presented to the sighted subject each instant.

As will be developed, humans are very limited in their capacities to be consciously aware of information, yet we seem to get by in a complex world. The illustration below provides a hint of how this might work: It highlights how perception is often based on very few discernments. A person walking is readily recognized from this sequence of images of a "point-light walker."

Importantly, "information" refers not just to the arrival of a new sensation. It can also arrive as a sudden absence of a sensation — such as the silence that is experienced when a refrigerator turns off. (The fact that absences can be as informational as presences highlights that we move through the world with sets of expectation. Interruptions of those expectations is one important form of information.)

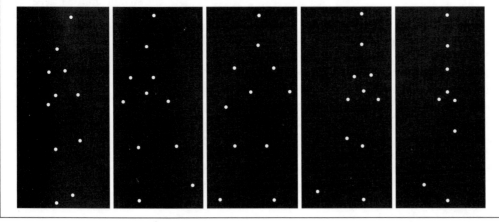

Conscious Awareness

When we open our eyes, do we see the world as it is?

Variations of this question have occupied philosophers and researchers for millenia. While theories and explanations have differed, overwhelmingly the answers have been the same: No.

Recent studies of perception have come to the same conclusion. In particular, they have demonstrated that humans are immersed in a vast sea of sensorial possibilities. The evidence actually suggests that, combined, our sense organs can register in the range of 11 million bits of information each second.

Only a small portion of these sensory possibilities ever reaches consciousness, however. In fact, it seems a typical person can be consciously aware of only 10 to 40 bits of information per second — that is, a person consciously notes about one out of every million sensory events.

Of course, consciousness seems much larger. If you lift your gaze from this text, it is obvious that you are capable of making far more than a few dozen discernments. A simple experiment, however, will give some insight into the pace at which such discernments can be made:

After reading these instructions, open this book to a different place, chosen more or less at random. Examine the pages for a few seconds. Then close the book and make a list of the things that you noticed on those pages. When done, return to this page.

Chances are that your list will be a fairly short one, even if you were familiar with the pages examined.

Another example: Stop to think about a familiar retail area. Is there a dry cleaner? A photography shop? You may have regularly walked past such specialty businesses without ever noticing them — until, of course, you needed one.

Yet another example, using a different sense: Pause from the reading to listen to your surroundings. There is likely a broad range of sounds that, for the most part, goes unnoticed as you move through your day — traffic, fluorescent lights, ventilation systems, hard drives, footfalls, leaves in the breeze, and so on.

The distinction that is being drawn here is between sensation and conscious perception. The former is vast, the latter is miniscule by comparison. In suggesting this difference, however, it is important to underscore that those

Fig. 1.3. Human consciousness is quite limited — and, in terms of perception, consciousness has been demonstrated as capable of handling only about one millionth of the events that actually impinge on the senses.

If consciousness is really so small, why does it seem so much larger? That is, if we humans are capable of perceiving so little information at so slow a pace, why do we feel so aware of so many features of the world?

One analogy that has been developed to explain this phenomenon is a comparison of consciousness to a spotlight.

Wherever its narrow beam is directed, the world is illuminated. In the same manner, detail is made available to consciousness wherever it is focused. At the same moment, however, previously illuminated details are pushed into conceptual oblivion.

The analogy is not meant to suggest that details that are not being consciously noted somehow do not matter. Quite the contrary, the evidence suggests that humans are powerfully attuned to and affected by events and circumstances that may never become conscious.

sensations that do not impinge on consciousness can still play a profound role in shaping what we think and do. Put differently, there seem to be two categories of awareness, conscious and nonconscious. Such fields as psychoanalysis and behaviorism have amply demonstrated the presence and the role of the latter. In fact, our awareness of what is around us seems to be mainly nonconscious.

By way of illustration, analyses of videotaped conversations have shown that human interactions involve far more than attending to the words spoken. Within such events, speech patterns are precisely synchronized with subtle body movements and are acutely sensitive to events in the surroundings. Yet the speakers are rarely aware of such movements or happenings, let alone of the complex choreography of their own bodily movements.

Similar studies have been made of parents' actions as they assist in their children's learning of language and various fine motor skills (e.g., piling blocks). Exquisite choreographies of activity emerge as a parent offers subtle cues and aid, maintaining a delicate and fragile balance between *too much* and *not enough* help. What is surprising, as highlighted in follow-up interviews with parents, is that this extraordinary process of adapting one's actions occurs *without conscious knowledge*. When asked about prompts given and assistance offered, overwhelmingly parents are unable to provide rationales for their actions. They are at an even greater loss when asked how and when they learned to teach in this complex, participatory manner.

In fact, follow-up interviews sometimes give rise to unexpected problems. It appears that drawing conscious attention to specific aspects of these sorts of interactions can actually cause them to fall apart — in just the same way that a musical recital or an athletic activity can falter when the performer's attention is deflected (especially when it is deflected onto the performer). Consciousness is often too small to accomodate both an engagement in an activity and awareness of one's self or one's actions. In fact, it is often reported that exemplary performances and profound engagements correspond to "forgetting" of self.

Such happenings are not limited to exceptional performances. On the contrary, people are constantly doing far more than consciousness can possibly be aware they are doing. Even now you are performing the very complex task of interpreting the marks on this page, and that is happening without consciously having to examine the shape of each letter or sounding out each syllable. If you had to be aware of the complexity of what you were doing, you would not be able to do it.

A tiny hint of this complexity is revealed with a singular change, such as inverting a line of text. While simple, it places a significantly greater demand on consciousness.

There are a number of important implications for educators here. Learning new things, for example, is largely a matter of conscious awareness. Enfolding such knowledge into one's life, however, is usually a less conscious event. For instance, conscious attention is usually needed to make sense of rules of grammar, to expand vocabulary, or to discern the standards of acceptable behavior in a new setting. At some point, however, such learnings must fade into one's fluid patterns of acting. Having to be conscious of the selection of each word or the construction of each sentence or the behavioral code of each setting would be completely debilitating.

When this matter is considered in the context of many schooling tasks, there is a powerful argument to be made for identification, practice, and mastery of specific competencies. Certain skills are needed for other tasks.

This is *not* to say that rote memorization or repetitive practice are appropriate tasks in and of themselves, however. Learners should, of course, also be able to appreciate processes and rules that underlie reading, arithmetic, and so on. The point being made is that, like walking, throwing, and speaking, some competencies must become automatic and transparent before they can be elaborated into more complex competencies.

Nor should the assertion be interpreted as a recommendation that skills be taught in isolation. On the contrary, humans are profoundly sensorial beings. Even in the most austere and focused settings, sensory organs are active. Inevitably, an array of nonconscious sensations will come to be folded into the learning outcomes that the teacher actually intended. In the context of the classroom, this means that the attempt to focus learner attention by concentrating on a single, isolated concept is not only naïve, but impossible. Research demonstrates that concepts learned in this manner are often difficult to connect to events outside of the classroom. Instead, concepts so learned are more often associated with inactivity, abstrac-

Fig. 1.4. When motion pictures were first invented, many educators saw them as having the potential to streamline instruction and to even out imbalances and inequities in schooling experience. In particular, it was widely held that important details and concepts could be presented uniformly and unambiguously, thus avoiding such educational "noise" as teacher error and social circumstance.

Similar (and even more grandiose) claims have been made of television and, more recently, of computers. But none of these hopes or expectations has been realized.

Why not?

One reason seems to be that such media operate at a low information level — one that

tion, fragmentation, and uncomfortable seats.

There are sound educational alternatives to reductive and fragmented teaching emphases, ones that both embrace the breadth of human sensation and that are accommodated to the limitations of human consciousness. Students might, for example, be immersed in rich, open sorts of activities while the teacher works to direct their attention toward particular aspects of those activities. In this way, the limited span of consciousness can be focused on certain elements while other, more tacit and less direct associations are being made. This recommendation is aligned with mounting evidence that *most* of what is learned never passes through consciousness. (In popular terms, such learnings are often described as "picking up habits," "absorbing things," or "learning by osmosis.")

There is an important caution here. The suggestion that learners be provided with rich learning settings does not mean that more stimulation is always better. On the contrary, too much or too varied stimulation is often distracting. A good example is the way a neighbor's blaring stereo can force itself into consciousness and make it impossible to focus on other matters. The notion of "richness" is presented here as a contrast to the style of teaching that focuses on singular, isolated, linearly sequenced concepts.

Along the same lines, an appreciation of the limitations of consciousness would suggest that, in terms of some of the more directive aspects of teaching, *less* is often better. Typically, humans can handle only a handful of novel instructions at a time, and so, for example, the practice of providing a detailed explanation before an exercise, can be frustrating to many students. (Consider the blind spot experiment presented in Fig. 1.1. Even though the instructions could be expressed in a few brief sentences, you may have had to read them several times.) Even more critical, concepts that require learners to make new discernments (such as noticing their blind spot) can be surprisingly frustrating. It is sometimes very difficult to learn to see something that has never been seen before.

By the same token, once procedures have been practiced and discernments have been learned, humans tend to be adept at performing and elaborating their competencies. The art in teaching is to maintain the difficult balance between richness of detail and narrowness of focus. In this light, effective teaching is more a matter of listen-

has been deliberately adjusted to suit what consciousness is able to accommodate. And so, while these technologies give access to immense stores of data, they operate at a very low level of stimulation.

Human sense organs, however, function at a capacity that is about one million times greater than conscious perception. As such, abundant use of the so-called "information technologies" may actually result in a starvation of the senses, an information poverty.

Traditional teaching strategies might also be criticized on the basis of such information poverty. These practices tend to be adjusted to the limitations of consciousness, but often fail to consider the breadth of human sensation.

Discovery Learning?

"Discovery learning" is a classroom emphasis that arose alongside holist theories of learning. (See Chapter 2A.) Like those theories, this approach to teaching emerged as a reaction to more fragmenting and fragmented practices.

For the most part, discovery strategies involve fairly high-stimulation learning settings. By way of example, a study of fractions might be developed around folding, cutting, and combining of pieces of paper — activities that could involve a range of mathematical notions.

Typically, it is intended that learners will come across important generalizations in their efforts to organize, explain, and predict observations. For example, one might hope that the idea of "equivalent fractions" would be discovered as a way to make sense of the fact that a half-piece of paper covers the same area as two fourth-pieces or three sixth-pieces.

Children do need these sorts of rich experiences as they make sense of their worlds. However, there have been some conceptual problems in the ways that discovery learning has been taken up. In particular, this emphasis often rests on the assumption that "knowledge is out there" — that is, that learning is mostly about finding pre-existent, unchanging facts that are tucked into a set of activities, much as an Easter egg might be hidden among bushes.

Studies of perception have demonstrated the untenability of such an assumption. Usually, there is a plurality of interpretive possibilities in any activity. It might thus be overly optimistic to hope that learners will home in on the specific quality or interpretation that the teacher has in mind.

In fact, close investigations have shown that the teacher often has to impose rather rigid and artificial boundaries on learners' activities in order to ensure "appropriate" interpretations. In other words, discovery learning events are often every bit as contrived and directive as more traditional teaching approaches.

An appreciation of the complex relationship between sensation and interpretation would support the intuition that learners need to be engaged in rich, explorative activities. However, it would also prompt an acknowledgment of the necessarily directive elements of teaching — of pointing, telling, highlighting. In fact, it could even be used to support the notion that, often, it is better just to explain an idea.

ing than telling — that is, of attending and responding to the sense learners are making, as opposed to trying to direct their interpretations.

Such matters have particular relevance in the context of learning to teach. Simply put, there is just too much to learn for everything to be made explicit, let alone announced beforehand. Even in settings where one's students are expected to be working privately and silently on standardized exercises, there is far more happening than a single teacher can possibly monitor.

Experienced teachers have learned where to focus their attentions — or, more precisely, perhaps, have established patterns of acting that free up their conscious awareness for other matters. Beginning teachers, in contrast, must grapple with the task of discerning where their limited attentions should be focused. For some, this project is overwhelming and even frightening. It is thus that, very often, one's entire concentration ends up being occupied by efforts to maintain control or cover content with little attention paid to what learners are actually learning.

There are many strategies to avoid such tendencies. One approach is for the beginning teacher to take on necessary but peripheral tasks (e.g., taking attendance, assisting during seatwork, etc.) and, from there, to work gradually toward fuller participation. This approach strikes a balance between immersing the new teacher in a rich learning setting and occupying her or his attention with manageable tasks. The novice teacher is able to develop particular competencies which can fade into automaticity while more complex responsibilities are taken on.

The suggestion here is not that a goal of teaching should be automaticity. On the contrary, a vital part of "being educated" is to be aware of what is being taken for granted and to be able to uncover what has faded into the backdrop of activity. The suggestion, then, is not that mindless application should be an aim of schooling, but that mindful practice often relies on well developed abilities to let other worries slide to the background.

In this vein, it is important for teachers not just to recognize that consciousness is limited, but to consider the conditions that contribute to what gets noticed. How is a trickle of perceptions selected out of the torrent of sensorial possibilities? How can we come to terms with the fact that conscious awareness is not presented with "raw data" about the world, but with a distillation, a summary, an interpretation.

Perceiving Realities

What contributes to this process of selection?

A broad range of opinions have been offered in response to this question. To oversimplify, they vary from the one extreme that perception is strictly a physiological event to the other extreme that all perception is socially determined.

Most opinions posit a shared contribution of heredity and environment. However, even though the most defensible position seems to be one that incorporates the influences of both nature and nurture, the actual story may be so complex as to problematize the commonsense habit of separating these into discrete components.

Fig. 1.5. The sense organs are highly differentiated in terms of both the amount of information that they might register and the amount of information from each that might become conscious. The following chart gives some rough approximations of these differences.

The Capacities of Human Sense Organs		
Sense Organ	# of Possible Sensory Events (per second)	# of Conscious Discernments (per second)
eyes	10,000,000	40
skin	1,000,000	5
ears	100,000	30
nose	100,000	1
tongue	1,000	1

Such data would help to account for such events as being dumbfounded, awestruck, at a loss for words, and so on — since both visual and auditory stimuli are sometimes able to occupy all of conscious awareness. They would also help to understand why auditory, gustatory, olfactory, and tactile perceptions can sometimes be enhanced by closing our eyes.

Nevertheless, there is always something to be learned by looking at the evidence that is used to support diverse opinions. That is how the discussion proceeds here.

Biology and Perception. Humans' sensory capacities are species-specific. That is, no other species is attuned to the world in quite the way we are. In general terms, the greater the evolutionary distance between a human and another organism, the larger the variations among sensory capacities and dispositions.

In fact, some other lifeforms have evolved radically different sense organs — so different that we can scarcely begin to imagine how they are attuned to their worlds. Some creatures, for example, are able to "see" heat, owing to the fact that they are sensitive to a much wider band of the electromagnetic spectrum than we are. Even more different, some birds may have a fourth, temporal dimension to their sight. (Humans see in three dimensions.) Other creatures, whose eyes are on opposite sides of their heads, have two distinct non-overlapping horizons, each of which is likely seen as two-dimensional or flat. Among insects, it is not even clear that "vision" is an appropriate word to use in reference to their sensitivities to light-related stimuli. Along the same lines, there are variations among other senses, there are senses that humans lack, and there may well be senses that we have not imagined.

In other words, we are physiologically constrained to sense the world in very specific and relatively narrow ways. The world we see when we open our eyes, for example, is not the world as it is. We are capable of observing only those aspects that are illuminated by a very narrow part of the electromagnetic spectrum.

Such a claim, however, is not meant to suggest that sensory abilities are consistent across humans. Quite the contrary, there are dramatic, physiologically based variations from person to person, ranging from familiar differences (e.g., colorblindness and extreme sensitivity to smells) to quite rare anomalies (e.g., synaesthesia, in which such varied sensations as color and flavor are fused). In fact, one need not look far to find variations among sensory capacities: Typically, one's own eyes and ears are differentiated, with varied sensitivities to brightness, color, volume, and tone. Not only do we see and hear differently from one another, our own eyes and ears don't match up

Fig. 1.6. With the invention of the telescope in the early 1600s, two astronomers turned their gazes toward the moon. In England, Thomas Harriot saw a "strange spottednesse" but could not offer an adequate account of his observations. (His sketch of the lunar surface is on the left.)

In Italy, using comparable equipment and looking at the same thing at about the same time, Galileo saw something quite different. (His sketch is on the right.)

perfectly with one another.

Further to this point, an individual's sensory capacities change as one ages — for the most part, in the direction of decreased sensitivity. These changes derive from two main sources. First, sense organs' losses of sensitivity are inevitable parts of the aging process as nerve fibres, tastebuds, and so on decline. Second, and perhaps more important, neurological pathways grow less flexible if they are not required to deal continuously with significant difference — that is, if they are not involved in *learning*.

Beyond such physiological conditions, it appears that our attentions are directed by what might be thought of as "built-in preferences." Recent research has demonstrated that newborns are able to differentiate among visual, auditory, and tactile stimuli from the instant of birth — and, more importantly, that there are some culture-independent preferences and dispositions. By way of example, most newborns can distinguish among vertical, horizontal, and slanted lines, and they show a decided preference for the vertical. (Neurological evidence indicates that adults are also more disposed to the vertical.) As well, newborns prefer face-like arrangements of dots over random orderings. On a related note, neonates give much more attention to symmetric forms over non-symmetric alternatives. Finally, week-old babies have been demonstrated to be capable of discerning differences among quantities.

Such pre-established habits and abilities have been well documented. For the most part, they have been explained biologically, in terms of the conditions in which humanity evolved. (The preference of vertical lines, for example, has been linked to the refuge offered by trees.) Each such innate preference, it has been suggested, would have afforded a survival advantage to our remote ancestors.

There also appear to be some culture-independent preferences that unfold later in life. For example, studies of various societies' strategies for categorizing colors — strategies that are often thought to be linguistically based — reveal that diverse peoples seem to gravitate toward the same broad divisions. Moreover, and somewhat surprisingly, there is a tendency for precisely the same shades of, for instance, blue or red to be identified as the most representative in particular categories.

Considered together, such evidence suggests that perception is overwhelmingly a biological event — one which

Why the differences in perception?

One hypothesis arises from the fact that Galileo was a trained artist, educated to interpret the play of light and shadow. He was thus able to see the strange spots in terms of mountains and craters and as illuminated by a distant sun.

There are many similar examples of this sort of insight in the history of Western science, demonstrating that one's knowledge and one's perceptions are inextricable.

is both conditioned by particular physiological constraints and oriented by a range of inborn preferences.

Culture and Perception. In spite of the similarities of our physiologies and our innate preferences, a good deal of research has shown that sensation (e.g., "visual ability") and perception (e.g., "sight") are not the same thing. For the most part, we must learn to perceive what we perceive.

Over the past few centuries, for example, several cases have been reported of persons who, through one means or another, have regained their vision after many years of blindness. Contrary to what might be expected, the restoration of vision is not always an occasion for celebration. Commonly, the reaction is more toward fear and frustration as the person is suddenly faced with making sense of a barrage of unfamiliar and fluid forms. It often takes years for such a person to learn to discern edges, to track movement, and to notice relevant differences — in brief, to see.

For human culture (and, possibly, among collectivities of several other species), there is another dimension. In addition to the necessity of learning to make distinctions, the perceiver must also learn the relevance of what is being distinguished. Ours is a complex context, structured around subtle codes and complicated webs of meaning. As anthropologists have demonstrated, vastly different worldviews are manifested across diverse societies. While different peoples may share almost identical physiologies, they clearly do not see the world in the same ways.

This is more than a statement about habits of interpretation. It is also a comment about what, literally, is allowed to impinge on the senses. In brief, interpretations of what is seen play a role in selecting where sensory abilities are directed. More is involved here than a natural unfolding of built-in potentialities and preferences. For sensation to make sense in the context of a human culture, the sensing person must interpret, and that interpretation will inevitably become entangled in subsequent sensorial events.

So profound are the variations in worldviews and mindsets across cultures, eras, religions, landscapes, and so on, that a good deal of academic discourse over the past 30 years has rested on the premise that all knowledge is socially constructed. Phrased differently, it is often asserted that perception is *entirely* determined by cultural circumstance. In particular, language is seen as selecting what is

Fig. 1.7. Among other things, "inkblot" tests have been used to study our irrespressible habit of making sense of objects of perception.

What do you see in the figure below? (Try to answer before reading on.)

If you had been told in advance that the image is intended to represent two persons sitting back-to-back, each holding a duck in their outstretched arms, you would likely have seen that. Although the image is not intended to represent anything in particular, such pre-interpretation can carve a rut for perception, one that is sometimes hard to escape. Every event of language influences perception in this manner, although not always so directly.

and is not perceptible. To state this perspective concisely, the belief is that what is named can be noticed; what is not named is unlikely to be seen.

It is fairly easy to demonstrate the tremendous influence of social situation and language on perception. Consider, for example, the following task: Take pencil and paper and go outside. By naming and / or sketching various shapes, compile a list of all the geometric forms that you are able to see embedded in the objects around you.

Take a moment to do this activity before reading on.

For the most part, persons given this sort of assignment return with lists of triangles, rectangles, circles, cones, and so on. Results, in fact, are strikingly similar across educational backgrounds and age levels.

Such consistency of outcome might be interpreted as evidence that we all see and classify the world in the same way, in terms of real, perception-independent shapes. Now consider the following twist:

First read the brief introduction to fractal geometry on page 16. When done, repeat the task of looking for geometric objects.

Chances are that there are a number of possibilities that, just a few moments ago, you did not see as geometric — trees, clouds, and so on. It may even be that you did not even see these forms at all — that is, that your range of observation was constrained by your cultural conditioning. More than likely, your gaze was directed mostly at human-made forms.

This sort of demonstration supports the assertion that habits of perception are deeply etched into the linguistic landscape. Our language focuses the spotlight of perception on particular details of the world, leaving other aspects virtually imperceptible. In other words, all perception — and, hence, all thought that relies on perceptions of the world — is languaged. Prevailing habits of association determine what is easy or hard to think.

Our language-based habits of perception underpin our activities and creations. Consider, for example, the ways classical geometry has been used to shape our living spaces. Modern cities are built around straight lines, countrysides are parsed into tidy rectangles. In turn, the predominance of these forms contributes to a tendency to interpret other aspects of existence in similar terms. (For example, lines

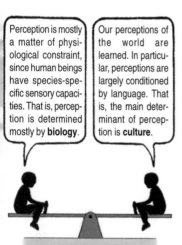

Perception is mostly a matter of physiological constraint, since human beings have species-specific sensory capacities. That is, perception is determined mostly by **biology**.

Our perceptions of the world are learned. In particular, perceptions are largely conditioned by language. That is, the main determinant of perception is **culture**.

SHAKY COMMON GROUND
Both positions assume that biological structure is separable from cultural influence — that is, biological influence is fixed whereas cultural influence is dynamic.

Fig. 1.8. Debates around the ways that humans perceive the world can often be traced to similar assumptions.

In particular, the belief that biological constitution is not influenced by experience (and vice versa) is a notion that tends to go unquestioned.

Recent research has demonstrated a much more complex relationship among the biological and the cultural.

and rectangles are prominent in popular conceptions of time, life, schedules, plans, and so on.)

The conclusion that perception is infused by language thus appears to be justified, at least in terms of those aspects of the world that enter awareness. Consciousness is simply too small to accommodate the fullness of sensation. Thus, humans have developed such strategies as lan-

Fractals

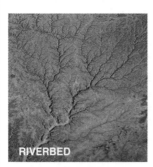
RIVERBED

Over the past several decades, a new branch of mathematics has emerged: Fractal Geometry. With it, the "fractal," a new category of geometric form has been identified.

page 72 for more information on self-similarity.) Other forms with this quality include broccoli, cauliflower, clouds, neurons, skin wrinkles, circulatory systems, and fern leaves.

TREE

A figure is fractal if it is *scale independent* — which means that the figure does not become simpler when magnified or reduced. For example, a mountainside demonstrates this quality. As you approach it, new features become evident so that the visual field always seems to be crowded with the same level of detail. In contrast, forms from classical geometry are not fractal. In the case of a circle, for example, when a part is magnified it appears to flatten out into a straight line segment — a form that is simpler than the original circle.

Several natural forms that demonstrate a degree of such scale independence are illustrated here. In each case, under magnification, these tree or tree-like forms reveal levels of detail that are as rich as that of the original.

Although such qualities have long been noticed, they were not recognized as mathematical until the 1960s. Since then, fractal geometry has burgeoned into one of the most active areas of mathematical research. It has contributed to and been influenced by such fields as Complexity Theory and Ecology. Fractal geometric principles have also been exploited by animators, information technologists, artists, medical researchers, and many others. In the process, whole new vistas of research and dramatically new ways of interpreting familiar phenomena are arising.

In other words, fractal geometry is transforming our perception — in very much the same way that classical geometry transformed the perceptions of our predecessors. In particular, this new

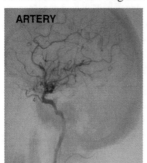
ARTERY

These particular images also demonstrate *self-similarity,* a quality shared by many fractal forms. A piece of any one of these images — like, a branch of the tree — will closely resemble the whole. (See

geometry is re-awakening perception to natural forms, rather than deflecting attention to an idealized realm of lines, circles, and other constructs that occur nowhere but in our imaginations.

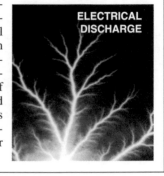
ELECTRICAL DISCHARGE

Fig. 1.9. What is the meaning of the symbol below?

Of course, the only sensible answer is, "It depends." The symbol might be an "I," an "L," a "1," a "/," or any number of other things — and each of these interpretations unfolds into another web of possibilities. We simply need to know more before we can begin to say what it means.

That is, the meaning is not in the symbol, but in the complex webs of associations that the symbol triggers when it is deployed in a particular context. Such is the power of letters, words, icons, and so on: They collect together an immensity of associations.

As such, symbols are a powerful and necessary technology for thinking. With them, we can chunk together a range of associations and "smuggle" more into consciousness than would otherwise be possible. Without them, consciousness would be something entirely different.

guage to compress information and to smuggle it into consciousness. The word "straight," for example, collects together an immense range of experiences and abstract qualities, but allows consciousness to operate without being overwhelmed by these details. In this way, our language greatly enables our capacities for thought and perception, even while it shuts out a vast range of possibilities.

In this sense, the dictum that "all knowledge is socially constructed" (and its corollary that all perception is culturally determined) is valid. But there is still a problem with the suggestion that all knowledge is lodged in or directly influenced by the social phenomenon of language.

Complexity and Perception. The abstract categories used by humans to perceive are not all language-based, as suggested by the fact that many other species can make use of similar categories. For example, a pigeon that is taught to peck at one lever when shown a picture of a cow and another when shown a picture of a truck can readily apply this training to cows and trucks it hasn't seen. That is, pigeons are among the many species that are capable of categorizing without the benefit of language.

More broadly, the suggestion that all knowledge is language-based — and, hence, formulated and explicit — would imply that agents must be aware (or capable of being aware) of their knowledge. As such, statements like "My dog knows how to dig holes" or "My heart knows how to beat" are nonsensical.

In other words, underpinning the claim that all knowledge is socially constructed is a presumption that "the human" is separable from the non- and sub-human. The same sort of separation is implicit in popular debates of nature versus nurture. It is also associated with the troublesome distinction of mental (thought) and physical (action). (These issues are taken up in Chapters 2 and 3.)

Another way of making this point is to examine the analogy that is often made between sensation and the inputting of computer data. Physical and biological conditions are commonly identified as "hardware," and these aspects are seen as more-or-less unchangeable. Social and experiential conditions, which are understood to be easily changed and influenced, are categorized as "software."

As it turns out, this analogy is wrong on the neurological level. Unlike computer chips, neurons and neural connections change in response to experience as the brain (along with the rest of the body) continuously regenerates itself. This rebuilding both affects and is affected by ongoing perceptions. Those perceptions play a central role in selecting and interpreting subsequent experiences and those experiences contribute to the ongoing transformations of brain structure — all in a complex and endless recursive cycle. Nature/nurture, mental/physical, human/natural, and all such dyads are, hence, sometimes troublesome when used to interpret matters of knowing and knowledge.

The computer analogy is also wrong on the social level. Learning not only implies a transformation of one's own body, it entails a change in activity and, hence, a transformation of the character of the collective. Learning is not a simple matter of adding onto a personal store of knowledge. It is implicated in the ways in which we act in and on the rest of the world.

Formal schooling, then, has deep moral and ethical ramifications. In particular, insofar as schooling efforts contribute to the maintenance of current worldviews and habits of perception, it is implicated in a host of crises that operate on the levels of the individual through the societal to the global. In a phrase, these are *crises of perception* — situations born of a particular way of seeing the world.

At the core of this worry is consciousness — or, more precisely, the habit of confusing the limited activities of consciousness with *all* of thought, perception, and action.

Perceiving Deceptions

Perhaps the most difficult conclusion of recent investigations into perception and consciousness is the challenge that this research presents to the conventional notion of "freedom." In particular, the ideal of *freedom of thought* seems to be almost contradicted by the assertions that our attentions and our interpretations are largely prespecified. Not only are we limited in terms of what we can notice, we don't have much say over the sense we make of our perceptions.

Is this indeed a challenge to freedom, as popularly understood?

The blunt answer is, Yes. However, there is an important qualification: Just as recent investigations into cogni-

Fig. 1.10. Have you ever uttered a phrase and then realized, a fraction of a second later, that you'd mispronounced a term or reversed two words?

Such events reveal one of the tricks of consciousness: It disguises the fact that it lags about a half-second behind worldly happenings. That lag is needed for nonconscious processes to sort through, interpret, and select what will become conscious. There is no way of avoiding it — but we're rarely aware of the fact that we're a few frames behind the action, as it were.

tion, consciousness, and perception have demonstrated popular understandings of these phenomena to be lacking, they have also suggested that such ideals as *freedom* and *individuality* might be reinterpreted.

A preponderance of neurological and sociological evidence supports the conclusion that we are not free to select what enters consciousness, any more than we are free to choose heart rate or body temperature. Such phenomena can be indirectly affected (by, for example, engaging in particular activities), but they generally cannot be directly controlled. Well before we become aware of a perception or a thought, complex nonconscious processes have sorted through and discarded information so that what enters consciousness has *already* been selected and has *already* been rendered meaningful. The point here may be startling: Consciousness appears to play very minor roles in choosing its foci and in making sense of things. Rather, consciousness seems to be limited to the role of monitoring the surface of cognition, of registering the sense that has already been made.

In fact, much of the time we operate not on the basis of conscious deliberation, but intuitively — that is, we make judgments and arrive at conclusions without really knowing why. If suddenly challenged by a question like, "Why do you say that?" the response is often hesitant, as we are faced with having to assemble a viable explanation for a notion that was not consciously derived.

Even more startling, perhaps, is the suggestion that our actions are not consciously selected. Even when we mull

Perceiving Stories

Perception is oriented to difference and surprise. More formally, neural systems are structured to alert us to things that are out of the ordinary. By as early as 8 months of age, in fact, children are already pointing at strange objects in familiar places and familiar objects in strange places. (An absence or delay of this ability is often a sign of a serious neurological problem.)

This feature of perception is reflected in the predominant structure of personal and cultural narratives. Our

stories tend to be about a strange object or happening that is cast against a backdrop of familiar forms or activities — or, conversely, a strange article or event within a familiar setting. Children as young as 2 and 3 years have been observed in the process of rehearsing, adapting, and inventing such narratives as they go about making sense of their lives. This prodigious talent clearly relies on, and may well be an elaboration of a biologically-based habit of perception.

Teaching Perspectives

Educators have been rather slow to appreciate the implications of recent insights into consciousness and perception. The corporate sector, in contrast, has been unabashed in its exploitation of this body of knowledge.

Advertisers want to influence habits of noticing — both in terms of what one attends to and the associations that one tends to draw. To achieve the goal of affecting *what* is noticed, commercials are tailored to the limitations of consciousness: They are brief, focused, repetitive, pervasive, surprising, and offer almost no explicit information. To influence *how* a product is perceived, advertisers strive to manipulate the sorts of nonconscious associations made by the consumer. The obvious message ("Buy me!") is usually embedded in images of success, normality, popularity, vibrancy, freedom, sexiness, and so on.

In terms of fostering critical thinking, formal education is usually characterized as having quite the opposite intentions of commercial advertising. Nevertheless, these two domains of activity share the desire to have others select particular details out of millions of sensorial possibilities. That is, like commercial advertising, teaching is centrally concerned with directing attention and affecting interpretations.

Discussions of the directive and focusing aspects of teaching, unfortunately, tend to get bogged down in debates over the importance of rote practice relative to rich experience. Advertisers, in contrast, have not fallen for this dichotomization. Every successful ad simultaneously aims to focus on the particular while embedding its explicit message in more generalized, contextual concerns.

The same sensibility can inform teaching. There is, for example, nothing wrong with a lesson on comma usage, so long as the topic is associated with situations in which the topic is relevant. (The issue might arise as a consistent area of difficulty in students' writings, for instance.) Conversely, having students engage in such complex activities as composing stories before they have mastered the alphabet — much less developed a broad written vocabulary — is vital for supporting more global understandings of, for example, conventional narrative structures.

The particular is embedded in the general; the general arises from the particular. This is a truism of life and a tenet of advertising, yet it is still a difficult idea for many teachers, parents, and politicians when it comes to formal learning.

Among the strategies available to teachers for focusing attention are repetition, well timed questions, highlights, and practice, along with such student activities as note-taking, discussion, and resymbolization or rephrasing of ideas. Pedagogical structures to avoid include elaborate explanations, extended instructions, and decontextualized formulations. As a general rule, most people cannot follow more than a few new ideas or directions at a time. Hence, one usually needs to build up to complicated activities — without, of course, fragmenting complex competencies into discrete, isolated skills. (Teachers can sometimes circumvent the limitations of consciousness and memory in this regard by offering mnemonics and other strategies to help students organize information.)

over possibilities and make deliberate decisions, it appears that the neurological and other bodily processes are in motion about a half-second before the "choice" or "decision" to act is consciously "made."

This is not to say that consciousness is merely an elaborate delusion. Clearly, consciousness is important to existence. Like a chalkboard in a classroom or a television station in a community, consciousness plays a vital role in allowing parts of the complex collective of neurons and neuronal structures to interact with one another and to be informed of activities across relatively large distances.

Nevertheless, the evidence suggests that we are constantly deceived by consciousness. It is as though a major part of its role is to dupe us into believing that it is in charge of things that are simply beyond its control. Instead of "director," then, a more appropriate metaphor for consciousness is "commentator." Just as sports broadcasters have virtually no impact on the events that unfold on an athletic field, so consciousness seems to do little more than piece together a coherent narrative of ongoing experiences. Consciousness doesn't initiate, it justifies.

Consciousness is so effective in this role that it even manages to deceive itself into believing that it is keeping pace with events. It always lags behind, however. Just as our blind spots are hidden from perception, we are generally unaware that conscious perception is a step behind ongoing events — including those activities that we believe we have deliberately (consciously) initiated.

The point here is not that there is no freedom or choice in life. It is, rather, that consciousness plays a less direct role in decisions and choices than is generally thought. Like all higher order processes, choice involves the *entire* brain — which means that, although we can and do make our own decisions, most of the mulling over, the weighing of options, the debating, and so on are simply not present to consciousness. But the fact that *I* might not be aware of such extensive and ongoing processes doesn't mean that it isn't *me* who is making the decisions.

Consider, for example, a familiar scenario: As anyone who has attempted to lose weight, quit smoking, or avoid alcohol will attest, the conscious decision to reduce consumption is not the same as controlling consumption. In fact, the simpler task of monitoring these behaviors can be an immense challenge: Most of us have had the experi-

Fig. 1.11. What do you see here?

Two rabbits looking to the right? Two birds looking to the left? A bunny and a bird facing one another? A bird and a bunny facing opposite directions? Something different?

We are capable of flipping among such interpretations, but we cannot consider more than one at a time.

It appears that consciousness is able to juggle about a half dozen interpretive possibilities (or discrete thoughts) at a time, but must flip back and forth among them.

Hands-On Learning

One of the major educational trends over recent decades has been "hands-on learning." Especially prominent in the teaching of mathematics and the sciences, this emphasis is developed around occasions for learners to manipulate and explore artifacts that are associated with particular concepts. Learning about fractions, for example, might be embedded in activities of folding, cutting, and arranging pieces of paper.

For the most part, such activities are seen to provide learners with concrete examples that they might attach to abstract principles. However, this popular rationale misses the essential point of a hands-on approach. There is a much more important reason for this teaching emphasis, one that derives from the realization that most of our learning is not conscious. As has become clear in recent demonstrations of the limits of human awareness, learning is mostly a nonconscious event.

It may be difficult to appreciate this claim. Can we really say that we've learned something if we're not consciously aware that we've learned it? The point to bear in mind, though, is that the thinking that passes through consciousness is only the surface of our embodied knowledge.

Some recent case studies of persons who lost their sight as young children and, through medical intervention, regained it as adults might help to illustrate this point. As mentioned earlier (p. 11), when their bandages are removed, these persons often cannot see — that is, they are unable to pull coherent images out of the visual "noise" that suddenly confronts them. They cannot discern edges, shapes, colors, and so on ... unless they have the opportunity to feel whatever it is they are looking at.

Such studies prompt the question, What would we see if we had never been able to touch the objects of vision? The answer appears to be, very little. Our perceptions of boundaries, depths, distances, sizes, and so on are all linked to our broad experiences in touching-while-seeing things. From these sensorially rich experiences, more explicit interpretations and generalizations can arise — but such knowings are always deeply rooted in bodily engagements with the world.

It is thus that teaching approaches that are focused only on formal concepts and symbol-use can be frustrating and readily forgotten. Very often, learners can make no *sense* of such abstractions. That is, such notions may remain meaningless and mechanical because they appear to have nothing to do with the knower's organic bodily sensations.

---

ence of catching ourselves about to swallow a piece of chocolate *after* resolving not to have more.

But that does not mean that we have no control or that we are puppets to circumstance. The person who made the *nonconscious* decision to pick up the chocolate was the person who suddenly became conscious that the chocolate was about to be swallowed. (It is at such points that we might assist consciousness by giving in to its limitations — that is, we might move away from the treat.) Simply put, consciousness is not responsible for initiating action. However, it does appear to play an important "executive" role in deciding whether or not an action, once begun, should be pursued.

In brief, people are not conscious of much. For the most part, we are aware of only the tiniest fragment of bodily sensation, we have access to only the surface of our thinking, we are attuned to only the gross superficialities of our actions. In other words, we are mostly unconscious.

There are some significant and immediate implications for teaching of the assertion that "conscious decisions" are, for the most part, neither conscious nor decisions (but, rather, after-the-fact justifications). Clearly, the common practice of describing teaching in terms of decision-making processes is problematic. Deliberate decision-making is a slow process, requiring a person first to become aware of what is going on, then to summon and weigh options, then to select and to initiate a particular action — all of which takes at least 2 seconds for the simplest of decisions. For the most part, persons simply do not proceed through life in this way, and teachers are not exceptions. Most of teaching action is a matter of getting caught up in a flow, of enacting sensibilities that are deeply inscribed in one's embodied habits of acting.

Learning to teach and transforming one's teaching practices, then, are not simple matters of deliberately selecting and enacting particular pedagogical strategies. They are, rather, complex matters of embodying different habits of perception, of speaking, of theorizing, and of acting. Although involving consciousness, such learning must be understood as vastly more complex than consciousness can possibly monitor (or that textbooks can possibly describe). Moreover, such transformations cannot be conceived strictly in terms of individual initiatives or personal responsibilities. As demonstrated by the successes of Alcoholics Anonymous and other organizations devoted to helping persons cope with addictions, efforts toward transformation are most effective when one's thought and activity are understood to be embedded in intertwining levels of biological-and-social organization.

The point seems to be that, in every event of learning or self-transformation, the learner is always and already entangled in a complex web of relationality. Change, then, needs to operate at more than a single level. Otherwise, as ineffective or inappropriate as some habits and practices might be, the forces of habit, tradition, and expectation will be difficult to overcome. Learning to teach, it follows, must be understood to involve one's students, their families, one's school, the surrounding community, and so on.

Many of these sensibilities were embodied in the "re-

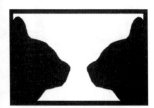

Fig. 1.12. Figure/ground studies have helped us to understand that some things must be pushed out of consciousness in order for other things to be perceived. Observing the bowl in this image, for example, means that the cat profiles must become the unseen ground of perception. And vice versa.

flective practice" movement that swept though teacher
education several years ago. They were also represented
in wide-ranging discussions of "metacognition" in the
1980s. Both these movements pointed to the need to be
critically aware of one's activities, physical and mental.
The guiding principle was that an ongoing monitoring of
one's actions would lead to greater effectiveness.

Such emphases marked an important break from educational strategies that focused on rule acquisition, classification schemes, memorization, skill development, and
so on as they invoked the human capacity to think about
thinking. Unfortunately, however, these movements appear to rely on exaggerated understandings of consciousness and of its role in effecting change. In general, consciousness is simply too small to accommodate *both* the
learning of a new activity *and* the monitoring of that learning. This is not to say that such monitoring is unnecessary
or useless, however. On the contrary, it is vital to change.
The problem is that consciousness can only effectively
monitor those actions that have become more-or-less automatic. Hence, trying to reflect on one's early efforts at
teaching or on one's developing subject matter knowledge
is difficult, if not impossible.

The question thus arises as to where one's analytic and
reflective capacities should be focused when learning to
teach. One suggestion that is gaining increased attention
is to invert the figure and ground of the issue — that is,
rather than worrying about one's teaching, the focus of
attention should be on students' learning.

The suggestion here is that the *obvious* (conscious)
worries are the wrong ones to be addressing. The more
appropriate emphasis might be on *transparent* (automatic
and nonconscious) activity. The assertion is that the teacher
should focus her or his attention more on what learners
are doing than on her or his own teaching activity. And,
although a focus on learning may seem obvious, a quick
review of the many "How to Teach" manuals that are currently available would demonstrate it to be a significant
departure from the common sense of teacher education.

Educating Perception

Further to the suggestion that educators should consider
inverting the figure and ground of schooling practices,

Fig. 1.13. Although the rectangles to the left are uniformly shaded, it looks as though each one is lighter where it borders with a darker block (and, for that matter, darker where it borders with a lighter block).

Even more surprising: Lay a pen on the border between two rectangles. The steps will appear to be much more alike in intensity than when they are not separated.

The main reason for these illusions is that visual perception works to make edges *pop out* — which isn't surprising, given that edges are the most useful information in the environment.

some important conclusions about perception and learning have recently arrived from an unexpected place: artificial intelligence research.

Early in the history of the electronic computer, it was shown that machines could be made to outperform humans on most school-related tasks — organizing, comparing, and compiling data, in particular. Such demonstrations contributed to a belief (and fear) that machines would soon be made that were smarter than humans.

Some 50 years later, it has become clear that these early expectations for artificial intelligence (AI) were ridiculously over-optimistic, largely because researchers were attending to the *figure* of collective knowledge rather than to the *ground* of knowing.

Most of what students are expected to master during their years of schooling is easily accomplished by electronic computers. However, what a child learns *before* coming to school is far more complex. Such "basic" and effortless competencies as using language, making comparisons, noting relationships, drawing analogies, composing narratives, and understanding humor are well beyond conventional machine technologies. These sorts of learnings rely on living in and moving though a complex social world — a world that can never be fully described, never fully conscious, and, hence, never fully programmed. In contrast, rule-based activities (like calculus and chess) place great demands on consciousness and thus *seem* exceedingly difficult. But they are relatively easily programmed.

Two mistakes were made by early AI researchers. The first was to regard conscious knowledge as more important than the complex web of experiences and interpretations that underlie one's conscious awareness. Second, humans were regarded as rule-based ("The brain is a computer!") creatures. Having recognized the inadequacy of such assumptions, current efforts to "teach" computers have shifted away from a focus on rules toward provision of examples and experiences. The most sophisticated chess programs, for instance, are structured to self-modify as new games are played. The smartest robots (which, at the time of writing, are reputed to have acquired insect-level intelligence) "learn" about their surroundings by exploring it — bumping, touching, and so on. The underlying idea, which is contributing to significantly greater successes, is that intelligent behavior relies on a broad and diverse body of experiences. Instead of attempting to be clear and explicit, the "education" of these machines involves ambiguity, unpredictability, and explorative activity.

Perhaps the most critical insight here is that intelligent behavior relies on complex experience. The inverse of this insight is that a deprivation of sensory engagement will lead to underdeveloped abilities to note relationships, to predict, to act — in short, to perceive. Indeed, as has been tragically demonstrated in cases where infants are deprived of movement, stimulation, and human contact, the capacity to develop abstract notions can be all but extinguished. (This matter is developed further in Chapter 3A.)

Knowing Looks

There is an obvious implication for teaching here, especially with regard to concepts that are generally considered more abstract: The meaningfulness of all knowledge, regardless of its level of abstraction, derives from one's experiences in the world. A key aspect of teaching, then, is to provide learners with the means of associating ideas with other events of their lives, whether by structuring rich activities, by pointing to related experiences, or otherwise.

So understood, teaching seems to be less about helping students to *know* what they don't know and more about helping them to *notice* what they haven't noticed. Teaching is about affecting perception — that is, about pointing to various aspects of the world in a deliberate attempt to foster different habits of perception/interpretation.

Every event of perception is caught up in the massive currents of our evolutionary-and-social histories. That is, every event of recognition is an event of cognition. It is a co-evolution with others, a participation in the world.

At the same time, it must be understood that we see things differently from one another, even when perspectives are shared. Our perceptions/interpretations emerge from our particular interactions and experiences over our lifetimes. There is, then, no singular "correct" way of seeing the world. In fact, the most privileged ways of seeing seem to underpin the greatest range of contempory problems.

Teaching, then, is not just about affecting perception. It also involves a study of perspectives, positionings, and points of view. It is all about knowing looks.

Fig. 1.14. Which of the embedded boxes is the darkest?

In fact, they're all the same shade. They seem different because perception *compares*, it doesn't make absolute judgments. That is, perception is about making sense of *relationships* among things. (This point is demonstrated each time you watch TV. The black parts of on-screen images aren't really black, since they can't be darker than the unactivated screen.)

All sensory capacities work this way. Whispers sound louder in libraries than at ball games, apples taste sweeter if eaten after potatoes than after chocolates, small worries can feel like crises in otherwise comfortable lives, etc.

I (Rebecca) placed a transparency of seemingly random dots on the overhead and switched on the lamp, waiting for the chat in the grade nine class to die down as they began to notice what was on the screen.

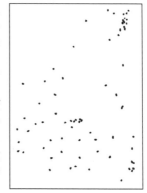

"What do you see?" I asked when I finally had their attention.

Their answers were predictable at first: A bunch of dots, ha ha. Fly specks on a window pane. Joe's answer sheet.

"Okay," I said. "Remember when you used coloring books? Sometimes they had pictures that asked you to connect the dots from one number to the next."

There were murmurs of agreement.

"Well, there are no numbers this time. Just a collection of dots. See if you can imagine lines that might connect them to form a picture."

They were silent for a moment, perhaps trying to decide if I was really serious. Then Marita spoke up. "I see a horse." I held up my hand to halt the guffaws from a group at the back. I asked Marita if she would come up and quickly trace the picture with her finger. When she did so, many of us could see the horse she imagined on the page.

Now there was a flood of suggestions, everyone seeing something different and being able to show the rest of us by tracing their fingers along the dots. Of course some of the visualizations were more powerful than others; some of the tracings stretched our imaginations further. Nevertheless, the students began to see that depending on how you chose to look at the dots on the page, you could find numerous possibilities to visualize.

"Why did Marita see a horse and Justin a plane?" I wondered. "Or Jenni see Pegasus?"

"I was reading about planes last night," Justin suggested. "I guess I was thinking about them."

"I thought of Pegasus after Marita because I could see using the dots a bit differently than she did," Jenni told us. "She gave me the initial idea but I didn't see it quite the same."

"I guess it depends on where you head's at," Luis said.

"This reminds me of the magic pictures in the newspaper," Willy said. "You know the ones that look just like some kind of wallpaper pattern and then you have to look real close to see a picture in them?"

"What do you have to do with your eyes when you look at those pictures?" I asked.

"You kinda have to let your eyes slack off, almost cross them," he suggested.

"Why do you have to do that?"

"So you can see it differently than you do usually."

"Did anyone do something different with their eyes to see the picture in the dots?" I asked. Some of the students admitted to squinting, others closed one eye, while some traced in the air with their finger. They agreed that, for the most part, they had consciously done something different from looking at the overhead as they usually would.

"Let's look at the pictures of someone who saw things differently too," I said, pulling out a picture book, *The Mysteries of Harris Burdick* by Chris Van Allsburg. In this book, Van Allsburg has drawn unusual pictures that he frames with a story about a mysterious author who brings the drawings and the first line of the stories that accompany each picture to a publisher. The man, Harris Burdick, leaves the portfolio with the publisher for his consideration but never returns to pick up the package. Despite all efforts of the publisher, there is no trace of Burdick. I set up the students' introduction to the book by telling them this story and then showing them the drawings. There are fourteen pictures and story openings in all, each of which takes an ordinary or "real" location and somehow makes it mysterious. For example, a picture of children skipping

 stones shows the water sparkling just a bit more brightly than it should in the sunlight. The caption reads: *A Strange Day in July. He threw with all his might, but the third stone came skipping back.* Another drawing shows a bedroom with wallpaper decorated with birds. If one looks closely, however, he or she notices that several of the birds are in the midst of flying from the paper. The caption for this drawing reads: *The Third-Floor Bedroom. It all began when someone left the window open.*

The students quickly forgot that they thought they were too old to be looking at picture books and got caught up in the speculation of who Harris Burdick might be and what he had been planning to write about. I did not tell them that Burdick is a fictional character that Van Allsburg created; at this point, they were enjoying the thought that he'd been a real person.

While I sometimes find that students write interesting stories when they use the first lines that Van Allsburg has offered, this time I wanted them to play with the notions of reality and imagination visually through photographs or drawings. I asked them to draw or use existing pictures to create their own Harris Burdick page. They were to find or draw a rather ordinary setting and then just change one detail that made the viewer take notice and feel a bit on edge as he or she realized that this was something different than what usually might be expected in such a place.

They came back with interesting and startling pictures, some drawn, some constructed from magazine pictures, some enhanced by computer programs, while others were photographs that they found in family collections or which they had taken specially and enlarged. One interesting example, created by Sara, was a photograph of a small pond by her house. The water was still except for small ripples from a breeze. Around the edge of the water grew willows and tall grasses except for an opening where a sandy incline lead into the water. Sara's caption read: All summer long it grew, feasting off the water. At first we looked for something hidden in the trees, searching the branches of willows for clues. Then someone noticed a dark shape beneath the water. What had at first seemed to be a darker reflection of the pond actually appeared to be a menacing figure beneath the surface. After some coaxing, Sara explained that she had created the effect by taking two slides, one of the water and another of a dark shape she set up in her bedroom. Then by putting the two pictures together, she made a slide "sandwich" that she then had made into a print.

What the students noticed as they created their pictures and text and presented them to classmates was the strong interconnection between image and word. Text helped them see and read the pictures differently just as the pictures changed their understanding of text. We talked about how they did not often think about how they looked at and "read" images, yet before human beings read alphabetic texts, they had understood images whether they were hieroglyphics drawn on pyramid walls or pictograms traced on stone in caves. The students understood that in looking at the pictures of Harris Burdick, they had seen a particular perspective; reading the text had given them another. When they considered both, they used visual and verbal skills interacting with each other to gain a fuller understanding of the book.

We spent some time looking at other picture books that created interesting relationships between image and text by writers such as Anthony Browne and David Macaulay. And we looked at other kinds of books where text and image were important such as Michael Ondaatje's *The Collected Works of Billy the Kid.*

To shift the students' perspective slightly, I suggested that we would spend the next few classes focusing on images only. "We're going to think about the visual grammar of pictures," I told them, "by looking at photography for several days."

I wanted them to realize that they could learn about interpreting and understanding pictures from thinking about the kinds of decision

making a photographer engages in. We were going to explore how photography was only one of many ways of perceiving the world.

We began by holding a "seeing" expedition. I cut out "slide frames"
for each student, making them oversized but of the same proportion as
actual slides (1:1.25). The students then went outside using their frames
to "take" pictures by holding them up to their eyes like the viewfinder of
a camera. They were also to keep fieldnotes about what they decided to
frame, what was left out, and why they made the decisions they did.
When the students returned and reported on their findings, they could
see that photographers make a number of decisions in creating the composition such as who or what should be framed and at what angle, thus
influencing the viewer's perceptions.

The students who included people in their pictures, noticed that the
participants in a photograph could also influence the visual impact by
choosing a particular pose or by portraying a certain sense of themselves.
We then looked at a number of pictures taken by famous photographers
and talked about what decisions might have been made. I asked them to
speculate about the relationships that were suggested by some of the
photographs and to determine how those traces existed in the pictures.
Students talked about the choices of lighting, color versus black and white,
and the positioning of those in the picture. They also pointed beyond the
frame, wondering what could lie outside it, and they considered the af-
fective dimension of the photograph, becoming aware of the depth and
array of meanings that can be possible with a work of art.

Richard Martin, a well known photographer, explains that one can
have all the technique in the world, but photographers can't take good
pictures if they can't see the possibilities. For example, they have to be
able to interpret that the mist rising from the lake may represent the feeling of solitary contentment that the fly fisherman feels being in the water
first thing in the morning. To encourage students to further recognize
such meaning in photography, I asked them to return to their card-
board slides and discover the metaphors of their pictures. What
does it look like if you frame the tip of a branch of a pine
tree? I asked. What feeling is created? What happens now
if you zoom back and look at the whole tree against the
bright sky? What feelings or meaning can be conveyed
by the picture?

As they compared notes, the students realized that
their "photographs" were ambiguous. There was never
a singular truth revealed by one choice. Perhaps the photographer thinks about the breathtaking sweep of an
archway against blue sky as an example of the wonder
of human accomplishment. The partner of the photographer sees the suggestion of a road disappearing into

the distance, a pointing to a journey. Later the photographer considers her picture again and remembers the swoop of Beethoven's music. As the students examined their photographs and those of others, they explored a range of possible responses and interpretations by considering what the photographer might see or imagine at the time the picture is taken (or afterwards), or what the camera, participant in the photograph, or the viewer sees.

Using a camera, particularly one that allows manual settings and focus, is an ambiguous process. Some settings on a camera will produce a photo that represents what the photographer sees through the viewfinder; other settings play with this vision, so the photographer has to imagine how letting in more light or less will impact the picture and how changing the aperture will affect the focus.

The students were no longer accepting their first glance at photographs. As they were doing with print text, they were learning to look closely and interpret visual images. They could also take their understanding of framing and choice in pictures and apply it to other texts they were reading particularly in pieces where pictures and text were in dialogue with each other.

I then asked them to use their understanding of photographs to move into some interpretive writing, using one of Margaret Bourke-White's photographs, "Taxi Dancers."

Margaret Bourke-White was an American photographer working primarily in the first half of this century. In 1936, publisher Henry Luce asked her to shoot the cover for the first issue of *Life* magazine. He sent her out to the northwest to photograph the multi-million dollar projects of the Columbia River Basin, including going to Montana to take photographs of one of Roosevelt's New Deal projects, the building of the Fort Peck Dam. Bourke-White was fascinated by the culture she discovered there — a ramshackle town built with the flavor of the Gold Rush in the long, lonely stretch of northern Montana inhabited by construction workers, engineers, welders, and all the people who are attracted to such opportunistic sites. Some of those who came were taxi dancers, women who would dance with the men for a dime.

Bourke-White's photograph of these women depicts two groupings of individuals: three couples dancing and two men and a woman poised for the camera. There is a certain languidness about the photo that suggests an artificiality about the whole event as if the participants knew this was not what people would consider "real" life. The women who are dancing have a vacant look of tolerance while in the bodies of the men is a certain tense eagerness. They are dressed up — not richly but neatly. Some of the men are in suits, some wear clean work shirts and dungarees; the women are all in dresses, some are suit-like while others are clearly cotton frocks. Everyone has the appearance of having "spiffed" up for the evening's entertainment. Even though the music can't be heard, one can tell from the bodies of the dancers, from the closeness they have in their proximity to each other, that the music is slow. One woman is posing with two men who each have a hand on her as if to hold her back as she leans into them. They smile slyly at the camera as if they know what people who view the picture might think. The photograph gives the impression that all these people would rather be somewhere else, doing something else, but that they think they should, at the same time, be excited to be on the edge of the frontier with these opportunities and possibilities.

I chose this picture to use with students for a number of reasons. First, Bourke-White was an extraordinary photographer who saw photography as a way to get people to see the world in ways that they had not done before. Her pictures have interesting compositions and are usually rich with possible stories, relationships, and interpretations. Second, by using a photograph that is historical and not part of the students' contemporary experience, they tend to focus more carefully on the details and grammar of the picture without leaping too quickly to assumptions. This is a culture that has some connection for them, but not so much that they can easily dismiss aspects that are overly familiar.

We began by looking at the photograph together and talking about what the students notice first. We looked at the lighting, focus, and the composition of the picture, and we talked about what Bourke-White may have kept out of the frame; for example, the band or source of music. What else might be going on? I asked, wanting them to see what the photograph might tells us about the relationships among the people at the dance. What did their bodies and their expressions reveal? What had Bourke-White chosen to capture in that moment? What might she have been thinking about this event?

Then students wrote. I asked them to choose a perspective: someone in the picture or outside, including the photographer and write from that individual's perspective. They also had to choose a listener. They could be a participant talking to the photographer, the photographer speaking to her subjects, and so on. Here are a few snippets written as if from the photographer's perspective speaking to herself.

Before the rising of the full moon, the town is shadowed and quiet except for the music of a bar on the outskirts, bright, noisy, a pocket of life in the Montana darkness. I am drawn from my car, even as I know a woman venturing into such a place in the midst of all this emptiness may be walking on the edge.

The dust from the shoes of dancers drifts through the open door along with sweat rising from damp wool and cotton. For a moment I'm just another body who shuffles, slides two-three-four through the crowd, sidling towards the bar and an empty stool where I can sit and balance my camera. It's when the first bulb flashes that they notice I'm not just another dancing skirt, and they two-pause-four shuffle onwards as the tempo barely takes a breath. Over here! a man calls as he pulls a young woman between the y of his legs. Another man — younger, her boyfriend? — drapes her like a proprietor one arm curves around the back of her neck and rests between her breasts. His other covers her chest, his left hand grasping the wrist of his right so she is locked in, trapped between legs and arms, posed for my lens. I look at the woman's floral print dress, crisp and new, and wonder where she found the money to buy that, considering her shoes are old and dusty, the heels worn from too many nights dancing. She smiles widely at me, a cigarette in her right hand, her left hidden among the men and for a moment I wonder who is being held.

When the students had written their monologue-style notes, we listened to the different voices that emerged in response to and from the photograph. As the characters began to have a presence, our understanding of the photograph became richer and more ambiguous. After every reading, we found ourselves returning to the picture to look for clues to the writer's interpretation. The students noticed details that they missed at first look and they understood that something they may have dismissed actually could take on some importance from someone else's perspective. They also realized that events are understood in light of the "frame" one brings to perceiving and interpreting. Their histories of learning and living created the conditions for their experiences. At the end of the reading, the students could acknowledge the diversity of perspective and the ambiguous truths of the photograph.

The final piece of this assignment was to write a poem from the voice notes. The work became an opportunity to talk about the visual importance of poetry on the page, no less considered than the composition of a photograph. When we write poems, we learn to discern what it is we see and imagine and then we must evoke those senses for readers or listeners. The flowers in the garden, the wind through the valley, the gray shade of the sky, the smell of new spring ground all matter. Like the careful photographer, the careful poet pays attention to detail: She smells the apple and licks it; she looks at the shadings of color and the shape that dips into hollows and rounds to curves; she tweaks the stem, feels the juice on her tongue and lets it roll down her throat. She comes to know the apple so well that she could choose it from amongst others.

Like a photograph, the framing of words in the poem is important as are the white spaces we create. Line breaks, open space, and word arrangement are a vital part of understanding a poem. When students attended to the line breaks and heard the breath of the poem, the rhythm of the voices, something not accessible just by looking at the photograph or taking notes, came to life such as in this excerpt from a piece about one of the taxi dancers.

> This time I have a dress navy with white flowers
> fresh cotton so I look crisp and clean
> something new; something worthwhile.
> Maybe tonight someone will pay double for a dance
> just for the chance to rub his calloused hands
> over the blue cotton on my back
> smell the scent of first-time dress
> and the lavender soap lingering on my soft neck.

One could spend a great deal more time with Bourke-White's photograph beyond the writing of poetry. At other times, students have taken their own photographs in response to Bourke-White and some have taken photographs of what might have happened just before or after she snapped "Taxi Dancers." Working in the medium of photography, students are able to immerse themselves in the kind of decision making Bourke-White might have made. Their photographs can be responded to by other students in similar ways to the writing done for "Taxi-Dancers," reinforcing the powerful play between image and text. Each time

we revisit the photograph using another activity, the students are surprised at what else can be learned from spending so much time with just one picture. In a setting where they are often hurried through one activity after another and where they often do not have time to really absorb the complexity of an artifact before being swiftly introduced to another, such an activity of lingering with a photograph and exploring different levels of interpretation can be an interesting respite for learning and learning to see.

1C   Framing Aims

A central theme developed in Section A of this chapter ("Knowing Looks") was that an event of conscious perception is always an interpretation — that is, a distillation of or a selection from among a myriad of sensorial possibilities. Every event of perception is framed by habits of association that are knitted through the language, by perceptual dispositions that are determined by our physiologies, and by personal experiences that are specific to the perceiver. Among other things, these points highlight that every event of learning affects one's perceptions of reality, whether or not an effect is intended.

In Section B ("Seeing Pictures"), a teaching episode that began with an appreciation of the relationship of experience to perception was presented. In this final section of the chapter, the aim is to interpret that episode and other teaching events in terms of frames of perception and the goals of teaching.

A central notion in this section is that perception and learning don't obey simple rules. What, then, is a teacher to do when faced with prescriptive curriculum demands, rigid time limits, and inflexible evaluation schemes? Specifically, in terms of the main focus of this section, how might one think about the intended outcomes of teaching?

Point 1 • FOCUSING FRAMES

Deliberate efforts at teaching need to be developed around focal events — that is, around specific objects or activities that are intended to gather and focus learners' attentions.

One of the first steps in any event of teaching is to identify the aims of instruction: What is hoped that students will learn by the year's end? By the unit's end? By the lesson's end?

For most of its history, the modern school has responded to such concerns through processes of fragmentation and linearization. By way of a specific example, most writers of mathematics curricula and textbooks for middle school students seem to have assumed that, in order for learners to adequately master the addition of two fractions, they must learn first to name fractional amounts, then to make equivalent fractions, then to simplify fractions — in that specific order. Similar examples could be readily drawn from other subject areas.

The thinking behind the fragmentation and linearization of concepts is actually sound. These practices are based on the realization that human consciousness is small: Learners can deal with only a handful of details at a time. The teacher must thus narrow the focus. For certain topics, a linearized, one-concept-at-a-time approach might seem like the only logical solution to the limitations of human awareness — even if we are faced with such unwanted consequences as decontextualization and demonstrated inabilities to generalize concepts to other subject areas or to contexts outside the classroom.

Focusing Attentions

After leading a class discussion on the apparent connections of industrialization to changes in global climate, Fiona met with her practicum supervisor to review the lesson.

The supervisor began by identifying some positive observations, offering particular praise for the way questions were distributed and for the orderliness of students. On the downside, however, the supervisor noted that it seemed that Fiona often did not pick up on student contributions. Many insightful points and important worries were allowed to drop — in large part, it appeared, because they didn't fit in with Fiona's line of questioning and her expectations of responses.

Upon reflection, Fiona had to agree that she'd by-passed several key opportunities to take the discussion to new and interesting places. Disturbed at this realization — since she saw such matters as more important to teaching than the planning and management skills that she did demonstrate — she began to wonder how she might become more attentive and responsive to student contributions.

She raised the concern in the staffroom at a lunch time meeting with the teachers she was working with in her practicum. Two suggestions arose.

 The first was simply to continue in the way she was already proceeding. Eventually, it was argued, she would become so good at the management side of things that it would occupy less of her attention. As that happened, she could begin to pay more attention to matters of learning.

"But by the time my management skills are automatic, my teaching practices might be automatic too," she protested. "What I want to be able to do is pay attention to students now."

With a bit more discussion, it was agreed that it would be possible to structure some experiences in which management would be much less a concern. After meeting with other student teachers at the school, a plan was devised for dividing up one of the classes that Fiona had been assigned to teach. During one period every day, she and several others would work together, each taking responsibility for 5 or 6 students in a small group setting. They hoped that this structure would allow them to focus more on the particularities and complexities of learners' interpretations. In another course, she would co-teach lessons with the regular classroom teacher. That would allow her a different sort of opportunity to focus on the relationship between her efforts to teach and students' learning.

In both situations, Fiona quickly noticed a dramatic change to interactive dynamics. Whereas her teaching in whole-class structures tended to involve a good deal of *discussion*, her work within these new structures seemed to be more *conversational*. There was more give-and-take, more listening, greater engagement. The emphasis was less on stating positions and making points, and more toward interpreting perspectives and seeking some sort of shared understandings. It was a manner of interaction, Fiona noted, that she would try to cultivate as she became more comfortable in the larger group settings.

A linearized curriculum isn't the only possibility, however. In fact, it might even be argued to be a poor choice. In contrast to the structures that are typical of many classroom settings, most of human learning occurs in sensorially rich, all-at-once sorts of situations. Isolated ideas, prespecified sequences, and contrived boundaries on experience clearly are not necessary for effective learning.

What is necessary, however, is the opportunity to focus — that is, to attend to something specific, yet something that is neither isolated nor decontextualized. The demands for specificity and sensorial richness need not be contradictory, provided that the teacher understands which discernments are important to a given concept and what sorts of artifacts and events might be useful in highlighting those distinctions.

In the teaching episode presented in the previous section, for instance, the teacher's explicit instructional aim was to have learners better appreciate habits of perception. The ensuing "unit," spread over several weeks, was not subdivided into discrete, lesson-sized pieces (e.g., "The Five Senses"; "Photographic Techniques"; etc.). Nor did the teacher attempt to address every exhausting detail of the topic. Rather, the teaching objective was woven through an array of interrelated experiences. In an important sense, in fact, the overarching goal of instruction was embedded and embodied in *every* aspect of the learning experiences — as opposed to being seen as a goal that awaited learners at the end of a sequence of instruction. As the teacher worked to point to particular elements, and as students worked to interpret relationships among the various activities, the aim of the instruction was realized in a manner that was not just effective, but that spilled over into other experiences, inside and outside the school.

The activities described in "Seeing Pictures" constituted a focal event — a moment of investigating something general by attending to something specific. (The same can be said of all the activities described in the Parts B of this book.) That event arose from an understanding of perception as something more than a process of "taking things in." Perception, rather, is a culminating event of interpretation, a gathering together of the histories of the species, the culture, and the individual.

  Connecting Thoughts

Think about a memorable event of learning from among your experiences as a student in a formal institution. What was learned? What were some of the focal events surrounding that learning? How was the learning knitted through your participation in the focal events?

Point 2 • UNDERSTANDING FRAMES

Frames matter.

As developed on the title page of this chapter (page 1), the term *frame* is used here to refer to constantly evolving senses of the world. The notion of framing is intended to collect together past, present, and future. A frame arises in a complex interplay of biological, cultural, and experiential histories. A frame infuses actions in the moment — and those actions and their consequences prompt changes in frames. Frames shape and are shaped by intentions and expectations.

Perceptually speaking, frames are matters of selection and interpretation. More bluntly, frames are matters of prejudice, partiality, and bias. Frames are never neutral or objective, but they are always necessary for understanding. One cannot step outside of one's frame — but it is possible to become more aware of it.

In fact, at least for educators, it would seem that there is actually a moral imperative to become more aware of one's frames. How one perceives the world matters. And those who participate so deliberately in structuring the experiences of others should be aware of what it is they're doing.

An example: For centuries the dominant worldview in Western societies has tended to regard Earth as a mindless resource, something separate from and at the disposal of humanity. Schools have participated in the development and maintenance of this sensibility in a variety of ways — the most obvious of which has been emphases on the acquisition of knowledge and use of various technologies, without an accompanying interrogation of the impacts of these particular disciplines and technologies.

Until recently, such attitudes and emphases appeared to be relatively unproblematic — until, of course, a burgeoning human population started to place extraordinary demands on the rest of the planet, demands that could no longer be ignored. It has become clear that the worldview that has dominated for centuries must change.

And it is changing. As disasters unfold and crises loom, on levels from the cellular to the planetary, a "new" appreciation for the ways that humanity is woven into the web of life is emerging. Rhetoric of domination, transcendence, mastery, ownership, management, and stewardship — that is, vocabulary that places humanity apart from and above other aspects the world — is starting to give way to sensibilities that are more tentative, participatory, embedded, and entangled. One might justly expect that future generations will look back at this time in the same way that this generation has tended to look upon the Scientific and Industrial Revolutions — as a time of enlightenment, hope, revisioning.

Some frames, then, are better than others. Unfortunately, it appears that there are no "best" frames, world

---

Reading Illustrations

Working with the school's teacher-librarian, Anne planned a picture book activity for her grade three students. The students began by reading different versions of stories written and illustrated by different people or they read several books by the same author or illustrator. For each set of books the students were given written directions that asked them to look for and do certain activities. For example, Anne asked students to read several versions of Little Red Riding Hood and then use a chart for comparison that asked the following questions: *In each version, how did Little Red Riding Hood get her name? Why did she get to her grandmother's? What did the wolf do and how did the story end? How does each book illustrate Red Riding Hood? The forest? The wolf?* Another grouping included several of Steven Kellogg's books where the students were asked to comment on the action and detail in his illustrations and why they thought he had chosen to portray the story in such a manner.

Meanwhile, the teacher-librarian worked with small groups of Anne's students, teaching them different styles of illustrating such as representational (realism), impressionistic, expressionistic, surrealistic, fantastic, folk, cartoon, and native art. The students then looked through picture books, identifying and critiquing the illustrations. By having Anne and the teacher-librarian point to the distinctions between illustration styles and then by offering a variety of media, the students were able to pick one of the styles and emulate it by creating one picture and then talking about the style they'd chosen. Whereas they had not paid much attention to the illustrations before, they now looked at the picture books they were reading with a new understanding and with a critical eye.

views, theories, or sensibilities — merely ones that are better fitted to constantly changing circumstances.

Every human participates in the evolution of these frames. Educators play a particular and central role in their development. In fact, formal schooling might be seen as a deliberate effort to affect frames, to instill particular habits of perception and interpretation.

This understanding places a certain moral responsibility on the teacher. To ignore matters of framing is to participate unconscientiously in the perpetuation of potentially troublesome worldviews, interpretations, and practices. As persons whose roles are defined in terms of affecting how learners see the world, it would seem that an attitude of mindfulness toward the ongoing evolution of sensibilities is a vital part of teaching.

This is not to say that every event of teaching should be explicitly about social justice, or ecological thought, or other critical issues. It is, rather, an imperative to be attentive to blind spots, to transparent assumptions, to unintended consequences. In English class, a mindful attitude toward a reading exercise might be realized in a discussion of the ways that characters are gendered. In mathematics class, it might be realized in the occasional departure from the text to look at recent trends and transitions in mathematics research, using those to open up discussions on the ways that changes in mathematics are associated with changes in ways some phenomena are seen. And so on.

●   **Connecting Thoughts**   ●

The teacher in Chapter 1B, "Seeing Pictures" was attempting to participate conscientiously in the ongoing evolutions of sensibilities. What sorts of assumptions might be challenged through this sort of learning event? How might such experiences contribute to learners' frames? How might that be different from the contributions of more traditional schooling experiences?

Point 3 • CHANGING FRAMES

Teaching practices emerge from deep-seated assumptions and beliefs — ones which may not be consciously known or even consciously accessible to the teacher.

Many, and perhaps *most* teachers begin their careers with the conviction that they will avoid those teaching practices that they found unhelpful or inappropriate when they were students: They will be less directive and more attentive; they will be less technocratic and more creative; and so on.

However, when the demands of full-time teaching are met, many, if not most beginning teachers quickly find themselves settling into patterns of teaching that are strikingly similar to the ones they intended to avoid.

Is there a way of sidestepping such a fate? Is it possible to insert oneself into a social institution that is steeped in unconscious habit and to act in ways that are more faithful to one's espoused goals for teaching? Or are we humans more likely to get caught up in the flow of established patterns?

Fortunately, history has demonstrated that change is possible. However, history has also demonstrated that change is rarely a simple matter of conscious decision. It must also involve ongoing interrogations of practices, of habits of association, and so on. This is particularly true of teaching practice. For the most part, teaching actions are not consciously considered and deliberately selected. There are simply so many demands on the teacher's limited attentions that most of what they do has to be "automatic."

This is not to say that teaching is thoughtless. Rather, it is an assertion that teaching is an ongoing enactment of embodied sensibilities, as opposed to a sequence of conscious decisions. Teaching actions arise from habits of perception and interpretation that are so deeply engrained that they're very difficult to even notice. Transforming practice, then, is hinged to the exercise of uncovering core assumptions and webs of belief about what knowledge is (an object? an action?), what learning is (acquisition? transformation?), what schools do (inform? enculturate?), and so on.

The project of uncovering assumptions and beliefs is a complex one. As psychologists have amply demonstrated, such matters cannot usually be addressed through direct questioning: What we say about what we believe is usually more a reflection of what we think we should believe than what is actually revealed in our actions. This is part of the reason that more indirect strategies for uncovering beliefs have been developed. Ink blot tests, dream analysis, word association, and so on are all aimed at circumventing conscious interpretation in order to get at hidden webs of meaning.

Less clinically, and perhaps more appropriate to teaching, another strategy for investigating one's assumptions is to ask indirect questions. For instance, the direct query, "What is science?" will almost certainly generate an interesting and appropriate range of responses in a teacher education seminar. However, responses to such tasks as "Recount an experience of learning science" or "Provide a rationale for science instruction" often reveal beliefs and assumptions that are incompatible with responses to direct questions. (That doesn't mean the explicit formulations are incorrect or untrue. It simply highlights that humans are more complex beings than is sometimes thought.)

In terms of what this might mean for someone interested in transforming his or her own teaching practices, then, the critical element is not a well-articulated position

---

Hair

"Write about your hair."

Denita could tell that most of the members of her teacher education class could not see the relevance of this prompt for their weekly writing exercise.

They were still wondering when they returned a week later with their page-long narratives in hand. As they read them to one another in their small groups, however, some consistent themes began to emerge. In particular, it became clear that almost everyone had mentioned that they had considered changes to their hair 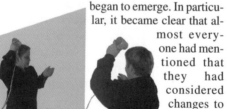 styles — changes that were linked to the upcoming practicum. Many of the men were considering more conservative styles. Some of the women were thinking about pulling their hair back. Several students had already made plans to re-dye their hair to more natural colors.

Shortly into the class, the groups reported on these emergent themes. Denita then posed the questions, "How are these thoughts connected to popular opinion, cultural myths, and personal views on the appearance of teachers?" and "What do those opinions, myths, and views have to say about what we think about schooling?"

The ensuing discussion wasn't focused on what others thought. Rather, the results of the hair exercise highlighted that everyone was complicit in the establishment and maintenance of norms — explicit and not-so-explicit alike.

statement, but capacities to notice contradictions in one's own actions and to interrogate the origins of conflicting impulses. Importantly, for change to happen, one must go beyond "reflection" on such matters, to consider the theories and philosophies that are embedded in one's habits of thought and action.

As well, change can also be effected by incorporating some deliberate changes to habits of acting. One might rearrange the desks in a classroom to alter the pattern of movement and interaction. The sequence of events in a lesson might be shifted around. Student responsibilities might be redefined. The teacher might self-impose a limit of 10 minutes for any lesson or exposition. All of these interventions emerge from an awareness that change requires rehearsal — that is, *thinking* about change usually isn't enough. It is important to become involved in other practices of living with different ways of acting.

 Connecting Thoughts

Return to the event that you thought about in response to the first "Connecting Thoughts" exercise — the one about a memorable learning event.

What, if anything, might that particular recollection reveal about your beliefs on the nature of teaching? The nature of subject matter? The purposes of schooling?

Point 4 • DEFINING FRAMES

It is important to specify the goals of any teaching event, but those intended goals should not be confused with the actual consequences of teaching. Teaching has no clear outcomes or end points.

When does teaching start and end?

One way of answering this question is to impose simple definitions. For instance, teaching might be defined strictly in terms of those instances when learners are under the direct influence of an instructor. So delineated, teaching begins and ends when a class begins and ends.

There are clear problems with this narrow definition. Think for a moment about some of your teachers. Did all of what you learned from them happen in their presence? Have you ever had an "Aha!" moment, long after the interaction with the person who might have prompted it?

The effects of teaching linger. Like all of life's events, one's experiences with a teacher are incorporated into one's evolving frame in complex, unruly, unpredictable ways.

One can never know the consequences of one's teaching — either in terms of the immediate outcomes or the long term effects. But this doesn't mean that the teacher should give up on the articulation of objectives for teaching, nor that such activity should be expanded to include consideration of all possible consequences of one's teaching actions. Rather, it is merely a statement that, just as conscious events of perception represent only the tip of the sensory iceberg, so explicit goals for learning are only a tiny aspect of the potential impact of teaching efforts.

One implication of this realization is that the emphasis in teaching shouldn't be on giving direction, but on

---

It's a St. Bernard

William puzzled over Kae, one of his kindergarten students whom he considered bright and capable. While she seemed to grasp most of the work quickly and easily, she continually made an unusual number of errors on her pre-reading sheets. William looked over the page again. Kae should have found it simple. The students were asked to look at groups of four pictures and circle the object that was different. In one box she had circled a pear instead of the bird. Hadn't she seen the banana and a slice of bread? Didn't she understand that they were all foods? He looked at her next answer. She had circled the dog instead of the clock. She had not realized that the cat, chicken and dog were a category. William shook his head. He might have more work to do with Kae than he expected when it came to pre-reading skills. He had assumed that she would learn to read with little effort.

"Kae," he asked, kneeling down beside her at the table. "Can you tell me why you've circled this picture?" He pointed to the dog.

"Uh-huh," she said. "That's because he's a St. Bernard."

"A St. Bernard?"

"Yes. A St. Bernard." Kae looked at Will with a frown that suggested she expected him to know this already.

"And this?" Will asked, pointing.

"A chicken. A cat. A calendar." Kae said, sounding bored with having to be so obvious for the teacher as she followed his finger down the page.

"Then why didn't you circle the calendar?" Will asked. "It's the only one that's not an animal."

"I know it's not." Kae frowned again. "But these are all 'c' words. "St. Bernard starts with an 's.'"

"Oh." Will paused for a moment and then point to the previous box. "And these are all 'b' words except for pear?"

"Yesss," Kae said, her attention drifting back to the Lego tower she was building, leaving Will holding the sheet and feeling sheepish about his earlier assumptions.

attending to the learning that is happening. Events of teaching are not about certain knowledge, but about tentative interpretations. Teaching, then, is more a matter of *listening* than of *telling*.

 Connecting Thoughts

An interview of a learner is a rare luxury for a teacher, but it can highlight some interesting interpretations. A useful exercise might be to set up a one-on-one discussion with a student about her or his responses on a formal examination.

Point 5 • NARRATING FRAMES

Narratives of experience are both important goals of and powerful means for learning.

Narratives of experience — that is, plausible and coherent accounts of noted events in one's life — are important conceptual tools in learning. Humans use narratives to weave together diverse experiences, to reinterpret previous events, to anticipate future activities, and to impose meaning on unexpected happenings. That is, narrative has a twofold function in learning: The act of composing a narrative is a tool for making sense of some aspect of the world, and the resulting narratives are used to frame one's knowledge. Narrative is both means and end.

Narrative is an important form on personal, social, and cultural levels. Culturally, narratives have long been used to render a complex and dynamic world comprehensible. Western societies' oldest surviving narratives, which originated at a time when people were more attuned to the rhythms of the earth, most often deal with important patterns: the passage from day into night, the changing of the seasons, the migration of animals. When one of these patterns was interrupted — by, for example, a late spring or a solar eclipse — the community created narratives to explain the anomalous event, in the process, weaving that explanation into an existing web of knowledge. Stories served, as they continue to serve, as a way of making the unusual, the unknown, and the unexpected understandable. Stories also served as a repository for cultural knowledge, as long lists of facts and interpretations could be embedded in these forms.

The same is true on the individual level. From birth, humans are agents in a storied world, where their actions and intentions are understood mainly through narrative structures. Narratives are used both to keep track of the regularities of one's existence and to make sense of strange, new experiences. Children quickly come to the realization that events have a beginning, a middle, and an end — and, in fact, have been observed to make use of a prodigious narrating talent in the preliminary stages of language development. But children are rarely (if ever) directly taught how to do this. More likely, their understandings of narrative forms arise as they listen to and rehearse cultural narratives, and as they begin to compose and revise their own stories of experience.

The use of narrative is so pervasive that it is sometimes difficult to notice its importance to comprehension. But consider what usually happens when a young learner has difficulty understanding an abstract set of symbols such as "7 – 4". In almost every case, a parent, teacher, or peer will begin by inventing a narrative: "Pretend there were seven people in a room and then four left"; "There were seven candies, but four were eaten"; and so on.

Narrating Insights

Karly is spending the afternoon playing with her Barbie dolls. She has gathered together on the kitchen table several of her dolls and some doll clothes, as well as doll-sized blankets, pillows, cars, kitchen, and appliances.

She begins her play, not unpredictably, by changing all the clothes on the dolls and then putting them to bed for a nap. As she pulls the blanket over one, she seems to remember that her great-grandmother is in the hospital with a broken hip. As she plays, she vocalizes this thought to her dolls:

"My Nana Celia is in the hospital with a broken bone. She fell and broke it. I went to see her yesterday and I brought her a present. When you break a bone, you have to go to the hospital. And you have to stay in bed."

As she continues, Karly elaborates the story of what happened to Nana Celia. As she does so, she adjusts the roles of the members of her doll community. One is named "Nurse" and another is designated the patient. Their interactions become a place for Karly to represent and make sense of her observations during her recent visit to the hospital. In the process, she rehearses and represents what she knows of broken bones, medical care, social roles, and so on.

Such usages tend to be incidental. That is, narrative forms are not always employed as deliberate and planned pedagogical structures in schools. In fact, sometimes the role of narrative is completely ignored, as is often the case in outdated mathematics instruction and in any curriculum area where the emphasis is on memorization of isolated facts. In other cases, narrative is sometimes used, but not as a tool for learning. Rather, cultural narratives are often imposed as "the way things are." This tendency is perhaps most obvious in some science classes where theories are frequently presented as the only plausible accounts for certain phenomena — as opposed to cultural narratives that are subject to ongoing revision and, from time-to-time, outright rejection.

The realization that humans are storying creatures is an important one for teachers — on many levels. In particular, a central element of teaching is to assist learners to understand how what they're studying is *about* them — where "about" is understood both in terms of being surrounded (as in "round about") and being implicated in (as in "about one's business"). The deliberate use of narrative structures — that is, telling and composing stories to incorporate new information into established understandings — is an important tool in this project, regardless of subject area.

● **Connecting Thoughts** ●

We, the authors, have used two very different rhetorical structures in this text: In some sections, we made deliberate use of narrative forms (i.e., Parts B and the boxed portions of Parts C); in other sections, we wrote in more standard academic prose (i.e., Parts A and the unboxed portions of Parts C).

Chances are that you "connected with" these contrasting styles in very different ways. It might be a useful exercise to glance back over parts of this chapter, looking at how dissimilar narrative forms might have affected your reading and learning.

Chapter 2

Learning and Teaching Structures

Structure is a prominent term in discussions of both building and biology. In reference to building, there are more deliberate senses of planning and step following — senses that are caught up in a web of associations which includes such notions as foundations, platforms, scaffolds, building blocks, hierarchies, frameworks, and so on.

The biological meaning of *structure* is quite different. Used in such phrases as "the structure of an organism" or "the structure of an ecosystem," the word points to the complex history of organic forms. Structure in this case is both caused and accidental, both familiar and unique.

The biologist's use of the term is more faithful to its original meaning. Linked to *strew* and *construe*, *structure* was first used to describe how things spread out or pile up in ways that can't be predetermined, but that aren't completely random either. When this notion was first applied to buildings some centuries ago, it made perfect sense. Such forms, for the most part, were not thought to be static or predetermined. Rather, they unfolded over years and decades as parts were added, destroyed, or otherwise altered. One built according to need, opportunity, or whimsy. The resulting edifices were thus not seen as permanent, but as evolving. That is, they were structures in the biological sense of ever-evolving forms.

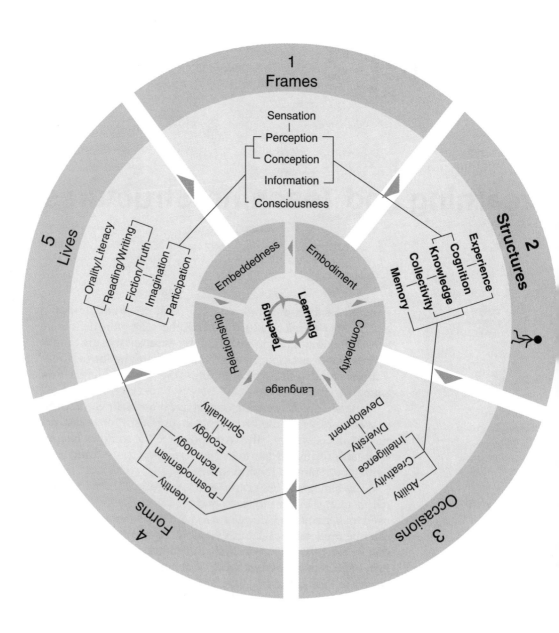

2A Learning Theories

An array of popular beliefs and common sense assumptions about the nature of thinking are embodied in such cultural icons as Rodin's *The Thinker*. Thinking, for example, is portrayed as solitary, personal, and private. Thinking is of the mind, best accomplished when the body is held still. Thinking demands strength and endurance: It is difficult, a manly struggle focused on reconciling one's inner world with the pregiven, unchanging outer world.

This chapter is a brief introduction to thinking about thinking — that is, to theories of cognition. It looks at past and current beliefs about how the mind works, what knowledge is, how learning happens, and what recent insights into thought might mean for teaching.

The premise of the writing is a simple one: All teaching rests on particular beliefs about learning. That is, as teachers, we all work from particular theories. (The word *theory* means, literally, a way of seeing.)

Such theories, however, are not often made explicit. Even though the language we use to discuss schooling is rife with assumptions and assertions about what learning is and how it happens, most people find it difficult to say what they actually believe. Indeed, much of the time, the prevailing wisdom seems to be that the processes of learning are so transparent, so commonsensical, that explicit formulation is unnecessary.

This is certainly the case among many discussions of teaching. By way of illustration, teaching practice is often characterized in terms of such categories of decision making as the content to be acquired, the activities through which students are to learn, and the teacher's role in facilitating the acquisition of content. An understanding of learning is presumed here. More pointedly, a theory of learning is being put forward in these sorts of statements. Learning is asserted to be a matter of *acquiring content* — a notion that assumes that knowledge is an object which is separate from and which must be apprehended by the learner. These principles are not made explicit, however, and they are difficult to uncover, in part because they reflect common sense. The notions that knowledge takes

Fig. 2.1. What is *thinking*?

Although it might seem that this question has an obvious answer, it is actually among the most complex issues ever investigated. Part of the difficulty of the question is that, by the time one is able to ask it, one's thinking is already conditioned by an array of cultural assumptions.

That means that thinking about thinking must involve a critical examination of what tends to be taken for granted. One strategy in this regard is to examine cultural artifacts, habits of speaking, and other forms for what they might reveal and conceal.

objective form and exists outside of knowing agents, and that learning is a matter of internalizing such knowledge, are knitted through our language. They are so pervasive that they're almost inaudible. Nevertheless, they have a profound shaping effect on teaching action.

The Language of Learning Theory

For centuries, a common habit among learning theorists has been to characterize cognitive processes in terms of prevailing technologies. Among the tools and machines that have been used to describe thinking are catapults, hydraulics, telegraphs, telephone switchboards, and, most recently, computers.

The further one goes back into history, the more inappropriate such comparisons seem. And, conversely, the more recent the metaphor, the easier it is to take it as a literal truth. Most of us would find the image of a catapult almost useless as a figurative device to understand learning, whereas we tend to slip uncritically into characterizing the brain as a computer. Consider, for example, com-

---

What is *theory*?

"The sun rises in the morning."

If pressed, few would actually agree with this statement's underlying premise that the sun is revolving around a stationary earth. Nevertheless, it is easier to interpret daybreak as being caused by a sun that rises than by an earth that spins us out of its own shadow.

The idea that the sun rises is an example of a theory. Derived from the Greek *theorein*, to gaze upon, the term *theory* refers to ways of seeing things. A theory is a system of interpretation that both helps us to make sense of experiences and, in turn, that focuses attention on particular events (while pushing others into the shadows).

Humans are irrepressible theorizers. We can't help but note similarities among diverse experiences, to see relationships among events, and to develop theories that explain these relationships (and that predict others). These theories — these ways of seeing — are necessary but limiting. We need them to make sense of a complex world. However, while enabling perception and interpretation, theory also determines what is (and is not) perceptible and comprehensible.

For the most part, like the idea that the sun rises, theories are transparent to the observer (and, hence, unavailable for critical examination). Usually this invisibility is unproblematic. At times, however, it becomes necessary to interrogate popular theories because they might fail to do the work they are intended to do. Such was certainly the case for the theory that the sun moves around the earth, and it is proving to be the case for many of the commonsensical notions about learning that underpin conventional teaching practice.

monplace references to learning as *acquiring and inputting data*, to learning difficulties as problems in *brain wiring*, to communication as *transmission and interfacing*, to thinking as *processing and compiling information*, to memorizing as *storing*, and to remembering as *retrieving and outputting*. Despite their seeming reasonableness, one might expect such notions to be a source of amusement to future generations in much the same way that references to other, now eclipsed technologies seem amusing today.

The fact that figurative language tends to slip into lit-

Where is knowledge?

The following classroom interaction, between a student and his teacher, was recently recorded during a mathematics lesson. It began when the teacher noticed that Sen was leaning forward in his desk, staring off to the side:

> "Sen, what are you doing?" the teacher asked.
> "Thinking," he responded.
> "What are you supposed to be doing?"
> "Working," Sen sighed, shifting back in his seat and picking up his pencil.

At first hearing, this exchange might seem unsettling. If one assumes that knowledge and understanding reside in the minds of knowers, and that human interaction can be understood in complicated (mechanical) figurative terms, then such an event must be interpreted as an instance of profound miscommunication. The cogs don't seem to be meshing here. Surely the teacher can't be suggesting that "thinking" is an inappropriate activity in a mathematics class!

Neither party in this interaction, however, interpreted this event as a breach in communication. Rather, it melted into the smooth flow of classroom events. That is, the meanings of the words spoken did not seem to reside in either of the speakers; rather, the meanings were shared. ("Shared" is not meant to suggest that Sen and his teacher had identical personal understandings of the words spoken. Rather, it is used in the sense that people can *share responsibility* or *share ownership*. The term "shared knowledge" is intended to suggest that knowledge does not

exist in one person or another, but in the capacity for joint activity.)

This incident demonstrates that knowledge, whether personal or collective, is not a "thing." For the most part, the images and metaphors that are used in discussing knowledge are object-based: Knowledge is something to be *acquired, grasped, held, possessed, exchanged,* and *wielded*. The metaphoric framing goes along with a habit of thinking that suggests knowledge can be located, either outside (*objective* knowledge) or inside the knower (*subjective* knowledge). In this figurative structure, learning becomes a process of bridge-building — a matter of connecting the external to the internal.

In contrast, more complex theories of knowing suggest that "where knowledge is" depends on the situation being examined. Sen clearly has particular personal interpretations of "thinking" and "working," as does his teacher — and so it's possible to see their understandings as "internal" (i.e., as part of their own complex subjectivities). However, in the instance described, word meanings seem to be dependent on actors-in-context — that is, the knowledge was part of the character of the Sen-and-teacher-in-math-class relationship, and this dynamic form has a particular character or identity. Knowledge, then, is not a *thing*. Rather, knowledge might better be thought in terms of potentiality, as a domain of possibilities. This metaphoric framing seems to be more useful when speaking of a social group's knowledge, or scientific knowledge, or personal knowledge, and so on.

eralness is both helpful and troublesome. On the one hand, by taking metaphors more literally (e.g., by thinking of the brain as though it really were a computer), we relieve ourselves of the need to re-think the purposes of the image every time it is invoked. On the other hand, as metaphors fade into transparency, they sometimes become mistaken as facts. Indeed, such is often the case with the "brain as computer" notion. Although the vibrant organic form of the brain actually has very little in common with the static architecture of an electronic computer — either structurally or dynamically — the belief that the two are alike is pervasive, resilient, and misleading.

Because of such tendencies, the task of thinking about thinking is a difficult one. While we rely on comparisons to understand this complex phenomenon, we must bear in mind that such stand-ins are always of limited utility. A particular analogy or metaphor might highlight some aspect of a phenomenon, but it will almost certainly push other aspects into conceptual oblivion. We must thus be mindful of the language being used. This brief introduction to learning theories, then, is not intended to be an exhaustive review of the history of cognitive studies. Rather, the intention is to examine the language of learning theories, attempting to identify key assumptions and assertions.

The approach taken is to briefly outline popular and recent perspectives on learning, highlighting their similarities and their differences. The particular focus is on those theories that are most prominent in conventional discussions of education, albeit that such theories tend to fade into an uncritical background.

Complicated versus Complex

There is one important distinction to be made at the outset, however, as it marks a recent and dramatic break in the tradition of thinking about thinking: *complicated* versus *complex*.

The distinction was first articulated by researchers working in the cross-disciplinary field of "complexity theory." They noted that, for the most part, understandings of virtually every phenomenon, from the functioning of a neuron to the emergence of the universe, have traditionally been founded on mechanical, cause-and-effect processes. That is, prompted by a notion first articulated by Isaac Newton and his contemporaries, there has been a

Acquire insight
Grasp a concept
Hold an opinion
Exchange ideas
Toss around ideas
etc.

Digest an idea
Ruminate
Raw data
Appetite for learning
Food for thought
etc.

Fig. 2.2. Beliefs and theories are not often made explicit. Rather, they tend to exist implicitly, in webs of association.

For instance, few people would be able to readily answer the question, "What is knowledge?" Yet, without having to give it any thought, we English speakers all use phrases like the ones here. In each case, a conception of personal knowledge as *some*

Solid foundations
The *basics*
Structure an argument
Build on ideas
Construct understandings
etc.

Flow of ideas
Drowning in details
Immersed in thought
Thirsting for knowledge
Soaking up information
etc.

sort of *physical object* is suggested — even though, on reflection, one must admit that there are problems with the metaphor.

Nevertheless, much of teaching practice is developed around the troublesome belief that knowledge is some *thing* — including that teaching is a matter of *delivering*, *relaying*, or *transmitting* and that learning is about *taking things in*.

habit of using clockwork and other machine-based metaphors to interpret events in the universe.

Complexity theorists describe clocks, refrigerators, and other human-produced mechanical systems as *complicated*. Such objects are the predictable sums of their parts. Their behaviors are planned, directed, and determined by their architectures. A familiarity with each of the components that are brought together in such machines is all that is required to predict the activity of the resulting wholes. These sorts of objects are intended to fulfill specific functions and they operate according to deliberate designs.

For a large part of the history of Western science, it has been assumed that most phenomena in the universe are similarly mechanical — that is, that understanding "how things work" and predicting their behaviors is a matter of reducing them to their fundamental parts. However, more recently, it has become apparent that this mindset is inappropriate for the study of, for example, large scale economies, brains, and weather systems. Researchers have realized that these systems are *not* comprised of inert cogs or switches or microchips, but are themselves collectives of other, smaller dynamical systems. Economies, for example, emerge from, but are not reducible to, the activities of citizens. The human body arises from, but is something more than, the interactions of a heart, a brain, and other organs. These organs, in turn, are comprised of and supersede collections of living cells and neurons. And so on.

These are *complex* systems. They exceed their components. They are more spontaneous, unpredictable, and volatile — that is, *alive* — than complicated systems. Unlike complicated (mechanical) systems, which are constructed with particular purposes in mind, complex systems are self-organizing, self-maintaining, dynamic, and adaptive. In brief, whereas complicated systems tend to be framed in the language of classical physics, complex systems draw more on biology. As such, terms like *organic*, *ecological*, and *evolutionary* have come to figure much more prominently in discussions of such social phenomena as learning, teaching, and schooling.

In terms of studies of learning and cognition, this distinction is vital to understanding recent changes in thinking. Traditional (and commonsensical) theories have cast learning as a complicated (mechanical) process, and this formulation has prompted efforts to dissect and prescribe classroom activities. More recent discussions, however, have sought to render learning (and teaching) more complex. These matters are elaborated below.

It is important at the outset to mention that, in the interests of brevity and clarity, it is only possible to offer a caricature of the most prominent ways of thinking about thinking. All of the varied discourses mentioned here are far more sophisticated than any brief analysis can suggest.

Complicated Learning Theories

In this section, popular 20th Century learning theories are discussed in terms of two main categories: *behaviorisms* and *mentalisms*. On the surface, these theories often appear to be flatly contradictory. They are grouped together, however, because they all rely on a complicated (mechanistic) interpretation of cognition. They also share other key assumptions — assumptions that, for the most part, seem commonsensical.

It is important to state at the outset that each of these theories has provided us with important insights into learning. The purpose here is not to demonstrate that they are wrong or inadequate, but to show how they rest on particular assumptions which both limit their utility and which, if taken up uncritically, can profoundly misinform teaching.

A key shared assumption of each of these theories, for example, is that thought happens deep inside the individual's body. The cognizing agent is seen as isolated and insulated — from other thinkers and from the world — and, hence, she or he is forced to generate unconfirmable hypotheses about the external (real) universe based on the information received through untrustworthy perceptual organs. Mental activity is assumed to be distinct from physical experience. This separation of the mind from the body sets up a cascade of other dichotomies that are taken for granted: thought versus action, self versus other, knower versus known world, subjective versus objective.

Behaviorisms. So profound is the assumed separation of mental (internal) activity and physical (external) experience that the dominant school of psychology for the first half of the 20th Century, behaviorism, actually began with

> What really matters is the match between outer reality and one's inner model of reality. Hence we must focus on the learner's internal **mental** models.

> All we have to work with are the external physical consequences of internal processes. Hence we must observe and seek to affect visible **behaviors**.

SHAKY COMMON GROUND

Mental is separate from physical; Learners are isolated and insulated from one another; Learning is a matter of internalizing a pregiven, external reality.

the premise that mental functioning should be ignored. Thinking is invisible and not directly accessible to the researcher or educator. Hence, it was argued, the attention of psychologists and teachers should be focused on observable and recordable gross behaviors.

The fact that behaviorism focuses on overt physical actions, however, does not mean that this framework rejects the inner workings of the mind. Rather, the case is that behaviorist theorists regard thought processes as subjective, idiosyncratic, and not directly accessible. In contrast, overt physical behaviors are obvious, measurable, and can be influenced through direct interventions. It follows that this category of behavior is the more appropriate location for scientific analysis.

A second assumption of behaviorism is that all behavior is lawful and determined, leading to a focus on straightforward causes and effects. Specifically, this framework seeks to identify and to train associations between particular events and particular behaviors. It was demonstrated, for example, that people tended to develop and act on associations among disparate phenomena — that is, they were self-trained in very much the same way that dogs can be trained to salivate at the ringing of a bell if, for a period, it is rung just before feeding time. Similarly, and once again supported by research on both humans and other species, it was demonstrated that long chains of complicated and counter-instinctive behaviors can be taught through careful administration of rewards, promises of reward, punishments, and threats of punishment.

One of behaviorism's major contributions to educational discourse is its demonstration that learning does not necessarily rely on explicit formulation or conscious awareness on the part of the learner. Rather, a good deal of unconscious learning, leading to significant and persistent changes in behavior, is constantly occurring. Competency in social settings, fluency in language, dexterity in sophisticated physical tasks — one's abilities to learn in such domains far exceeds human capacity for conscious observation and interpretation. This fact, behaviorism argues, should prompt educators' main focus toward the environmental circumstances — and, specifically, the usually unnoticed structures of reward and punishment — that work to shape the learner's activities.

For these sorts of reasons, behaviorism has tended to

Fig. 2.3. Popular theories of learning, although often appearing incompatible or even flatly contradictory, tend to rely on similar assumptions. Mentalism and behaviorism, for example, share a fairly mechanistic, cause-and-effect world view. As well, both rely on a series of interrelated and commonsensical, but problematic, dichotomies — including mind/body, internal/external, self/other, individual/collective, whole/part, and human/nature.

frame its recommendations for teaching in terms of feedback and reward systems, of well-sequenced and incremental learning structures, of clearly articulated learning goals, and of unambiguous and consistent teacher (or trainer) actions — in short, of control. These culminated in the radical assertion that virtually any learner could be trained to fulfill virtually any role, provided that the learning experiences were sufficiently well structured.

In terms of discussions of formal education, this learning-as-training motif has now been largely rejected, in part because of the way that it deliberately overlooks the distinctly human capacities to imagine possibilities and to radically change behaviors on the basis of such imaginings.

Nevertheless, many aspects of behaviorism have settled into the common sense of schooling practices. Two places where behaviorist sensibilities continue to be prominent are lesson planning and classroom management. For example, the practice of structuring syllabi and programs of learning in terms of sequential lists of isolated facts or competencies, while predating the theory, was given a scientific basis by behaviorism. Such curriculum structures assumed and helped to further entrench the beliefs that learning is linear and that personal knowledge is cumulative, both of which are problematic.

Formal curricula that are structured around these assumptions of accumulation and linearity are tied to popular conceptions of "lessons" and "lesson planning." In many teacher education programs, for instance, lesson writing activities begin with the statement of concise and prescriptive "learning objectives." (In many cases, these are still called "behavioral objectives.") Subsequently, prospective teachers are asked to parse the imagined lesson into discrete sections and to pre-specify both their own and learners' activities in detail. Teaching and planning for teaching are, in this frame, truly conceived as complicated (that is, mechanical) processes.

The same mindset is evident in popular discourse around discipline and classroom management. Rather than considering such concerns in terms of complex human dynamics, these topics are often addressed in terms of programs by which rigid standards of behavior are identified and enforced through equally rigid programs of reward and punishment. With its ability to mask its prescriptions in terms of scientific research, these behaviorist manage-

CLASSICAL CONDITIONING

1: Natural Association

2: Conditioning Process

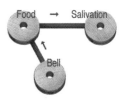

3: Conditioned Association

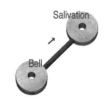

Fig. 2.4. *Behaviorism* refers to those theories of learning that are principally concerned with observable behaviors — or, more specifically, with constructing associations between particular stimuli and particular responses.

Two manners of forming such links are illustrated. On the left is a case of "classical conditioning," whereby a neutral stimulus (a bell) comes to elicit the same involuntary response (salivation) as a nonneutral stimulus (food). On the

OPERANT CONDITIONING

1: Desired Association

Command: "SPEAK!" → Barking

2: Conditioning Process

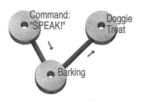

Command: "SPEAK!"   Doggie Treat

Barking

3: Conditioned Association

Command "SPEAK!"

Barking

right, an instance of "operant conditioning" is illustrated. A reward (doggie treat) is used in an effort to increase the probability that a stimulus (the command "Speak") will elicit a particular voluntary response (barking).

Such learning mechanisms, it is asserted, can be used to create long and very complicated chains of behavior. This theory of learning underpins teaching practices that focus on mastery of isolated skills which have been linearly sequenced.

ment programs have often been presented as the only fair-minded, even-handed, and emotionally neutral approaches to maintaining orderly classrooms.

Once again, the reduction of human relationality to mechanical interactions is evident. It is important to note, however, that behaviorism did not define this mindset. Rather, its implicit cause-and-effect logic, like the belief that human behavior is subject to prediction and control, was never interrogated. These assumptions were part of the common sense of the moment. Indeed, for most theorists, they may have been beyond question at the time.

Before leaving this topic, it should be re-emphasized that behaviorism is not "wrong." In fact, its principles have been used to great success in many situations, especially those that involve suppressing or overriding inhibitions, phobias, and resistances. Fear of spiders, smoking habits, nervous gestures, and so on can be greatly ammeliorated through focused and consistent responses. As well, those human activities that are largely unmediated by language, including automatic and nonconscious responses, are good candidates for behaviorist conditioning. Further, virtually all current animal training is informed by behaviorist principles.

Such strategies are successful in large part because behaviorists have been willing to address the role of nonconscious processes and automaticity in learning. However, in focusing *only* on such processes, behaviorism places humans in the same category as rats and birds.

More specifically, the problem is that behaviorism rests on the premise that the universe is mechanical and ultimately predictable — that is, complicated. This assumption is adequate for affecting some behaviors, especially in less complex species. However, it becomes increasingly problematic as it is applied to more and more complex phenomena. For example, the implicit linear and causal logic of behaviorism is useless for making sense of children's early mastery of language, much less the complex webs of association and meaning that quickly arise as young children begin to experiment with words and stories.

Mentalisms. Although dominant for much of the 20th Century, behaviorism has always had its detractors. In particular, while acknowledging that visible activity might provide evidence that learning is occurring, many argued that one must focus one's analyses on internal processes in order to understand the *mental* phenomena of learning and thinking.

Of course, the idea that studies of mental phenomena must focus on mental activity is not a new one. Nor is it one that directly contradicts the behaviorist approach to studying learning and cognition. Both attitudes, in fact, can be traced back to the earliest of written records. Each relies on the idea that the mental is separate from the physical — and this was a well-established notion in the writings of the ancient Greeks, among others. The difference between focusing on external behaviors and focusing on the internal activity, then, is more a matter of emphasis than of mindset. Nevertheless, despite the similarity of their assumptions, the two frameworks offer very different prescriptions for educational practice.

Behaviorism's predominance in the 20th Century is something of an historical anomaly. Most discussions of learning and cognition, prior to and since behaviorism's dominance, have been concerned with trying to understand how the mind works. Among these discussions, by far the most prominent perspective — in both historic and contemporary terms — is that learning is a matter of assembling an internal representation (or mental model) of an external world. Working from the assumption that cognition is a brain-based event (notably, *mind* and *brain* tend to be treated synonymously), these mentalist discourses focus on the fit between the "real world" and the learner's subjective, internal constructions of that world. Put differently, for the mentalist, learning is a process through which learners piece together a subjective model of an objective reality.

Historically, the imagined process of assembling this inner model was described in terms of sculpting, painting, writing, theorizing, and/or projecting. More recently, the process has come to be framed in terms of computer metaphors. Rather than imagining personal conceptions in terms of actual models or theories, the predominant current interpretation casts these inner representations and models in terms of digital encodings in neurological networks. In spite of this shift in figurative framing, though, the distinction between internal and external is preserved.

It is this perspective on learning and thinking — this learning theory — that serves as the backdrop for most

Fig. 2.5. *Mentalism* refers to a broad range of theories, all of which rely on the premise that learning is a matter of building an internal model or representation of an external, pregiven reality.

Historically, these theories have drawn on prevailing technologies as sources of descriptive analogies. Early in the 20th Century, for example, movie technology was used:

current discussions of cognition. It has become, as mentioned, commonsensical. In particular, it is this theory that is most persistently enacted in the conventional classroom, where teaching is overwhelmingly cast as an attempt to have learners *internalize* an array of external, ostensibly objective knowledge. Despite the fact that such metaphors as "mind as sponge" or "learner as empty vessel" are widely rejected, the project of schooling tends to be interpreted in terms of doing precisely what these sorts of metaphors suggest: somehow ensuring that something that begins on the outside gets inside the learner.

That is, many conventional practices — including the delineation of what learners are to *acquire* and the administration of standardized tests — rest on the assumption that learning is a process of "taking things in," "grasping ideas," "building solid foundations," and "dealing with cold, hard facts." Once again, in spite of clearly figurative natures of such notions, they have become so literal that it is sometimes difficult to think about alternatives.

One of the most problematic consequences of this manner of thinking about learning has been a proliferation of uncritical discussions of "learner types" and "learning styles." Such terms as *visual* or *auditory learners*, or *concrete* or *abstract thinkers* are constructions that rely on the assumption that learning is a matter of filtering knowledge from the outside to the inside in order to build internal models. While it is almost certainly the case that different learners make varied uses of their sensory modalities — and that people, for the most part, do not think alike — such discussions often reduce the complexities of learning and teaching to simplistic prescriptions.

With regard to the practical implications of mentalism for schooling, the principal task of teaching is most often described in terms of ensuring that learner conceptualizations (which are seen as fallible and dynamic) match with external reality (which tends to be treated as pregiven and unchanging). In fact, "understanding" is generally defined in terms of the extent of match between internal model and external reality. As with behaviorism, a host of dichotomies are assumed and enacted in this conception: learner versus world, knower versus knowledge, teacher versus learner, and so on.

Also like behaviorism, schooling is seen as a linear process, one which seeks to minimize ambiguity through a

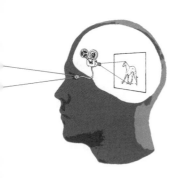

eyes were seen as cameras, memory as recorded images, imagination and thought as projection, and so on. (A problem here is that a second, internal observer is implied — one who, presumably, has her or his own internal observer.)

More recently, electronic technologies have been taken up, leading to a different (but similarly problematic) set of metaphors for cognition.

highly structured pedagogical style. Teaching is seen as highly complicated, but *only* complicated. Its complexities tend to go unappreciated.

Common Ground. Although they are usually presented as opposites, behaviorism and mentalism are better thought of as flip sides of the same coin. The simple fact that both lines of thought seem to comfortably co-exist in most textbooks, curriculum guides, and classrooms indicates a deeper compatibility than might be expected.

There is, in fact, a significant school of thought, often referred to as *neobehaviorism,* that is concerned with both observable stimuli and responses (the domain of behaviorism) *and* with the neurophysiological events that mediate between them (the domain of mentalism).

These theories of learning share the same fundamental premise: that behavior and cognition are mechanical processes — and, hence, law-abiding. Good teaching is thus highly technical work, involving abilities to isolate factors, monitor circumstances, and manipulate causes. Learning to teach, then, comes to be seen as a process of mastering a set of prespecified skills — competencies which are often gathered together on checklists and in teaching manuals. As with the underlying theory of learning, this conception of teaching is a complicated one. There is an appreciation of the difficulty of the task, but this difficulty is interpreted overwhelmingly in terms of classical mechanics. So conceived, the teacher's principal worries are with order, control, prediction of outcomes, and so on.

Complex Learning Theories

While such views on learning and teaching were predominant through most of the 20th Century, other perspectives have also been represented in discussions of education. In particular, *holist* philosophies have figured prominently.

A holistic understanding of a phenomenon involves seeing that phenonenon in its entirety. In contrast, behaviorist and mentalist theories rest on the assumption that full understandings of a learning event can be obtained by reducing it to its most basic components.

Holist theories underpinned the broad movement toward "child-centered teaching" that rose to some prominence in the 1970s. Unfortunately, however, these perspec-

Fig. 2.6. The terms *complicated, holist,* and *complex* are being used here to refer to three different mindsets or worldviews.

A *complicated* theory is one that aims to reduce phenomena to elemental components, root causes, and fundamental laws. In this view, a full understanding of a clock would arise from a detailed knowledge of each of its parts. (In fact, the clock serves as the most popular image for this worldview. The idea of a "clockwork universe" arose when the mechanical clock was the most sophisticated human technology available.)

A *holist* view of a clock would see it as a functional whole, something that is more than the sum of its parts. This includes an appreciation of the interdependencies of its parts.

A *complex* theory embraces both complicated and holist views, but also argues that an understanding of a clock demands an attention to the fact that the clock is embedded in social and natural environments — which compels considerations of the roles that a clock plays in shaping social lives, the historical conditions that supported its invention, the materials involved in its construction, the effects of its use on the natural environment, and so on.

tives lacked a scientific basis and, as a result, never really congealed into a coherent theory of learning and teaching. It was not until the late 1980s that a broader shift in thinking opened the door to this possibility. Over the past decade, radically new theories of learning and cognition have emerged, theories that work from a very different set of assumptions from previous models.

In particular, new theoretical offerings problematize the reliances of behaviorist and mentalist theories on an array of dichotomies. While acknowledging that all thinking depends on the ability to draw distinctions, these more recent (and more complex) theories have sought to instill awarenesses of the figurative devices used and the assumptions made. The principal critique offered of behaviorist and mentalist models is *not* that they are incorrect, but that they are not mindful of what is taken for granted.

For example, the commonsensical separation of mind and body (or mental and physical, or thought and action) within popular theories is largely rejected within more recent discourses. Rather than casting thought as a phe-

Learning Systems

At the core of complex learning theories is a particular perspective on what constitutes a "learner" or a "learning system." Perhaps the best way to make the point is to provide an example of one such system:

Sometime in the late 1970s or early 1980s, zebra mussels — tiny, but prolific mollusks — were introduced to the Great Lakes in North America. No one is sure how it happened, but its likely occurred when a cargo ship from Europe purged it ballast tanks after delivering a shipment.

Having no natural enemies, the mussels thrived, quickly spreading through all of the Great Lakes. As their population grew, many ominous predictions were made about irreversible environmental disasters. The mussels, it was asserted, would almost certainly upset a fragile and delicate balance.

So what's happened?

There have been two main consequences so far. First, it has cost a few billion dollars to clear the mollusks from underwater grates and valves. Second, the mussels have actually helped to *clarify* the turgid waters of the Great Lakes, straining out great quantities of suspended matter as they pump lake water through their systems.

In other words, the net result has been far short of the predicted disaster.

Why?

Simply because the ecological web of life in the Great Lakes does *not* exist in a delicate balance. Rather, it is a dynamic, robust, ever-evolving, and constantly learning system. And zebra mussels have now been incorporated (i.e., *embodied*) into that system. Put differently, the form, the qualities, the responses, and the sorts of patterns that the system follows have all changed. That is, *the system has learned* — in the same way that humans, immune systems, societies, species, and so on, learn.

The point: Any complex system that can adapt itself to changing circumstances is a learning system.

nomenon that is *about* the world, thinking is recognized to be *part of* the universe. Although it may seem like a small shift in conception, the implications of this notion are profound. Within theories that assume a separation of the world and the knower, the universe is seen to remain constant while conceptions change. For theories that reject this dichotomy, the universe is understood to change when a thought changes, because that thought is not merely in the universe or about the universe. Rather, it is a dynamic part of an ever-changing reality.

That is, learning is not seen as a "taking in" or a "theorizing about" a reality that is external to and separate from the learner. Rather, learning is coming to be understood as a participation in the world, a co-evolution of knower and known that transforms both. This change in emphasis is consistent with a shift in thinking across virtually every realm of academic inquiry, away from machine-based metaphors and toward more organic, biologically-based notions. (The same transition in thinking is announced by the distinction drawn between complicated objects and complex forms.) A living being cannot be understood solely, or even principally, in terms of an assemblage of parts. Rather, it must be seen, simultaneously, as a collectivity of interacting subsystems *and* as a unity that transcends those subsystems *and* as a dynamic element within a grander unity. The actions of a complex form, then, are never entirely predictable.

Complex learning theories are ones that regard the learner in such complex terms. This change in focus implies a different dynamic and very different pedagogical emphases. In particular, such theories suggest that learning is *dependent on*, but cannot be *determined by* teaching.

The following introduction to some of these theories is arranged according to the main focus of each, beginning with the complex form of the individual learner, then to the complex form of collective knowledge, then to the complex forms of culture and society. Finally the camera is pulled back to consider the complex form of life itself.

The discussion of each framework is followed by a brief examination of some of the teaching concerns that might be prompted by that framework. These examinations are developed around a topic that is found in most middle school curricula: an introduction to various models of the solar system.

Fig. 2.7. In popular terms, evolution is regarded as a steady progression toward perfection. This movement is usually thought to be linear and upward, as suggested by metaphors of *ladders* or *trees* of evolution — and as seems to be assumed by those illustrations that portray a smooth ascent from scrambling simian to weapon-toting Caucasian male.

Recently, an alternative theory has arisen — one that is based on *adequacy* rather than *perfection* (i.e., "survival of the fit" rather than "survival of the fittest"). In this frame, evolu-

Constructivism. A first category of complex learning theories focuses on issues of individual cognition. These "constructivist" discourses work from the premise that the learner's basis of meaning is found in her or his direct experience with a dynamic and responsive world. Put differently, these theories assert that we can only form concepts through our bodily actions. Hence, *every* understanding that one might have of oneself, others, or the world is abstracted from the bodily, physical sensations that arise through perceptual and motor actions.

Constructivism challenges such dichotomies as mind-versus-body and knower-versus-knowledge. Cognition is understood as a process of maintaining an adequate fit with one's ever-changing circumstances, as opposed to assembling an internal mental model of an external world — and it is this notion that marks the most radical departure from commonsensical theories of learning.

This shift in thinking about thinking is not a subtle one. Learning is no longer seen as a process of "taking things in" but of adapting one's actions to ever-changing circumstances. Important, "action" in this context refers to more than observable behaviors. Brain activity, perceptions, and other dynamical processes are also included.

In the same way that the notion of action is expanded, so is the concept of "knowing." Popularly, knowing and knowledge are used to refer to concepts and ideas that have been explicitly stated, whether subjective interpretations or objective facts. Constructivism works from the premise that this understanding of knowing is greatly impoverished, as it ignores a wealth of unformulated knowings that are enacted in every moment of our existences. Most of the time we don't know what we know.

A thought experiment: You have been put in charge of an android that is capable of the same range of physical movement as most humans, but which is, as yet, unprogrammed. Your task is to provide this robot with everything it needs to know to go to the nearest supermarket, purchase the items necessary for this evening's meal, and proceed home where it will prepare dinner.

Such daily routines present little challenge to most humans. Even those raised in dramatically different cultural settings are quickly able to learn what is needed to accomplish such feats. But beneath the surface of the obvious activity are such competencies as walking, opening

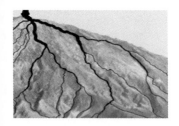

tion is not seen to be linear, nor to be driven by competition and selection. Rather, evolution is a creative process that is prompted by and that contributes to a dynamic and evolving landscape of possibility. This post-Darwinian theory sees change as principally a matter of *co-evolution* of agent and setting. The guiding image is not an upward climb toward a pre-given goal, but a drift or flow that leads to a grand diversity of viable possibilities.

It is this perspective on evolution that infuses current discussions of cognition.

doors, identifying supermarkets — competencies that are clearly parts of what we *know*, but which are not usually considered when discussing one's knowledge. As developed in Chapter 1, they are the unseen part of the iceberg of our knowledge. We know more than we know we know.

More important, with this conception of cognition, knowing does not reside in the brain. Rather, as hinted by the ways that bodies *know* how to walk, that hearts *know* how to beat rhythmically, and so on, cognition is understood as *embodied*. That is, the biological body is not a structure through which one learns, but a structure that learns. In this way, constructivism embraces an important behaviorist insight. However, constructivism rejects the assertion that such learning is reducible to structures of reward and punishment and places more emphasis on the flexible creativity of the learner to adapt to complex and dynamic circumstances.

In some ways, this emphasis appears to be more closely aligned with mentalist sensibilities as it seems to indicate a focus on the mental. There is a profound difference, however. For the constructivist, formal learning is a matter of interpreting and re-interpreting one's primal body experiences — and, hence, a main concern of teaching is the provision of rich activities that might be interpreted. Constructivism thus rejects the ideal of a body held still and forced to face one direction in a rigid desk — a model of the learner that rests on the notion that learning is a mental activity which requires the suppression (rather than the participation) of the physical.

Implicit in this conception of embodied knowing is an acknowledgment that bodily action is not simply an external demonstration of internalized understanding. Rather, bodily action *is* understanding as the knower seeks to maintain fit with her or his circumstances.

Of course, such circumstances are as dynamic as one's knowings/doings, and this realization has prompted some to suggest that, just as cognition is spread through one's body, so it is distributed across the objects of one's world. That is, departing from the commonsensical notion that thought and memory reside in the brain, cognition is stretched beyond neural processes and bodily action to include more worldly objects. Our thinking, for example, can be greatly enabled by books, pencils, internet access, and so on.

Fig. 2.8. Motivating learners to learn is one of the most prominent issues in current discussions of teaching.

This *complicated* worry makes sense if learning is thought to be a movement along a straight path. It fits with concerns for keeping learners on track, getting on with things, and achieving prespecified goals.

Complex learning theories, however, suggest that the idea of *motivating learners to learn* is much like *motivating water to flow downhill*. We are all learning, constantly and inevitably.

The metaphor of flowing water can also be extended to highlight a theme that is woven through every chapter of this book: The path of learning can never by *determined by* the teacher. However, the path of learning is *dependent on* the teacher — along with a host of other contingencies.

Constructivism and the Solar System

What might a constructivist say is important when teaching about models of the solar system?

Working from the premise that personal knowledge derives from one's experiences in the world, the teacher whose practice is informed by constructivist ideas might begin by wondering about the sorts of observations that led our ancestors to develop their theories of the universe.

Except for the last few centuries, the most popular models of the universe have been *geocentric* — that is, earth-centered. This isn't really surprising. One of the easiest ways to make sense of the movements of heavenly bodies is to imagine that they are spinning around a stationary earth.

Even though most middle school students will be well acquainted with more current *heliocentric* (sun-centered) models of our solar system, some would be hard pressed to explain how such models account for day and night, not to mention the seasons, variations in day-length, eclipses, phases of the moon, and other celestial phenomena. In fact, quizzing young adolescents on such matters often reveals that they are working from a predominantly geocentric perspective, in spite of the knowledge that the earth moves around the sun.

Such personal theories are derived from years of experience, and so it's unlikely that the straightforward presentation of a new theoretical framework will do much to interrupt well established habits of thinking. A more effective instructional emphasis might be a series of activities designed to highlight the relationships among the movements of the earth, the sun, and other bodies — in the process demonstrating the power of a sun-centered model of the solar system.

For example, the connection between earth's rotation and sunrise might be explored with a globe and a flashlight. From there, students might examine lunar phases by positioning a moon (e.g., a ball) in various locations around the earth (i.e., a student observer) as both are illuminated by a distant sun (e.g., a flashlight). Similar activities could be set up to examine other astronomical events, and many of these could be structured by the students themselves.

In each case, students would be asked to express their observations and to offer theoretical accounts for what was noticed. In addition, discussions and assignments might be developed around critical readings of other theories, including those suggested by everyday phrases (e.g., "sunrise"). In the process, students might begin to better appreciate that a heliocentric model is actually far more sophisticated than it might first appear.

Social Constructionism. As well, we are usually better thinkers in the presence of others, particularly others whose competencies are more developed.

This extending of cognition beyond the skin marks the overlap of constructivism and social constructionism, which focuses more on small groups (such as pairs of students, teacher-learner interactions, and classroom groupings) as learners build understandings and come to shared conclusions. Much less concerned with individual sense-making, social constructionism focuses on conversation patterns, relational dynamics, and collective characters. Cognition, in this frame, is always collective: embedded in, enabled by, and constrained by the social phenomenon of language; caught up in layers of history and tradition; confined by well-established boundaries of acceptability.

In other words, rather than focusing on the biological body, social constructionisms focus on social bodies. Following complexity theory, the use of the term "body" here is more than figurative. Rather, the suggestion is that collectives of persons are capable of actions and understandings that transcend the capabilities of the individuals on their own, in the same way that cells come together to form organs, and organs to form biological bodies. Collective integrities — that is, characters or identities of collectivities — emerge, defined by joint interests, shared assumptions, common sense.

Social constructionism has a great deal in common with constructivism. Both focus on bodies (for constructivism, the body biologic; for social constructionism, more collective bodies, including student bodies and bodies of knowledge). In terms of the relationships between these different bodies, it is understood that the whole (in this case, a collectivity) is enfolded in and unfolds from the part (in this case, the individual) — and this sensibility marks a

---

Social Constructionism and the Solar System

What might a social constructionist highlight when teaching about models of the solar system?

A possible emphasis in the context of a science class is the way that this particular topic might be used to frame the question, What is science? In particular, through an examination of the evolution of models of the solar system, one might also study the ways in which scientific theories emerge, the twists and turns in their development, the criteria for their success, and so on.

One might ask, How did Euclid's geometry enable Ptolemy to develop his particular geocentric model? What sorts of observations prompted Copernicus to propose a heliocentric model? How have fractal geometry and chaos theory prompted revisions of the model created by Copernicus? What do these instances tell us about the nature of "scientific proof"? What makes one theory better than another theory?

More broadly, What does science do? How does scientific inquiry differ from other modes of thought and re-search? What are the roles of discussion, debate, and experiment in science? How might in-class activities reflect the work of scientists?

Notably, the history of heliocentrism is a troubled one. When first introduced, the ideas were scorned by scientific and non-scientific establishments alike. It might be interesting to contrast this history with that of other theories, such as Continental Drift, Evolution, the Gaia Hypothesis, and Chaos Theory — all of which were met with tremendous skepticism, yet all of which have since become part of the scientific mainstream.

It would not be necessary — in fact, it might even be ill-advised — to take on these sorts of questions and issues directly. Instead, they might be better considered a sort of persistent undercurrent of science class. While the explicit foci of lessons move from topics in biology to chemistry to astronomy and so on, the teacher should always be aware of what holds such ideas together. Otherwise there is a risk that "science," which is a particular way of asking questions about the world, might be reduced to a collection of facts to be mastered and models to be memorized.

profound departure from complicated or mechanical approaches to thinking about thinking.

In terms of other commonalties between constructivism and social constructionism, both draw on evolutionary and ecological metaphors to describe the dynamical characters (that is, the "knowing") of bodies. And both highlight the ways that what an agent knows is inseparable from what that agent does, which is in turn inseparable from what or who that agent is. Knowing is doing is being.

Cultural and Critical Discourses. This sort of assertion pushes the discussion toward an even grander corpus: society. Over the past few decades, a number of educational researchers working from a range of philosophical perspectives have sought to demonstrate that learning and knowing, whether focusing on the level of the individual or the social group, can only be understood when considered in the broader cultural context.

These cultural and critical discourses have worked to interrupt narrowly focused discussion of formal education by shifting the topic of conversation from the individual's

Cultural and Critical Discourses and the Solar System

What might cultural and critical discourses have to say about models of the solar system as a topic of study?

Historically, the transition from a geocentric to a heliocentric model of the solar system marks some dramatic transitions in Western sensibilities. It occurred at the dawn of the modern scientific era, and the rise of science was coupled to the emergences of capitalism, industrialization, urbanization, European imperialism, and other events.

Cultural and critical theorists might be interested in the social and societal movements that contributed to and that emerged from these sorts of historical transitions. In this case, one might question the impact of science on various social structures. One might inquire into who was in the authority and how they got there. One might wonder why all the main players in this history are European and male.

The emergence of heliocentrism  corresponded with and contributed to a break between religion and science. Prevailing religious doctrine could not readily accommodate displacement of the earth from the center of the universe, and history has recorded many tales of menace and torture as intellectual authority shifted from priests to scientists.

A question that might be asked here is, How is a world structured by religious faith different from one structured by scientific doubt? And how are they the same? More pointedly, How has the overwhelming success of modern science been woven into contemporary world views? How have these world views supported the cultural imperialism that has unfolded over the past several centuries?

Such questions give a preliminary sense of the issues that might be addressed in an ongoing examination of how personal perceptions are shaped by collective sensibilities.

efforts to shape an understanding of the world to the manners in which the world shapes the understanding of the individual. In particular, with reference to formal schooling, some of the issues examined by these theorists have included the ideal of individual autonomy, the creation and maintenance of societal norms (gender, racial, class, etc.), and the privileging of certain domains of knowledge.

These discourses also make use of evolutionary and ecological notions — albeit that these tend to be coupled to other interpretive discourses (e.g., Marxism, various feminisms, psychoanalysis, queer theory, etc.). And, like constructivism and social constructionism, they also focus their analyses on a particular body — in this case, the body politic. As with the other discourses, cognition is not seen as something that is located *in* a body, but rather as a means of describing the relationships that afford that body a coherence or that enable that body to maintain its viability and integrity within a larger, similarly dynamic and responsive context. (This rather difficult idea is developed further in Chapter 5A.) Individual knowing, collective knowledge, and culture become three nested, self-similar levels of one phenomenon. As such, bodily identities — whether individual, communal, or cultural — are never unitary, never stable, never neatly bounded, and, hence, never able to be fully represented.

Ecological Theories. The same themes that link constructivist, constructionist, and cultural theories can be (and have been) extended in both microscopic and macroscopic directions. Such extensions to smaller and larger bodies have helped to demonstrate that cognition is not just a human and social phenomenon, but a biological event.

On the subhuman level, for example, much of recent medical research has been developed around a conception of individual bodily organs as cognitive. In particular, HIV/ AIDS-prompted studies have demonstrated that the immune system learns, forgets, recognizes, hypothesizes, errs, and recovers in a complex dance with other (bodily and non-bodily) systems. Neither fully autonomous nor a mere mechanical component of a larger whole, it seems that one's immune system is related to oneself in the same way that the individual is related to the collective. That is, the immune system (and other sub-bodily systems) can and should be seen as a cognizing body in its own right.

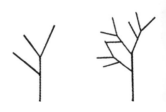

Fig. 2.9. Fractal images — like those on pages 16, 65, and 72 — can be generated using a special sort of *recursive* process.

A recursive process can be thought of in terms of a series of elaborations, where the starting place of each stage is the ending place of the previous stage.

For example, the parsley image above is generated by starting with a 3-pronged fork. The first step in the recursive growth process is to apply 3 tines to each of the prongs of the original image. The same happens to the new tines in the next step, and so on until the image is complete.

Fractal forms illustrate how surprising detail can quickly emerge from simple beginnings. Extended to a discussion of learning, the notion of recursion can help us to understand how learners are able to elaborate simple experiences and naïve understandings into sophisticated insights, sometimes with amazing speed.

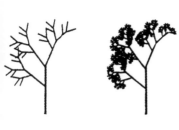

Similar developments have been occurring among neurological studies of the brain. One startling conclusion has been that cognition, even when understood narrowly as brain functioning, does not seem to be a globally emergent process. Rather, as one moves through the nested layers of brain organization, it appears that all levels of functioning are similarly patterned — and, importantly, describable in terms of the same evolutionary and ecological metaphors used by constructivist, constructionist, and cultural theorist. In other words, the neuron is cognitive in the same way the brain is cognitive. Both co-evolve with their dynamic contexts.

The same usage of evolutionary and ecological notions is occurring among those interested in global ecology. Perhaps finding its clearest articulation in the "Gaia Hypothesis," and gaining in popularity as a way to understand humanity's role in the biosphere, this conception of life on Earth regards our species as a mere subsystem of a larger

---

Ecological Theories and the Solar System

What might an ecological theorist highlight in a study of different models of the solar system?

One might begin with the question, What happened to beliefs about the nature of the universe when the earth — and humanity with it — lost its status as the center of creation to become a minor planet that orbits an average star on the edge of a typical galaxy?

Historically, the shift to a heliocentric conception of the solar system corresponded to a dramatic reconfiguration of humanity's relationship to the nonhuman. In particular, the change in world view contributed to a redefinition of humanity's role in the universe: less as participants in an unfolding creation, and more as detached observers of a believed-to-be-stable reality. (There was no simple causal relation here. See Chapter 4A for an elaborated discussion of the topic.)

By way of specific example, the word *planet* derives from a Greek word meaning "wanderer," so-named by early astronomers because of the sometimes erratic paths that they seem to take in the night sky. Such unpredictability prompted our ancestors to personify the planets — hence their current names, after gods in the Greco-Roman pantheon. By contrast, in scientific accounts, planets are reduced to inert lumps whose motions are governed by momentum and the force of gravity. More than a change in perspective is represented here. There is a change in the star gazers's personal relationship to the universe.

As ecological theorists have developed, this transition was neither simple nor innocent. These theories demand an attitude of tentativeness and attentiveness toward habitual ways of seeing and acting. Prompted by a range of crises, from the immunological through the personal and cultural to the planetary, an ecological mindset calls for us to be aware of how our thinking about thinking is entangled in the events unfolding around us.

For the ecological theorist, a change in thinking is a change in the world. In terms of the relevance of ecological perspectives in the classroom, then, one might ask, How might various models of the solar system be enfolded in prevailing beliefs about humanity's relationship to the non-human?

You are here.

Self-Similarity

Current theorizing across a range of social phenomena, from thought processes to large-scale economies, tends to invoke organic, ecological, and evolutionary metaphors. One notion that is key to understanding some of the interrelationships of the emerging theories is *self-similarity*, a quality of many fractal images (see page 16).

Self-similarity might be thought of as an extension of the mathematical notion of *similarity*. Two figures are similar if, by enlargement or reduction (and maybe some sliding around), one can be made to fit exactly on top of the other. (For example, all circles are similar to one another.)

It has recently been noticed that some figures are similar to themselves. That is, for a special collection of forms such as the fern leaf in the diagram, the parts resemble the wholes. Enlarging a part will produce an image that closely matches the original figure. In the case of the illustrated fern leaf, this process can actually be accomplished at several levels, as is typical of self-similar figures.

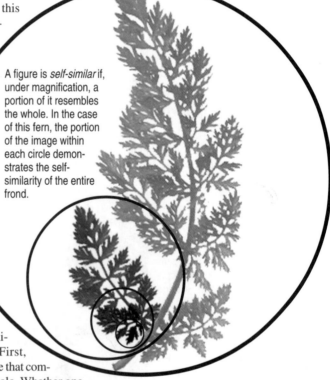

A figure is *self-similar* if, under magnification, a portion of it resembles the whole. In the case of this fern, the portion of the image within each circle demonstrates the self-similarity of the entire frond.

Self-similarity is a quality of many natural forms. Some examples include the structures of trees, cauliflower, and clouds, or the surfaces of river beds, tree bark, and water ripples, or the edges of coastlines, mountainous horizons, and breaking waves.

The property of self-similarity has helped to highlight two important qualities of many phenomena. First, self-similar forms demonstrate that complexity is not a function of scale. Whether one moves in on or pulls back from such forms, the same level of detail presents itself.

Second, there is value in examining the part. In the example of the fern leaf, one could learn a great deal about the fern plant by looking at only the structure within one of the smaller circles. (It is also important to note that such partial viewings could never be adequate to understanding the nature of the larger form. Rather, the point being made it that such partial studies are no simpler and no less informative than studies of the whole.)

Complex Learning Theories

Recent discussions of cognition have examined learning at a range of levels, from bodily subsystems to planetary dynamics. These discourses tend to share a number of assumptions, all of which might be linked to a metaphoric commitment to a "body" as a focus of inquiry.

Such bodies are seen as complex collectives whose boundaries are never tidy or fixed. Although each is seen as having its own proper integrity or identity, there are no breaks between or among the levels of these perceived bodies.

regard the learner as an autonomous agent working to fit in with her or his context, as a component of a larger social order, as a complex collective of dynamic bodily subsystems, and so on. (In this way, such popularly held dichotomies as mind/body, self/other, individual/collective, and human/natural are replaced with the assertion that such phenomena are enfolded in and unfold from one another.)

While these bodies do not much resemble one another, in terms of their physical appearances, they have much in common in terms of their dynamics. In particular, complex learning theories all draw on evolutionary thought to describe how these bodies change and adapt. At each level, cognition is seen as a complex process of co-evolution — that is, of agents (whether species, societies, social groups, persons, or cells) adapting to and affecting one another and their dynamic circumstances. This is not a mechanical process, but a complex choreography.

In other words, these learning theories argue that phenomena such as personal cognition and collective knowledge are tightly interrelated and, in terms of their dynamics, self-similar. However, pervasive uses of such metaphors as "knowledge as object" make it hard to understand the relationships among these phenomena. Instead of "knowledge as object," these theories suggest notions that are more toward "knowledge as action." That is, a body's knowledge might be thought to encompass the habits and behaviors out of which that body's character or integrity emerges. In this sense, *learning* is a process through which one becomes capable of more sophisticated, more flexible, more creative action.

The Biosphere, or the Planetary Body (Ecological Theories)

The Species (Biology and Evolutionary Theory)

Society, or the Body Politic (Anthropology, Cultural Studies, and Critical Discourses)

Collectivities: Social Bodies, Bodies of Knowledge, and so on (Sociology and Social Constructionism)

The Person, or Body Biologic (Psychology and Constructivism)

Bodily Subsystems: Organs and Cells (Recent studies in Immunology, Neurology, and related domains)

Put differently, the relationships among these bodies are analogous to the levels of a self-similar figure: Each layer or body can be simultaneously seen as a whole, a part of a whole, or as a complex compilation of smaller wholes. An implication is that, to understand the phenomenon of personal cognition, one must simultaneously

and more complex web of relations — that is, as part of a grander body whose cognitive processes are seen by humans as ongoing co-evolutions of species and habitats.

A new understanding of cognition is thus implied. Rather than being cast as a locatable process or phenomenon, cognition has been reinterpreted as a joint participation, a choreography. An agent's knowing, in this sense, are those patterns of acting that afford it a coherence — that is, that make it discernible as a unity, a wholeness, identity. The question, "Where does cognition happen?" is thus equivalent to, "Who or what is perceived to be acting?" In this way, a rain forest is cognitive — and humanity is necessarily participating in its cogitations/evolutions. That is, our habits of thought are entwined and implicated in unfolding global conditions.

Ecological theories, then, make use of the same sorts of logics, metaphors, and images as other complex learning theories, extending to phenomena that range from subcellular events to planetary dynamics. In a nutshell, what these overlapping and nested theories suggest is that our (personal and collective) knowledge fits with the world for the same reason that our lungs match the earth's atmosphere: They evolved and are evolving together.

Fig. 2.10. The typical human brain has about 50 billion neurons (brain cells). There are several types, but they all share a similar branching structure. They communicate with each other through *synapses* at the tips of their branches. Each neuron has between 1,000 and 10,000 such connectors.

Neurons and their interconnections are constantly changing, as new synapses grow and other synapses are lost.

Memory

Some of the significance of these embodied and embedded notions can be illustrated through a brief look at an important aspect of learning: memory.

Little is actually known about how memory works. It is clear, however, that this phenomenon is far more complex than is typically acknowledged. It is now known, for instance, that a memory is not a mental model or a program or any other "thing" that is stored in the brain.

In fact, it appears that this common conception of memory couldn't be further from the truth. It is wrong on at least two counts: first, the idea that memories are neatly bounded objects; second, the assumption that memory is internal. Both these issues are addressed below.

Personal Memory. The two main categories of personal memory are short-term and long-term. Both have to do with patterns of activity among neurons. Short-term (or "working") memories are associated with temporary fluctuations in neuronal activities. These patterns tend to fade in a matter of minutes and do not much affect neuronal structures. Long-term memories are more stable patterns that are linked to actual changes in brain structure.

Short-term memory is what we use to keep track of where we are in a conversation, to dial a phone number, and so on. It amounts to what we have "in mind" at any given moment. Most persons can juggle 5 or 6 items in short-term memory. It is this multi-tasking capacity that enables us, for example, to monitor speed, watch for pedestrians, follow directions, and think about dinner while driving a car.

Long-term memories are stable patterns of activity among neurons. Their resistance to fading is linked to the fact that they are associated with actual changes in neuronal structure. Particular clusters of neurons are generally involved in many memories, which means that we have little control over the ways our memories come to be organized. They spill into, subsume, and trigger one another in complex and unpredictable ways — which is both a curse and a blessing. It means that long-term memory is not directly controllable, but it also opens the door to interesting and novel associations.

Because of this associative structure, straight recall is notoriously unreliable, especially in decontextualized settings (such as writing an exam in a strange place). As well, because memories are patterns of interconnected activity, they can easily interfere with one another. (This is especially true when learners try to memorize largely meaningless procedures. Because of superficial similarities, such sequences of activity can easily become confused.)

No one is sure how long-term memories come about. The most popular theory is that they involve the formation, loss, and / or alteration of synapses (neuronal connections). Experiments on organisms with vastly simpler neurological structures suggest that there are two main processes at work here: *habituation* and *sensitization*. Habituation is a process of familiarization that is associated with predictability and repetition. Neurologically speaking, habituation corresponds to a pruning of synapses — which, in effect, leads to a reduction in the range of possible associations one might make with a particular memory. Sensitization, in contrast, is associated with the growth of new connections among neurons. Such changes are prompted

Fig. 2.11. Humanity has devised a number of technologies that serve to lessen the demands on the brain for retaining and organizing memories. Among these strategies, perhaps the most important is writing — a technology that enables us to offload memories into the environment as it prompts us to organize our thinking in more linear sorts of ways.

by novelty and challenge and they appear to give rise to more flexible and adaptive behavior.

In terms of the issue of intellectual potential, these lines of thinking suggest that repetitive and predictable activity can actually "dumb you down," whereas participation in unfamiliar structures that demand adaptation — that is, places where learning is required — literally, can make you smarter. Further, there is ample evidence that such engagements not only improve intellectual ability, but help to reduce or mitigate neurological and degenerative disorders associated with aging and injury.

Of course, the educational implications of this insight into brain structure aren't really so simple. Constant novelty may promote greater flexibility of thought, but it can also engender insecurity in the learner. Conversely, although repetition can work to limit adaptability of thought, it can foster security as it makes contexts more predictable to the learner. As well, there are many skills that must simply become automatic for them to be useful, and repetition can help to achieve this goal.

In terms of how we might go about supporting the development of long-term memories, we know very little. We are aware that rest, proper nutrition, and exercise are important elements. In some cases, rehearsal and repetition are helpful. In others, deliberately "overlapping" established memories (such as memorizing the human anatomy by associating muscle groups with close friends) is effective. However, by far the most powerful "aids" to memory are relevance and emotional significance. Relevance is important because it means that whatever is to be committed to memory can be readily located within a complex web of established associations. Emotional impact is important because, to oversimplify, the same hormones that are associated with extreme emotions are also linked to memory development. (This is, of course, not all that surprising. An organism able to retain memories of traumatic and blissful events would have a decided survival advantage over a more forgetful counterpart.)

In this sort of discussion of memory, however, it is important to bear in mind that not everything we know is bounded by our skin.

Collective Memory. It is a biological truism that creatures tend to use the least "costly" way to preserve knowledge

Fig. 2.12. Saying something out loud — like repeating the name of a person you just met — can greatly enable memory, even if done only once.

Why?

Part of the reason is that the activity of the brain "mirrors" the activity of the rest of the body. The physical interactions of the body parts associated with an articulation are reflected in the interactions among neurons and brain regions — which, of course, are the starting places of memories.

Hearing or thinking a word has a similar, but generally less pronounced effect on brain processes, which means that opportunities to verbalize are important for learning. Neurologically speaking, being able to say things out loud — to recite, to explain, to repeat, etc. — is often a far more powerful learning strategy than listening quietly or doing work in silence.

Among the unfortunate aspects of this phenomenon is that saying something incorrectly (e.g., getting a name or a number fact wrong) can set up an unwanted but resilient resonance pattern among neurons. You have to be careful about what you say!

— and one of the most efficient strategies to keep track of things is to structure the environment in ways that reduce demands on personal memory. Humanity has taken this preference for offloading to its extreme. We use many external memory systems, including ones that are more subtle and pervasive than our notes to ourselves and our books. Our knowledge is also invested in our tools, in our language, in our customs, in the structures of our homes and cities, and so on. In other words, memory is a collective event, especially for such a social, language-using, and technologically reliant species as humanity.

In particular, our shared language allows us to offload much of the work of memory onto the world. Two key aspects of language, in this regard, are its built-in webs of association and its accompanying technology of the written word. Our language is mostly inherited and is infused with habits of association that, for the most part, are invisible to us. (Interestingly, they tend to be more obvious to second language learners whose first languages often have very different webs of association.) A variety of linguistic devices, such as metaphor, metonymy, and analogy enable us to map one category of experience onto another. We do this constantly, as revealed by such prominent notions as the "clockwork universe" and "brain as computer." Such associative strategies greatly reduce the demands on our brains. In effect, it means that much of the hard work of thinking has already been done for us by our ancestors who first noticed relationships and structured their observations in their habits of speaking. (An unfortunate side of this phenomenon is that the built-in associations of language can support troublesome and resilient beliefs.)

The written word (and, more recently, electronic technologies) have also become important aspects of personal and collective memory. In particular, thanks largely to the invention of an alphabet which can be used to organize ideas and information in a way that greatly reduces the demands on personal memory, we have ready access to almost infinite amounts of information.

Of course, the availability of such strategies does have its downsides. Cross-cultural comparisons, for example, show that citizens of literate cultures (like ours) have much lessened retention and recall capacities than persons from oral traditions. Our unaided memories, in fact, would be pathetically inadequate to cope in their circumstances. The trade-off, however, is that our mind-space has been freed up because our information storage technologies (especially writing) allow us to get by without committing much to personal memory.

Collective memory is more than a set of strategies for offloading personal memory. Rather, these two domains of memory are intricately intertwined. In fact, they seem to be self-similar — that is, the same sorts of processes seem to be at work at the collective and individual memory levels. In particular, long- and short-term memories appear to be related to one another in the same way that cultural customs and passing fads are linked. Like long-term memories, customs are stable patterns of activity that are molded into the structure of a collectivity (whether brain or society). Similarly, like short-term memories, fads are specific patterns among interacting agents (neurons or people) that tend to fade away, leaving little obvious trace or lasting impression.

An implication of this realization is that every complex form — whether cell, organ, person, social group, society, species, planet, or other — has memory. Memories, then, are discernible patterns of activity among the agents that come together in more complex collectivities.

Learning Theories

Complex theories of learning suggest that learning is not about acquiring or accumulating information. Rather, learning is principally a matter of keeping pace with one's evolving circumstances. The learning agent — whether immune system, person, collective, culture, or species — is constantly revising its memories, its capacity for action, its range of possibilities. Knowledge is contingent, contextual, and evolving; never absolute, universal, or fixed.

Learning, in this sense, is more a reaching out than a taking in. It is a participation. It is a process of *remembering* — in the word's original sense of pulling together the parts of a body into a more complex unity. That is, even though it is often convenient to speak of an agent's knowledge as though it resided within the agent, that knowledge is what defines the agent's relationship to the rest of the world. The agent's activity and identity are inseparable from his, her, or its knowledge. Knowing is doing is being.

Fig. 2.13. Another category of memory that is not often mentioned in discussions of learning is sensory memory. You can test out the visual version by staring intensely at the dot in the middle of the leaf for 20 seconds and then shifting your gaze to an open white space.

You should see a distinct after-image as collectives of cells continue to be activated.

Whether or not particular sensations are consciously noticed, our sense organs have a sort of memory of any sufficiently intense stimulation. Usually, these fade in a few seconds as the activity of the stimulated cells fades.

(This experiment also demonstrates how perceptions and memories are about relationships and patterns of activity among active cells.)

How does one begin writing a story? It might be difficult to move beyond the simple recounting of an experience to a shaping and reinterpretation of that experience, but somehow the writer has to know how stories work so that the stories can be worked.

A good place to begin is with what is known and most familiar — something like buttons for instance. Since my (Rebecca's) grandmother's death, her button jar has sat on my shelf: a two-quart sealer like the ones she used for canning dill pickles or carrots or raspberries.

As long as I can remember, she loved to sew; she made all her own clothes, many of my grandfather's, and numerous outfits for my sisters and me. The button jar was an important part of that process. If there was one button left on the card when she finished making a dress for me, that button went into the jar just in case. When clothes wore out, she carefully snipped their buttons into the jar before using the cloth for rags. Jackets, dresses, and trousers that were worn long before my birth are remembered in that jar, and when I spin it around, I have memories of moments, impressions, and feelings. The white plastic buttons like the ones my grandfather had on his flannel pyjamas remind me of the nights that he held me to his chest when I was sleepless and afraid until the warmth of the material and his heartbeat lulled me to sleep. I see the green fabric-covered button from the suit my grandmother wore at my uncle's wedding–the one where I was a flower girl and got car sick in my grandfather's new Pontiac StratoChief. Even buttons that I do not recognize remind me of other clothes and other times.

As I spill them onto a blanket, I tell students my button story and invite them to come and choose one. At first, they do not understand the significance of their choice, but then they begin to write. The shape, color, design of that button held in the palm of their hands takes them somewhere to a memory or cluster of memories as they bring a new significance to that which they may have forgotten they knew.

Every time I open the jar and every time I choose a button, another story is discovered, another memory drawn from the small circle or square. It matters what button I choose, the color of blanket I spill them on, the people that are watching me. Sometimes I will go for the safe button, the one that has the memory already rising to the surface of my telling; sometimes the look on one of my students' faces will tell me to choose the brown leather one instead of the white sailor button. We are as caught up in each other's button stories as the threads that attached them to cloth.

Last week I began to read a short story by David Henderson called "The Conjurer's Assistant." I was reading at home in my favorite chair by the large window that opens up to a wide expanse of sky. The story began as a journey with a young man, Adrian, setting out to drive eastward across the continent to temporarily escape marriage and other responsibilities. Near the west edge of a mountain pass, his car breaks down. The nearest garage tells him that the parts for his repairs will have to be ordered and since that could take weeks, Adrian decides to take a job at a nearby roadhouse. In my reading, I imagine that Adrian has driven from Vancouver, eastward toward Alberta where I've seen roadhouses along the highway just like this one–a bar and grill, 24-hour coffee shop and motel by a trailer park. But, while I can envisage the setting and am intrigued by the appearance of a conjurer as an unlikely entertainer for a clientele of mostly truckers, miners, and loggers, I'm not convinced I want to continue reading. Is there enough of a story here to engage me? Since I'm on the way to the Laundromat for my weekly outing for clean clothes, I decide to bring the story with me and keep reading while I wait for the washing.

When my clothes are deposited in two Maytag washers, one labelled "Rosi," the other "Jean," I settle down to pick up the tale. But as I read, a strange thing begins to happen. As the conjurer and his assistant work their magic, drawing out the subliminal desires of the other characters 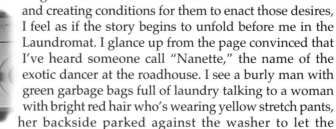 and creating conditions for them to enact those desires, I feel as if the story begins to unfold before me in the Laundromat. I glance up from the page convinced that I've heard someone call "Nanette," the name of the exotic dancer at the roadhouse. I see a burly man with green garbage bags full of laundry talking to a woman with bright red hair who's wearing yellow stretch pants, her backside parked against the washer to let the vibrations of the spin cycle sink deep into her bones as if it were this week's only pleasure. I watch her in my peripheral vision deciding that she could be Nanette during the day — before dancing on stage. Not far from her, a young man has propped himself against the wall, a pulpy paperback folded back on its cover in his hands. He reads intently only glancing up when the whir of a machine stops. He takes a moment to glance at "Nanette." As my attention moves from the page to the Laundromat and back to the page, I realize that reading this story in this place helps me understand the story in a way that was not possible at home. Laundromats are transitory places as are roadhouses. Both attract unusual and interesting characters, people who are dropping in on their way to somewhere else.

I sense that the next time I'm in the Laundromat, the feeling of the story will still linger. There will be another Nanette and another Adrian playing out their momentary desires. The story and the Laundromat will always be entwined for me: the story coloring the place as the place staged the story.

Where and how things are done matters. Thinking of the button jar, I ask students to bring an object from home — any article as long as it has significance for them and as long as they can tell its story. When they bring their choices, there is energy in the classroom. Something important has come with them; something they will be able to speak about and show. Someone laughs and tells me that this reminds them of show and tell. It is show and tell, I think, and they are responding with as much enthusiasm as young children. Why do we think we should stop show and tell once students are no longer primary?

The students move into small groups and take turns showing their objects and telling the group members the story. No one seems to have trouble participating or talking. Even students who are very quiet seem animated when they speak. Once they've each told their story, they put the objects in the centre of their table, a beginning point for another story, a collective one. Moving around the group, each person contributing a sentence at a time, they create a group story that incorporates all the articles in a new role. They find this a funny process since the stories are by no means polished; nevertheless, the group story brings the articles together in some kind of relation to each other. Afterwards, everyone writes about the new story of their object: the connection between their individual and in-the-group telling.

Several days later, I ask them to think about their objects again. Every item that they brought is connected to some place. I want them to think about the place with which they associate their object and then to write about it, using specific sensory details. What do they hear, smell, taste, see, feel in that place? What else do they sense? Write a "thick" description I tell them.

I begin to write about the living room in the house where my grandparents lived, where the button jar was, where my grandfather in his flannel pyjamas held me in the quiet frightening nights:

> The living room where I slept when I visited my grandparents was a large square room with two double-hung windows on two of the walls. During the summer when those windows were opened to let in breezes, the green foliage from the poplars and Bam trees planted around the house rippled green shadow across the white plaster walls. My grandmother planted blue delphinium below those windows so the perfume of their blossoms would invade the room, and hummingbird wings would compete with the buzz of bees as they drew nectar from the flowers. The ceiling in that room was higher than rooms are now —

at least ten feet. Whoever built the house in early 1900 must have thought that there would be large gatherings in the kitchen and the living room because, except for my grandparents' bedroom off to one side, the main floor was only those two rooms. I remember my father telling me once that they'd held dances there, and I could imagine them when I ran from one room to the other, my feet would echo against the green faux marble linoleum. My grandmother had had special shelves made that would support all their books and her gifts from her cousin, who travelled in his job. Crystal from France, china from England, Hummel figurines from Germany. Things of delicate beauty that made the room exotic against the plainness of the furniture and their daily life as farmers. But it was the night times I remember most vividly. The room would be so dark and quiet when my grandparents would wrap me in a blanket and settle me for the night on the chesterfield. I felt like I was sleeping at the bottom of a huge, black cave. Only my frightened whimpers would ensure that my grandfather would pad out in the darkness and let me settle against his flannel chest, listening to his heartbeat until I fell asleep.

Everyone writes about places to which their objects were deeply connected, but while such writing may be interesting, it is only a beginning for moving toward fictionalizing. To create the sense of moving further into that process, the students choose a character to enter their place from among four possibilities: an older man who has just fallen in love, an older woman who is leaving a horrific situation, a middle-aged man who has just committed a crime, and a young woman who has just learned she has inherited a great deal of money. We write about our places only from this character's point of view without specifically mentioning the love, the situation, the crime, or the money in the descriptions; rather our characters "tell" the story.

I've read and reread the novel, *Moon Tiger*, where Penelope Lively writes about Claudia Hampton, a journalist, historian, and writer, who is dying as the story begins. Claudia announces that she is "writing a history of the world" and begins telling about her life and the times she has lived through, including both world wars. One moment we see an incident from a third person limited view of Claudia, then the first person Claudia, before we slip into the first or third person perspective of other players in the scene such as Claudia's brother or daughter or sister-in-law. The recounting of Claudia's life is driven by the images, incidents and relations of her living — a lifetime as an instant or a holographic image where her voice, as well as the perspectives and voices of those she knows, interacts with and shapes her identity. The novel is structured to develop this idea, not chronologically but from memory to memory and from voice to voice, revealing that a sense of life being linear is only true if one chooses to think about it as such and history is really about who is interpreting what at every moment: There are many possible histories in every event. It all depends on one's point of view.

I decide to write from the point of view of an older man who has just fallen in love:

> The room was soft with the tea colored light of early dawn as he settled in the sofa near the windows to watch the rising of the sun. He had awoken early with an energy that he had not felt for years, even the pain that had been plaguing his hip had diminished. His body was renewed.
>
> He slid up the window to feel the coming warmth of the day and to hear the birds loudly anticipating the sun. Usually such noise irritated him, making him put the pillow over his head. But today, the songs reminded him that he was alive still, very alive, on this mid-summer day, his face flushed with excitement.
>
> He ran his hands along the books carefully arranged in alphabetic order, small puffs of dust rising beneath his fingers. "Leaves of Grass" by Walt Whitman would have the words to express the anticipation he was feeling and it would be a book to be shared. He returned to his place by the window and began to read, the page brightening as the sun rose and spilled green into the room. The blue flowers beneath the window opened their blooms wider to the light and an early humming bird ducked his long beak into the heart of the delphinium, seeking his breakfast nectar.
>
> It was a day beginning just as he had hoped ...

That living room has changed. Any of the darkness that I felt as a child has disappeared with this character who sees only the color, light, and beauty of that room. His reading of that place enriches my positive understandings of the living room, but also uses my memories to create another place. That living room is and is not the room in my grandparents' house. Introducing someone with a different perspective moves the memory away from the personal narrative into the realm of literary fiction.

I'm looking at my bookshelf for a story I remember in an anthology by Jane Urquhart. It is another story about a woman dying called "Storm Glass." The woman spends her final days in her bedroom from which she can see the lake that has had a significant place in the lives of her family. She remembers and reinterprets the relationships between her and her children and between her and her husband as they played out in conjunction with times at the beach. When I find the book, I choose phrases from Urquhart's story and lay them out like a found poem:

> beach stones
> unexpected sand
> beach smaller and higher

smooth softness of water
strong spring winds
urged lake
to push stones into several banks
like large steps up
to grass
a natural ampitheatre
grey stone, white stone shining
pre-Cambrian magic
small bay
clean dry bones of seagulls
delicate
storm glass

If I read closely, I can still see the trace of the characters but they are not easily visible. There is room, I think, for others to inhabit this place. What kind of character lives here? I ask. Write about who comes here, who may be coming.

The writers follow the mood of the lake, the sweep of sand, the rocky outcroppings, the discovery of storm glass and imagine the footsteps of those who walked there. They read the landscape to find the shadows of characters to which they give color and movement and language. And, while everyone creates a different personage living by that lake, there is a connection between them all, including Urquhart's characters. The shades of blue water, the sound of waves, the curve of sand and rock flows through each one.

In pairs, the students receive a large brown envelope that is filled with clippings — pictures from Anthony Browne's children's book, *Gorilla*, without the text. They spill the clippings onto the table and silently begin to choose pictures, first one then the other. When each pair has eight pictures, they return the rest to their envelope. Still without speaking and beginning with one person, they choose from the eight pictures the one that they believe would start a story.

This work makes the students uncomfortable. They are used to being able to speak, to exert some control in the decision making of a group process. This time, they can only respond by choosing a picture to follow their silent partner's choice. The process seems arbitrary to them. Afterwards, each person lists the points of the plot they imagine the pictures reveal.

Finally, they speak to each other, comparing plots and describing the process of having to create a story in such a way. They comment on the frustration of only having partial control over the story, but they are interested in comparing their version with that of their partner. We talk about intertextuality, places where their stories touched other stories that they know. We discuss how in creating such a story one is not sure of where the connections will take you or what will happen next, but there is a desire to create meaning, no matter what. They point out how one partner notices details that they missed, realizing that interpretation depends so much on what they pay attention to. They feel they have a new understanding for how story can be created.

We return to the pieces of story we have been working with. There are pieces from places they remember, pieces where other characters entered, pieces taking place by Urquhart's lake, or the button and object stories. Each person picks the writing that he or she wants to pursue and makes a quick list of the plot that could unfold from what's already written. Then they exchange these lists with others in the writing group and see if someone else's plot will give them an interesting perspective on their story. Sometimes they go back to their first plot, sometimes they ask to use their partner's, or sometimes they write a third possibility that uses elements from each.

I imagine what plot might emerge from my older man sitting in the living room reading Walt Whitman as he thinks about his loved one and looks forward to that person's arrival. I still don't know much about his beloved, but I know the feeling that exists in this room, the sunlight, the flowers, the sounds of summer outside the window. In that warm and inviting place, with a book of poetry on his lap, my character, Robert, suddenly stops at one line of the poem. He reads and rereads that line: The smoke of my own breath .... The image takes him back to an earlier time during one winter when he was younger, a time when he was jilted by someone he loved. I can begin to see how this story may connect through memory, from one incident to another, from one time and space to another, a story of several loves that have led him to this room to where the story opens.

I am drawn to stories that push the expected, that move our anticipation of stories somewhere else, that use structures and forms that arise from the needs of the story rather than some reliance on convention and the expected. Audrey Thomas, for example, uses dramatic conventions in her story, "The Man with Clam Eyes." A lonely woman who has just been rejected by a lover comes to a seaside cabin. The story is described in small scenes, interspersed by sound directions in parenthesis that recall the setting through the repetition of waves, wind, and seagulls. The interruption of the story by such instructions creates the fragmented sense of existence that the woman is feeling, but also, the repetition of sound works like a rhythmic beat in poetry or a chant that helps lead the story into its magic realism ending. In the same collection, Claire Harris begins her story with a poem that actually represents the dream of the main character and she, too, creates a sense of interruption in the writing by shifting voices and rhythms.

The students and I draw different story structures on the board. Some stories spiral, some peak, while others drop down from a line like giant raindrops. My story about Robert could have such a structure. The day in which the story opens could follow through and be the line from which other memories "drop." Everyone draws the shape of his or her story and then we imagine what our stories would be like if we changed the shape, tried to create something different. Just like changing the location, the characters, or the plot matters, so does changing the structure. In every story there is the potential of many other stories.

I return to my bookshelf one last time, thinking how structured and formulaic this exploration of writing short stories seems in one way, but on the other, learning how to work stories can help you discover the magic, that inexplicable pleasure of being taken into a story. David Arnason in "A Girl's Story" acknowledges that very thing as he plays with the readers' expectations about story and their understandings of literary traditions. He begins by inviting the reader, whom he's sure has always wondered what it must be like to be a character in a story, to become one in his. But no sooner do we take the invitation then he changes us, dictating our appearance and our gender. We realize that who we think we are is never the same as who we are in a text. Arnason continues by creating a setting for the character and announcing his use of foreshadowing in that location. He also boldly anticipates readers' responses, something writers usually do more privately, as he toys with plotting the events that happen to the character in the setting he has established. As Arnason keeps pulling back the curtain to show a writer at work, we begin to think that perhaps we can see how stories are put together, how some writers make decisions. But then we realize with a start that we are taken into the story about Linda and Greg, wondering what they will do next and how their tale might end. We have become part of the story without seeing how we got there. Arnason, even with showing us his sleight of hand, has still managed to create the magic that we cannot see. So, while one can talk about ways of experimenting with story and ways of approaching writing, there is no way of describing the effect of a story working. We can only find that by working the story.

The process of structuring classroom activities is a complex one. In this section, this task is characterized as a matter of *liberating constraints* — a phrase that describes the balance between freedom and restraint that creates conditions for learning and creativity. The balance is a fine one since weakly defined boundaries and overly rigid expectations alike can adversely affect the possibilities for learning. But, when the limitations and boundaries for classroom activities are set, as they must be, teachers can consider how such constraints can liberate their students' thinking rather than limit it.

Point 1 • LIBERATING STRUCTURES

Teachers can enhance creative activity by placing appropriate constraints on the range of possibilities.

Imagine being presented with a jar full of buttons. You are to chose one and then write about it.

At first hearing, this task may seem like an odd starting place for an assignment. The structure might be seen as contrived, overly restrictive, and hardly supportive of the sort of freedom that is normally associated with *creative* writing. Yet, as detailed in "Working Stories," this sort of limitation can serve as a powerful starting place for creativity.

Well-crafted learning activities are ones that maintain a balance between enough organization to orient students' actions and sufficient openness to allow for the varieties of experience, ability, and interest that are represented in any classroom. That is, learning activities must simultaneously limit and enable possibilities. The idea of selecting and writing about a button is one possible example of such liberating constraints. The writer focuses only on one button but can write about any memories or connections she or he realizes in that writing.

The notion of liberating constraints emerges from an appreciation that learning is not a simple matter of "taking things in" or of accumulating information. Rather, learning is a complex process of incorporating or embodying a diversity of experiences. This insight, in turn, demands that classroom activities be considered in more complex terms, not as rigidly defined tasks but as structures.

One often hears the term *structure* in discussions of formal education — in reference to lesson *structures, knowledge structures*, in*struc*tion, and so on. Across such usages, there are sometimes two very different meanings at play. On one hand, there is a complicated, technocratic sense; on the other, there is a more complex organic sense. The latter is intended here. (See page 49, the title page for this chapter.)

The traditional lesson plan has tended to be understood in technocratic terms. In fact, many manuals for teachers offer rather rigid lesson plan guidelines — and sometimes even fill-in-the blank templates — that are recommended for use across virtually every subject area and for virtually any group of learners.

More complex appreciations of learning and learners prompt the suggestion that learning structures need to be understood in more vibrant, adaptable, and flexible terms. This is precisely what is intended by the notion of *liberating constraints*.

A few out-of-school examples of liberating constraints might help to illustrate what is meant by the term. Virtually any domain of human activity might be chosen. A soccer game, for instance, is subject to very narrow constraints. Players must abide by specific guidelines (i.e., rules) that greatly limit what they are permitted to do. Yet, within those constraints, there is space for an extraordinary range of creative possibility. The constraints are utterly necessary, as revealed when they are relaxed only a little (by, for example, poor refereeing). Without them, events quickly decay into mayhem.

The same is true of a script for a stage play, or of the legal and ethical codes that structure social interactions, or of the environment inhabited by a species. In each of these cases, the creativity and originality of the game, the performance, the culture, or the emergent ecology arises as a result of — not in spite of — the defining constraints.

Of course, constraints can be too constraining to allow for much creativity. Such, in fact, has been a problem with many classroom practices, particularly those that have focused on right-or-wrong, fill-in-the-blanks exercises as a mainstay rather than as a backdrop for more meaningful engagements. Perhaps the most familiar of overly restrictive constraints is the traditional mathematics class, organized around standardized textbooks and unvarying routines. Such contexts tend to allow for little variation or imagination.

Curiously, these sorts of inflexible classroom conditions do not reflect the structures in which mathematicians, writers, and other creative professionals work. The constraints that these persons place around their activities are ones that liberate their thinking.

 Connecting Thoughts

Think about a memorable learning event in your own schooling experience. What sorts of constraints were set out by your teacher? How were those constraints liberating?

Or, alternatively, think about an ineffective classroom event. Does the principle of liberating constraints help to understand why it might not have worked?

Learning Theories and Writing Stories

There are many ways to teach people to write, and each approach is associated with particular beliefs about learning.

A common method is to read a number of short stories, analyzing them for the elements of plot, theme, character, and setting as well as for techniques such as foreshadowing and symbolism. This activity is followed by a request that students write a short story about anything they wish but with some structural provisos. For example, the teacher may tell the students that the story must have at least one character involved in a conflict, sometimes still described by the dated (and sexist) adage of man versus man, man versus himself, or man versus the environment. Or the teacher may draw a plot diagram on the blackboard, pointing out that the writer begins with an initial incident that changes the path of the character and puts him in some kind of conflict. The conflict in such a story builds through a number of incidents until it reaches a high point, a climax, where things must be resolved. The story then ends quickly with a dénouement and some kind of resolution.

By choosing such a technique for story writing, the teacher is able to check students' understandings of the short story elements. Can they create characters who face some conflict and work through rising action to some kind of resolution? Is there a sense of a universal theme present? What does the story teach or say about the "human condition"? Later, when students return to reading short stories in anthologies, the expectation is that they will be able to identify the elements in these models.

Such teaching demonstrates a complicated theory of learning. If the students can identify the "parts" of the short story, if they can work on such parts individually and then put them together, many believe they will have written a short story. Stories are simply the sum of those parts that were created in isolation of each other. Students often manage to write what passes for short stories using this technique, but many find it difficult, floundering in their search for an opening scene of a story without really understanding how a short story evolves more complexly than simply imitating a form from beginning to end. When writing this way, students often feel more resistant to revising their stories because it seems too difficult to begin again, and so they persist on the one path they've discovered. No matter how boring and conventional they may feel their story is, they continue rather than facing the uncertainty of starting over. Sometimes students do write interesting stories from the working-on-parts theory of writing, but on closer investigation, this success is largely due to their deviating from the structure or ignoring it entirely.

Another way to teach story writing also relies on reading short stories and learning to identify and recognize the elements. Students still search for plot, character, setting, and theme, but the teacher broadens the possibilities for understanding one's experience for writing. Perhaps the teacher plays music for the students' response or passes around fragrant and pungent objects to stimulate their sense of smell and stir memory. Or a teacher may take students outside to explore the changing colors of autumn, searching for details to make their writing rich. Involving students in activities that call upon their senses, that remind them of other times and places, is suggestive of a more constructivist perspective. Students often come to such writing able to evoke strong imagery and to remember experiences that can become shaped into a story. The same difficulties, however, remain as they try to struggle with the material to make it fit a given structure — to write A Short Story in the defined style.

A third possibility for teaching writing in school evolved during the 1980s with the rise of "the writing process." Classrooms were set up like workshops and students shared texts and ideas, editing each other's work, making revision suggestions, and celebrating accomplishments by public (class) readings. Like the constructivism-inspired approach, students were given opportunities to have various experiences that could stimulate writing. However, the big difference was the interaction among students. Rather than writing quietly in their desks, the workshop approach encouraged conversation and group learning, a structure that incorporated social constructionist theories of learning. Groups of students were asked to identify effective imagery, interesting plots, character traits as well as other aspects of writing as a way of beginning to make distinctions between "good" and "bad" writing. Ideas of creating interpretative communities that would establish some literary standards for the class were prominent.

The thinking was that students could then use these standards and the skills of identifying technique when they wrote their individual stories.

Such an approach to writing broadened the possibilities for students. Writing was recognized as a complex process that needed support, time, and opportunity to develop. Teachers also realized that students can learn from working with each other and seeing texts other than their own or those published in books. The difficulty with this approach to writing is that often there was too little structure for students. They had opportunities to write about whatever interested them and they could sometimes not find what it was they wanted to write about. Sometimes, too, the feedback they were given by peers, when those peers had been given no guidance, was not helpful. While a great deal of writing tended to get done in comparison with the more structured approaches to teaching writing, the quality of that writing was often questionable.

None of these approaches to the teaching of writing fully acknowledges the complex and emergent quality of writing. Knowing possibilities for structures and forms of stories is important, but not an adherence to one set of characteristics nor the reliance of thinking that the parts make a whole. Realizing that writers draw on their experiences to write fictions is also important, for how else can writers know what to write about? But experience alone is not enough; it must be challenged and reinterpreted in fiction. The importance of how others participate in the creation and understanding of our texts is also an element of writing. But the process for teaching people to write must go beyond such techniques and cannot be limited to one or the other. Writing what one already knows in a predictable and piecemeal form does little to advance learning, especially when the same form is used over and over again and the depth of one's experience is limited. Writing stories should help us learn new things and come to understand differently. By taking an ecological perspective to the teaching of writing, such learning becomes possible. Conditions for writing need to include opportunities for experiences that stir the body and touch memory as well as to create contexts for students to explore multiple possibilities in their writing, contexts that move writers from habituation to sensitization.

Point 2 • INTERPRETING STRUCTURES

The key aspect of any learning event is interpretation — that is, the juxtaposition of different categories of experience and the reading of those experiences against one another.

"Good teaching" is often described as if it were a simple matter of clear, unambiguous communication from teacher to learner. This conception seems to rely on a belief that knowledge is some sort of substance that can be passed from one person to another.

Complex theories of learning have demonstrated the untenability of this belief. One's personal knowledge is now understood as an ever-evolving weave of interpretation. As such, an event of teaching in any classroom will prompt an incredible diversity of opinion and interpretation. Or, in other words, there is no such thing as a clear, unambiguous explanation.

The key question for teacher preparing to teach, then, cannot be, "How can I best explain this concept?", but "What sorts of experiences might this concept be used to interpret?" And the teacher's main task is to assist learners in the continuous process of understanding previous experiences and knowledge in terms of new events and circumstances. (The middle sections of the chapters in this text are intended to provide examples of this point.)

An appreciation of what is intended by the word *interpretation* is important here. In brief, to interpret is to read one experience against another. The word *interpretation* derives from the Latin *inter-* (meaning "between" or "among") and the Sanskrit *prath-* (meaning "to spread abroad"). That is, as originally intended, interpretation occurs between seemingly disparate moments or happenings, events that are spread out in one's life. (In this sense, the term is closely aligned with the notions of *frame* and *structure*, developed earlier.)

The vital quality of an interpretation is that it enables one to draw connections from one set of experiences to another. Some examples: The concept of "adjective" might be used to interpret experiences of describing images of different people. The concept of "density" might be read against experiences with objects that float or sink. And so on.

This suggests that, when seeking to develop a new concept, the teacher must either find ways of enabling learners to draw on their personal experiences or structure in-class experiences that might be collectively interpreted. Examples of both approaches are offered in Chapter 2B, "Working Stories." Students were asked to engage in experiences that helped them remember and then reinterpret that memory by writing collective stories or using a different structure for the writing. Beginning with buttons, the teacher invited students to engage with the familiar and the habitual — where the color, shape, size, and textures of those buttons recalled earlier experiences. The buttons, the teacher's own story, and the ritual of spilling of them onto a blanket, created conditions for such recollection, even while constraining what was remembered. The students were surprised how a small object like a button could stir memories that seemed almost forgotten.

Teaching writing in this way was not a series of piece-meal activities that were then "put together" into a story

---

Acting Structures

Max teaches drama at a secondary school. Many evenings throughout the winter he also participates in a community theatre group that performs at least two plays each year. A number of his Grade 11 and 12 students are as interested in drama as he is and participate in a club that has one major production each year as well as some smaller events. Some of the classes Max teaches, however, have students who are not particularly interested in the course but who have ended up there by default because they need an option. With such classes, Max wants to create conditions where the students feel able to take a risk and participate in a play by becoming a character and taking on a role. He realizes that even if they don't go on to act in plays or work in theatres, by involving themselves in 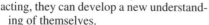 acting, they can develop a new understanding of themselves.

 Max invites these students to participate through an experience with melodrama. Initially he asks them to view some familiar Bugs Bunny cartoons. They talk about how body movement, voice, and appearance are used to characterize the simple figures. He then shows students some clips of early silent melodramas and asks them to begin to make connections between the cartoon figures and the actors. He follows up such work by asking students to explore their notion of stereotypical figures such as heroes and villains by listing the characteristics of such icons. Within such a context, Max teaches them simple and exaggerated body movements: They slink like villains, they stride like heroes, and they faint like damsels in distress. When the students begin to choose bits of costume, such as a black stovepipe hat or a feather boa, and develop voices for the characters, roles begin to emerge. Max then presents each group with a prepared, short melodramatic script. He asks the students to take their knowledge of cartoons, their newly learned skills of movement, costuming, and voice, and develop these roles within the confines of a script. Working in a form that is readily understandable and fun to participate in, students learn how one can become a character.

structure. Instead, the students were brought into their experiences, which they then interpreted and reinterpreted through different but connected activities. With every new event, the emerging story revealed new facets, other directions, different possibilities. The students had the opportunity to think and think again about what is important in their evolving story and to see what surprising aspects appear.

An important caveat should be made here. The path of learning that unfolds in a classroom will be particular to that context. Learning events are highly specific, and so one should not expect a structure that worked well in one setting to be generalizable to another. As is commonly reported, teaching ideas that were "magical" with one group of children sometimes fail completely with others. Such events highlight the specific personalities of classroom collectives and serve as cogent reminders that there are no generic teaching methods and no perfect lessons.

Such events should also serve as a further reminder that teaching should never be reduced to matters of clear communication or "telling." If anything, teaching becomes more about attentive response — of listening — to the complexities and the possibilities that present themselves in a classroom of learners.

 Connecting Thoughts

Review the account presented in Chapter 2B, "Working Stories." Identify some moments of interpretation — that is, instances where the teacher asked learners to juxtapose two categories of experience and to read those experiences against one another. How did the teacher structure this juxtaposition?

 Point 3 • UNDERSTANDING STRUCTURES

Teachers need a well developed relationship with a subject matter in order to structure liberating constraints.

It's almost a truism to suggest that the most significant constraints on one's teaching practices are the ways one was taught and one's history with the subject matter. In brief, one's teaching methods tend to reflect one's own history as a student.

One of the key reasons for this situation is that teachers of writing (or reading, or mathematics, etc.) often do little writing (or reading, or mathematics, etc.) themselves. That is, their relationship to a discipline is often limited to their own schooling experiences, rather than by an engagements with its creative aspects.

The net effect has been a certain perpetuation of teaching methods and curriculum objectives. Much of current instructional practice and curriculum was developed centuries ago with the explicit intention of preparing a workforce of clerics and factory laborers. Although mechanical proficiency and the capacities to cope with repetition and tedium are no longer so necessary qualities, outdated topics and methods persist.

The context has changed — so much so, in fact, that the reasons particular topics were originally included in course syllabi have been all but forgotten. Whereas once it was easy to respond to the question, "Why are we doing this?", today the all-too-frequent response is, "Because it's in the curriculum."

It is against this backdrop that a new emphasis has arisen in teacher education: Teachers must themselves know what it means to engage in a particular practice before they can teach it. Whether writing poetry, conducting a scientific inquiry, or whatever, being able to engage learners in disciplined study demands a well developed sense of what is involved in such engagements. One needs more than a textbook and a teacher's manual. To teach how to write, one must have written. To teach mathematics concepts, one must have participated in mathematical inquiry.

This is not to say, for instance, that every science teacher has to be a scientist. This sort of situation is hardly practical, and perhaps not even desirable. But it does mean that one's ability to structure liberating constraints is greatly enabled by involvement in the sorts of creative and inquiry-based activities that are particular to various disciplines.

Further to this point, teachers are less likely to treat various concepts (e.g., spelling, factoring, etc.) as isolated technical competencies if they have experience with and knowledge of the ways such focused topics arise in the course of engaged study. As is illustrated in each of the teaching episodes presented in this text, technical compe-

Designing Structures

Lois approaches life with a curiosity for how things work; she is passionate about the process of inquiry. When she was interested in the technology of the garage door opener, she dismantled it to see how it worked. When she wanted alternative ways of teaching, she participated in cooperative learning workshops and became a leader. In her junior high science classes, Lois invites her students' own questions about the world and then involves them in exploring the possibilities of such questions. When her grade seven students study principles of design, she sends them out first to pay attention to structures in their community. What do you see? she asks them. What do you wonder about? When the students return with their notes, she fills the blackboard with their questions and observations. From there, she teaches them about design: how one determines the strength of a structure; the role of shapes in creating support. Now that her students have a context and some understanding for the decision-making required in design, Lois tells them that they will be using a few materials to design a bridge within certain specifications. Every group has to build a bridge of a specified span that will support a golf ball rolled along it. The materials for such a bridge are two paper cups and two index cards. These limited elements for building will require students to really begin to interpret the kinds of designing decisions that she has prepared them for. Through such work, they have a deeper understanding of what it means to plan and design a bridge.

Lois prepares a similar activity for her Grade 8 unit exam. The students have spent several weeks studying the principles of machines and building examples within certain constraints. For the test, Lois divides everyone in pairs and gives each group some blocks, several straws, a few strips of tape, a 30 cm ruler and elastic bands. Using what they have learned about machines, each pair is to build a functioning catapult to pass the test.

tency is vital to inquiry and creativity. Such competencies need rarely to be developed in isolation, however.

A broad experience in a subject domain is critical in making decisions about liberating constraints. Lacking such background, many teachers are compelled to plod through prefabricated textbooks, ones that ignore both the complexities of a subject matter and the particularities of a group of learners.

Some specific advice can be offered to prospective and practicing teachers on this matter. To begin, when and where possible teachers should participate in events appropriate to their subject areas — ones that are structured by disciplinary specialists, such as writing workshops, mathematics and science fairs, and so on. As well, given the impact of our experiences as students on our practices as teachers, educators should take full advantage of opportunities to observe the pedagogy of teachers who are experts in various subject areas. How do they structure tasks? How do they address key concepts? How do they engage with students? What do they seem to believe about learners, and how are those beliefs enfolded in their teaching? How do their practices reflect or differ from your own? What sorts of liberating constraints do they use?

 Connecting Thoughts

In most formal curricula, there are categories of specific technical competencies that are presented for mastery. Review a curriculum document and identify some of these competencies. Then discuss with others why those particular topics and not others might have been selected.

Point 4 • PLANNING STRUCTURES

Liberating constraints are not lesson plans. They are starting places for possible paths, not the routes to be followed. The space of possibilities opens up only in the actual moment of teaching.

The nature of liberating constraints is such that the task of structuring them should be among the last activities taken on by the beginning teacher. The suggestion that educators should take advantage of opportunities to observe other educators is reflective of a common feature of the preparatory experiences for many occupations and professions — namely, that the task of planning should be among the last that is taken on by the beginner. It should be undertaken only after there has been ample opportunity to become familiar with the many facets of one's role.

The main reason for this sequencing is, on the surface, a simple one: Until one is sufficiently familiar with the many demands of a complex task, it makes little sense to attempt to structure it. Compelling a beginner to take responsibility for planning a complex event would more than likely force an attention to superficialities (such as explanations and time allotments) and deflect attention from the critical elements (such as the deep engagements of learners with a subject matter). To draw an analogy, the last responsibility that is taken on by an apprentice tailor is the cutting of the cloth — a task for which one must consider the function of the final garment, the accommodations needed for seams and hems, the weave and other

Beans

Yuen was clearly overwhelmed. The extended practicum was a few weeks away, and she had just been given the task of preparing an integrated unit to span the 4-week experience.

As she explained to her seminar group, her mentor teacher had identified the topic of "beans" and had led her to a filing cabinet overflowing with possible activities. Unfortunately, for Yuen, the range of choices presented by the topic and the support materials was simply too broad. She didn't know where to begin.

That worry was compounded by the fact that she hadn't had sufficient time to become familiar with the various Grade 2 curricula. What were students expected to learn in science class, and how might beans be used as a focal point in that study? What about language arts? Mathematics? Art? She felt lost.

As it was too late in the day's session to take on the topic, JoAnn, the course instructor, promised to get back to it the following week.

After class, she took advantage of a chance meeting with a few colleagues to brainstorm around the topic of beans. JoAnn kept a list of the books (e.g., *Jack and the Beanstalk*, *The Princess and the Pea*), objects (e.g., bean bags, types of beans), and phrases (e.g., "spill the beans," "full of beans") that came up.

A few days later, JoAnn visited the resource library to pick up copies of children's books involving beans. Her next stop was a bulk food store, where she selected several different varieties of dried beans — along with, on a whim, jelly beans.

As she prepared for the next seminar session, JoAnn wondered about how she might help her students think about liberating constraints: How might she begin with a condition that was debilitating because it was so broad and open (i.e., structuring a unit around beans), and impose boundaries that would support creative and productive thought. She settled on three orienting activities.

In the next class, students found mounds of beans in the centers of their tables. JoAnn instructed them to spend several minutes devising different means of grouping their beans in — an activity that was as much intended to have students look closely at what was in front of them as to highlight the mathematics curriculum topics of attribute identification and set-making.

To frame the second activity, JoAnn explained: "You're going to create images in your groups." "Taking turns, and without speaking, choose one bean from the pile and place it somewhere on the table." This particular activity was one that JoAnn had used in a variety of situations. Here she intended it as a starting place for a discussion of the surprises and the frustrations of collective work. From experience she knew that interesting and unexpected structures would emerge. As they were being assembled, however, there would be moments of tension and silent disagreement, as different group members' contributions diverged from other members' desires for the image.

The third activity was a writing exercise. It began with three instructions: Name a location. Name an article of clothing. Select a bean from the pile. The group task was then to devise a storyline that involved all three.

In the ensuing discussion, JoAnn asked about responses to and products of these three activities, jotting notes on the chalkboard as different comments were made and ideas were announced. After some initial reporting, she invited class members to brainstorm with her around a bean theme. Further ideas were listed on the board.

It was about an hour into the class when she asked students to turn to their curriculum guides. "Let's start with math," she suggested. "What sorts of curriculum objectives have we addressed here?" A surprising range of possibilities was highlighted. In fact, it became clear that *most* of what children were expected to study in Grade 2 mathematics could be addressed through activities like the ones they'd just explored. The same seemed to be true of curricula for language arts, science, and art.

To bring some closure to the event, JoAnn returned to the notion of "liberating constraints." Referencing to each of the day's activities, she re-emphasized the importance of imposing enough structure to orient learners' activities, but in a way that would enable creative possibility.

qualities of the material, and so on. It is only through a knowledge of such elements that the task of cutting the pattern can be accomplished with understanding.

Traditional approaches to teacher education have tended to locate lesson planning among the first tasks addressed. This sequencing is hinged to linear conceptions of learning and teaching, views that cast pedagogy more as a matter of control than of engagement.

That the topic of creating learning structures is presented near the start of this text (rather than nearer the end, as we seem to be arguing should be the case) is intended to highlight the importance of focusing attention on the specifics of preparing to teach — in effect, to provide prospective teachers with a set of issues to orient and interpret their observations of particular events of teaching. As such, if parts of the text are being read in sequence, it would be inappropriate to ask readers to devise liberating constraints for, say, a lesson on momentum for middle school science students. A more appropriate activity might be to observe a lesson prepared by an experienced teacher, participating where appropriate, but focusing the most attention on the structure of the task and the manner in which that structure supports or frustrates students' actions. From there, the teacher candidate might discuss classroom events with the teacher, using the notion of liberating constraints to orient analyses.

 Connecting Thoughts

As authors, we've attempted to make this text an example of what it attempts to teach — that is, we've tried to make use of the principle of liberating constraints. Does it work? Does it enable thought and support discussion about teaching?

Point 5 • EXPERIMENTING STRUCTURES

A "lesson plan" is a *thought experiment*.

As developed in the previous point, lesson planning is among the most complex of the teacher's tasks. It demands a familiarity with a subject matter, an understanding of learning processes, a knowledge of one's students, and a sense of how these and other elements come together in the complexity of the teaching moment.

As such, and as mentioned, the task of planning a full-blown lesson is perhaps better left for the latter stages of one's pre-service preparation. That being said, there are some activities that might be taken up earlier on as one moves toward full-class responsibilities.

A first question is, What is a lesson plan?

Going by the sorts of templates, guidelines, and sample lessons that are presented in most manuals intended to support teaching, it seems reasonable to suggest that lesson plans are most often conceived in terms of itineraries — that is, of step-by-step listings of specific activities, their durations, and their prespecified outcomes. In the extreme, some lesson plan formats are so specific as to prescribe almost every aspect of the teacher's and learners' activities (e.g., homework checks, formal lesson, two examples, seat work, etc.), timed to the precise minute.

Such rubrics project a conception of lesson planning as a fill-in-the-blanks activity. As well, these formal structures seem to leave little room for learners to affect the unfolding of a lesson or for lessons to spill beyond their intended boundaries. They might even run the risk of reducing teaching to a scripted performance, as opposed to a complex engagement with students.

An alternative frame for lesson plans is to think of them in terms of *thought experiments* — that is, as occasions for thinking through some of the possibilities for particular activities with particular learners in particular contexts. There are no hard and fast rules for such experiments. They may well involve some sort of lesson plan template (which could serve as a useful reminder of some necessary considerations), or they might be more freely structured. They might be mostly a matter of adapting lessons taught elsewhere, or they might involve newly imagined activities. The key quality of lesson planning, in this sense, is that it should support a sense of the dynamic and complex possibilities that might arise.

The questions that guide such thought experiments include, Who am I teaching? Are there any special considerations or accommodations that might need to be made? Where and when will this lesson occur? How might such contextual details influence what happens? What do I hope will be learned? How might the various theories of learning inform my decisions around curriculum objectives? What resources are available? How might these resources influence the learning that occurs?

These are weighty questions — ones that a relatively inexperienced teacher candidate should be considering, but likely not ones that they can always answer on their own. A possible preliminary step in developing one's competencies in this regard might be to assist an experienced teacher through the planning process, bearing in mind that many of the "decisions" made by experienced teachers will be occurring on a nonconscious level, arising from a deep

Teaching Structures

Angie, a professor of mathematics education, was recently faced with the task of restructuring her students' practicum experiences, due mainly to a sudden increase in enrollment in her classes. After years of working with 10 to 15 students wishing to be elementary school mathematics specialists, Angie found herself with a class of 31 — and with no time to find classroom teachers who would be willing and able to host these teacher candidates on such short notice.

In the education program at Angie's university, the practicum occurs during the autumn semester and is structured as follows: 3 weeks of on-campus study, then a 2-week practicum block, then 3 more weeks on campus, culminating in an extended 5-week practicum block. Since she only learned about the increase in enrollment in August, when schools were closed, Angie simply had no opportunity to contact prospective host teachers. This situation was compounded by the fact that teachers themselves were very busy at the start of the school year.

Angie made a quick decision to "buy time" by restructuring the 2-week practicum block near the start of the term. Instead of sending each teacher candidate to a different classroom, she arranged for them all to be placed in the same school. With the assitance of two Grade 4 teachers, Angie subdivided two classes of students into 15 groups of 2 to 5 learners. In pairs, teacher candidates were then matched to these small groups and given primary teaching responsibilities for

about one third of the school day. The remainders of their schedules were taken up in observation tasks and assisting responsibilities in other parts of the school.

The responses to this structure were overwhelmingly positive, from all parties. The two regular classroom teachers reported that they were delighted to have some opportunity to "float" among their students, offering advice, becoming better acquainted with specific difficulties and strengths, and so on. The Grade 4 students seemed to benefit from the focused attention in mathematics. And teacher candidates reported that they learned a great deal about what it means to plan a lesson — largely due to the fact that they weren't overwhelmed with the prospect of having to occupy 30 people all at once. With the increased opportunity to attend to student responses, teacher candidates acknowledged a much intensified appreciation of the complex relationship between their efforts to teach and the learning that happened.

The activity was so successful, in fact, that even though enroll-ment has since returned to previous levels, Angie has kept this structure for the 2-week practicum.

familiarity with the circumstances of their teaching.

Another structure that might be useful in the project of developing one's lesson planning abilities is to start out by taking responsibility for only two or three learners, rather than for an entire class. This sort of arrangement should reduce the demands for thinking through possible contingencies while it enables teacher candidates to pay closer attention to the consequences of their efforts to teach. Teacher candidates would likely feel far more at ease — indeed, they might even feel more compelled — to stray from planned activities and preformulated explanations when working with only a few learners. In the process, better appreciations might emerge of the complex relationship between planning and teaching.

● **Connecting Thoughts** ●

What sorts of planning — that is, what sorts of thought experiments — might have preceded the teaching events described in Chapter 2B, "Working Stories"?

Chapter 3

Learning and Teaching Occasions

Occasion comes to us from a Latin term that was used to describe the way that surprising possibilities can arise when things are allowed to fall together.

Conventionally, occasion is used mainly as a noun to refer to a happening, an opportunity, or a chance event. Its more archaic verb form, though, suggests something richer: "To occasion" is to bring something about, but not always deliberately. An occasioned event is one that may be incidental or by chance.

This sense of the term is closely related to the root meanings of *frame*, *structure*, and *interpret*, developed in previous chapters. The term is used here to describe the way that rich and diverse possibilities for activity and understanding are always presented in an event of teaching.

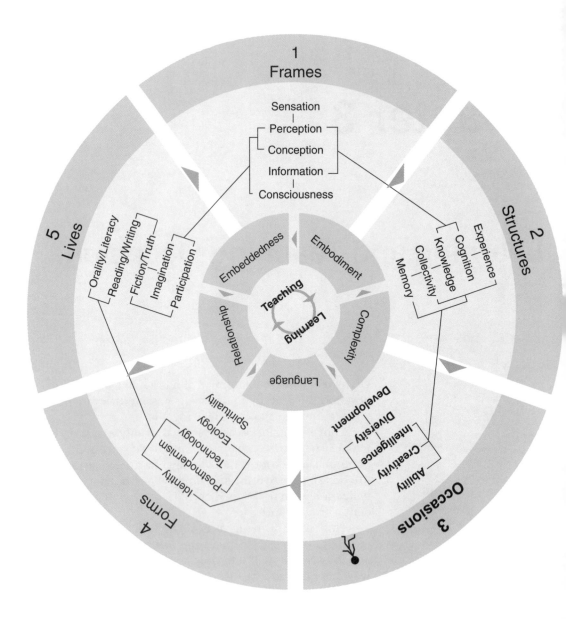

People are different from one another.

As much a platitude as this statement seems, it highlights one of formal education's greatest dilemmas: On the one hand, schooling is often seen as a place where one's talents might be nurtured and one's deficits minimized. On the other, formal education seems to have great difficulty dealing with individual difference, structured as it is by curricula, teaching methods, and testing regimes that are aimed at the "normal" or "average" child.

The understanding of normality that underlies this dilemma is, as it turns out, quite recent. The purpose of this chapter is to examine some of the issues around matters of difference among learners — differences that are often grouped together under such categories as intelligence, creativity, exceptionality, deficit, dysfunction, and so on. What are these? How have teaching and schooling become implicated in them? What does an appreciation of diversity contribute to questions of assessment and evaluation? And, how can we think about difference without getting caught up in a debate over teacher-centered versus child-centered classroom practices?

This chapter continues to build on the notion that "learning" is not a singular general process. Learning is more than making associations or committing them to memory. Rather, it is always contextualized, sensorial, interpretive, and bodily. Learning is a constant reconfiguration of one's existence that involves discerning what is relevant and how such discernments might be entangled in one another.

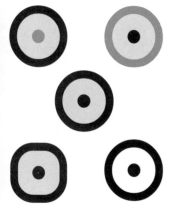

Fig. 3.1. Which figure is the most different? (The answer is on the next page.)

Inventing Normality

Underlying almost all discussions of ability and difference is an assumption of normality — of *average* talent, of *expected* development, of *typical* circumstances, and so on. In consequence, much of schooling practice revolves around deep-seated beliefs about what is and is not normal for a child at a given age. What is not well known is that the notion of normality, as it is deployed in discussions of development and schooling, is scarcely a century old.

Norma, the Latin root of normal, originally referred to the carpenter's square, the instrument used to measure and to create right angles for buildings. When incorporated into the English language, *normal* was used in very much the same way, in reference to the extent to which particular cuts or corners conformed to a preset standard of 90°.

(*Normal* is actually a part of a broad web of associations. The root *rect* — as in *correct, rectify, direct*, etc. — and the word *right* share almost identical histories to *normal*. As well, the words *true* and *regular* originally referred to the extent to which an object was straight and balanced.)

By the early 1800s, the term was being used more broadly to refer not just to actual constructions, but to standardized models and patterns. No longer limited to precise right angles, a figure or form was regarded as normal if it matched with predetermined specifications. This notion was of mounting importance in an era of rapid industrialization and mass production. There was an increased demand for standardized (normal) parts for machines, since these were much less costly than individually manufactured replacement pieces.

This need for standardization supported the emergence of a new field of inquiry, statistics, which drew on developments in mathematics and several applied sciences (astronomy, geology, and biology, in particular). By the mid-1800s, a number of statistical methods had been developed to help cope with the scientific and industrial needs for systematic means of summarizing data and making predictions on the basis of those summaries. Most prominently, these methods were used in determining typical values (for tree growth, production levels, etc.) and for analyzing deviations from these values. It was quickly realized that measurements of a good many natural and human-made forms — such as height, lung capacity, and manufacturing error — seemed to cluster around particular average values. Moreover, the manner in which such measurements deviated from the average appeared to be remarkably consistent, regardless of the phenomenon under investigation.

In their efforts to characterize these variations, statisticians soon developed a quantitative interpretation: The "Normal Curve" (or, more popularly, the "bell curve"). This development contributed to a dramatic transformation of

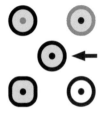

Fig. 3.1. (Continued from the previous page)

The middle figure is the most different. Each of the others differs from the "norm" in one way: The upper left has a gray dot; the upper right has a gray border, the lower left is squarish, and the lower right has a white background. The middle figure has no unique trait, making it the most different ... even though it seems the most normal.

This item, which is a parody of the sorts of questions used on tests of intelligence, points to a logical flaw in the conventional notion of normality: In a species made up of highly differentiated beings, a truly *normal* specimen would be truly *abnormal*.

the meaning of *normal*. No longer referring to the level of match to predetermined specifications, normality quickly came to be regarded as the nearness of a measurement (of virtually *any* form, whether natural or human-made) to a mathematically determined average value.

At first, this conception of normality was applied only to physical attributes or behaviors that could be unambiguously measured. However, near the end of the 1800s, there was a rather abrupt change to the ways statistical tools were employed as social scientists began to look to these methods as means of making sense of now vast amounts of data on human beliefs and interactions. Also motivated in large part by a desire to place themselves on par with those engaged in the "hard" sciences (i.e., physics and chemistry), social scientists took up statistical methods in earnest just over 100 years ago.

Before long, those means of analysis that had been developed to study concrete phenomena were being applied to more abstract constructs, such as personality traits, intelligence, tolerance of ambiguity, and so on. It was at this stage, in the early 1900s, that the notion of the "normal person" began to be widely used. (More accurately, the original construct was the "normal man," as the persons studied were almost always adult males — who also tended to be white and from the upper middle class.) At the same time, and closely related to this emergent notion, there were broad movements toward standardization in schooling. Common curricula, homogeneous classrooms, uniform teaching methods, age-appropriate routines, and standardized examinations soon became commonplace — all of which rested on the assumption of the normal child while further entrenching the notion in schooling practices.

Although a fiction (i.e., there are no "normal" children), the "normal child" has become an invisible but pervasive aspect of educational discourse. Even when such terms as *normal, average, standard, typical, grade-appropriate* and *age-appropriate* are not explicitly invoked, the assumption of normality is implicit in such labels as *abnormal, unusual, disabled, disorderly, dysfunctional, maladaptive, hyperactive, delayed, retarded, challenged, handicapped, inadequate,* or *gifted*. Each of these notions presumes a standard, pre-determined, and measurable norm.

More recently, and partly in response to this problem, such phrases as *differently abled* and *exceptionality* have been

Fig. 3.2. A "Normal Curve" (or "bell curve") is used to illustrate the distribution of many naturally occurring phenomena, such as the heights of adult women in North America, the masses of potatoes in a field, and so on.

The shape of the curve highlights how most data points (i.e., measurements) tend to cluster around an average value (the *mean*, μ). As one moves away from the mean, the probability of particular measurements decreases sharply (meaning, e.g., that really small potatoes and really immense potatoes are much less likely than average-sized potatoes).

With this curve, "normality" is defined in terms of nearness to the mean. Typically, those points within one *standard deviation* of μ (the dark grey region in the figure are considered normal).

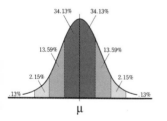

taken up, accompanied by educational imperatives for accommodating students with special needs in regular classrooms. (The two most prominent of such efforts are referred to as *mainstreaming* and *inclusive education*.) Unfortunately, assumptions about normal ability, normal development, and normal behavior have persisted, leaving difference and diversity as qualities to be "tolerated" or "accommodated" rather than appreciated and embraced.

Labeling Problems

Once *normal* is defined, so too is *not normal*, opening the door to a host of exceptionalities. It is no surprise, then, that widespread practices of labeling — that is, of classifying deviations from established norms — have arisen. Such practices are often justified as necessary for determining appropriate interventions and for securing educational resources. Conversely, they are often condemned as stigmatizing, stereotyping, focused on weakness, and influential of expectation.

A number of classification schemes and disorders have been proposed in recent years. Instead of attempting to review the range of possibilities, the strategy in this chapter is to focus on one "disorder," hyperactivity, and to use it as a sort of case study for the practices of defining differences, assigning labels, and structuring interventions.

Hyperactivity (and a cluster of associated diagnoses, including Attention Deficit Disorder, ADD, and Attention Deficit Hyperactive Disorder, ADHD) is regarded by many as something of an epidemic. Production of the drug most often prescribed for hyperactivity, Ritalin, increased by 500% through the first half of the 1990s. Currently, from 3 to 5% of school-aged children in North America (and more than 10% of boys in elementary school) take Ritalin or other drugs for hyper behavior, making hyperactivity one of the most prominent categories of diagnosed dysfunction. In some jurisdictions, the rate is as high as 20%.

Drug therapies are not the only response to hyperactivity. Dietary regimes (e.g., limiting sugar or protein) and behavior modification programs (i.e., rigid structures of reward and punishment) are also widely employed. Less commonly used strategies include neuro-feedback, small group learning structures, and direct parent involvement in classrooms. In every case, success is varied.

Fig. 3.3. While recognized dysfunctions are far too numerous and diverse to survey, a sense of their range can be gleaned from a glimpse at the *Diagnostic and Statistical Manual of Mental Disorders*, published by the American Psychiatric Association. More than 800 pages long, this regularly revised document lists the thousands of labels that are currently in use, along with the established diagnoses as determined through majority votes of the Association.

Despite its apparent pervasiveness, the symptoms of hyperactivity are rather vaguely defined, covering such qualities as restlessness, inattention, poor concentration, fidgityness, and so on. One reason that has been proposed for the apparent lack of precision in these symptoms is that hyperactive behavior may itself be a symptom of various underlying, less obvious problems. That is, overactivity and inattention might not always be disorders in and of themselves, but are caused by something else. As such, strategies of drug therapy and other interventions might sometimes do nothing more than mask undiagnosed problems.

There is hardly consensus on this opinion, however. One prominent theory on hyperactivity suggests that some cases are caused by a lack of a certain neurotransmitter from the pre-frontal lobes (seen as the "head office" of the brain) to other parts of the brain, causing the "employees" to run around in circles due to a lack of direction. Ritalin and similar drugs are believed to improve the efficacy of these neurotransmitters — meaning that, in these sorts of cases, the bases of the disorder are indeed being treated.

At best, however, such cases account for a fraction of diagnosed instances of hyperactivity. It seems that a more likely "cause" of the rise in diagnoses is a pervasive assumption that there is some normal level of behavior that can and should be expected of all children — an assumption that may be contributing to maskings of underlying problems rather than to seeking proper treatments. This conclusion is supported by statistics which show that use of behavior-control drugs falls off precipitously when the school year ends.

Professionals are split on the nature of less obvious causes, with some focusing on biopsychological problems and others offering sociological explanations. Among the array of possible biopsychological causes are low-grade poisoning (lead, mercury, manganese, carbon dioxide, or other substances), malnutrition and nutrient deficiencies, chemical dependencies (cocaine, solvent sniffing, alcohol, etc.), and exposures to pollutants (released by mold, mothballs, disinfectants, pesticides, air fresheners, furniture polish, cigarette smoke, insect repellent, and so on). Other possibilities are brain tumors, head injuries, diabetes, allergies, petit mal seizures, and deformities of organs (e.g., heart, lung, digestive system) — any of which can seri-

Fig. 3.4. The following are among the many persons who as children are reputed to have been identified as "inattentive," "uncreative," "developmentally delayed," or even "stupid": Ludwig von Beethoven, Cher, Winston Churchill, Tom Cruise, Charles Darwin, Thomas Edison, Albert Einstein, Whoopi Goldberg, Florence Nightingale, Carl Jung, Louis Pasteur, Isaac Newton, Auguste Rodin, Vincent van Gogh, James Whistler, Virginia Woolf.

ously handicap the brain by not providing it with adequate levels of oxygen, hormones, neurotransmitters, and so on.

Sociologically speaking, children's behavioral problems might stem from difficulties at home or among peers. They may be linked to difficulties with classroom tasks or with efforts to divert attention away from low academic achievement. More broadly, as evidenced by the dramatic increase in diagnoses of hyperactivity, expectations of normal behavior might simply be too restrictive in many instances, especially when opportunities for exercise are limited or activities are not sufficiently varied. In fact, changes in expectation on what constitutes "normal behavior" are usually cited as the most likely reason for the rise in Ritalin sales. An inadequately explored option to drug interventions, it is often argued, is a broadened conception of acceptable behavior, accompanied by more diversified and active learning contexts for children.

What is obvious across these discussions is that many issues must be addressed when considering any category of difference — including interactions of biological and social circumstances, the societal habit of imposing quick-fix solutions on troublesome situations, the role of difference in the viability of any complex organization, and widespread discomfort with the idea that individuals be allowed to operate outside the statistically determined parameters of normality.

Such worries are hardly specific to hyperactivity and attention deficits. Those differences among individuals that are gathered together under the title of *learning disabilities* (LDs), for example, share a similar history to hyperactivity and are oriented by the same sorts of normalizing impulses. The defining quality of a learning disability is some manner of sharp contrast in one's learning profile — that is, a clear weakness in some specific domain with typical or strong abilities in most others. Like hyperactivity, then, learning disabilities are defined in terms of deviations from pre-established norms; like hyperactivity, the "symptoms" of LDs are generally vague; like hyperactivity, LDs are usually identified in terms of dysfunction.

The similarities arise from the fact that hyperactivity and learning disabilities most often are not disorders in and of themselves, but indicators of other problems. (The list of possible causes and triggers for LDs is similar to the list for hyperactivity, presented above.) Such is also true

Behaviors Associated with HYPERACTIVITY

- poorly sustained attenti
- low task-persistence whe no immediate conseque
- impulsivity; inability to de gratification
- inability to adhere to instructions
- more active and more restless than most childre
- difficulty abiding by rules

Fig. 3.5. A quick comparison of some of the most often mentioned "symptoms" of hyperac-

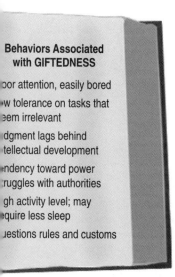

**Behaviors Associated
with GIFTEDNESS**

oor attention, easily bored

w tolerance on tasks that
em irrelevant

dgment lags behind
tellectual development

ndency toward power
ruggles with authorities

gh activity level; may
quire less sleep

uestions rules and customs

tivity and "qualities" of
giftedness should give educators some pause.

of childhood depression and anxiety disorders. In each such case, the overwhelming medical and educational responses have been to minimize the symptoms by imposing some regime intended to push the "offending" behaviors back into the established bounds of normality.

Of course, some interventions are quite effective. Consider, for example, dyslexia, a reading disability that might affect up to 4% of people. It seems to be associated with neuronal activity that differs from what happens in most human brains. Dyslexics can, however, become competent, even outstanding readers — but they usually have to develop different strategies for making sense of written texts.

In brief, there are constitutional differences among people, some of them dramatic. To ignore such differences would be to seriously handicap some learners, especially when defensible and effective intervention strategies have been developed. These interventions are an important part of current educational knowledge, and the practicing teacher should have some familiarity with their literatures.

However, the belief structure that underpins most of the discourse around difference needs to be interrogated, beginning with the obvious prejudices instilled by the terminology of disability, dysfunction, disorder, abnormality, deviance, impairment, and deficit. Such vocabulary casts difference as a lack, something to be overcome, compensated for, remediated.

There *is* another way of thinking about such categories of difference. But before developing this point, it is helpful to consider another domain of exceptionality that sits at the opposite pole of social approval: giftedness.

Labeling Talents

From 2 to 5% of children deviate sufficiently from the norm in some category of performance or achievement to be labeled "gifted."

There are as many categories of giftedness as there are domains of human activity. As might be expected, the sorts of abilities that tend to be noticed in this regard are as much a reflection of cultural bias as they are of individual exceptionality. In Western countries, for instance, an overwhelming majority of the children who are identified as prodigies have exceptional abilities in calculation, visual arts, music, or memory — categories for which prowess can be demonstrated without interpretation of results. By contrast, in other settings and other eras, persons are or were more often singled out as exceptional for social skills, wisdom, compassion, story-telling, and insight (often mystical or prophetic).

Giftedness tends to be uneven. Although there are instances of persons with abilities that are exceptional across-the-board, most children identified as prodigies (perhaps 95%) are outstanding in only one domain. In particular, among prodigies, there tend to be marked disparities between mathematical and verbal abilities. The most extreme of such cases are *savants*, who typically excel in drawing, music, or calculation, but who tend to have severe language and social deficits. Conversely, there are those with advanced linguistic and social abilities who have great difficulty with logico-mathematical and performance-oriented tasks.

Recent neurological research has shed some light on the origins of such discrepancies. Like human communities, brains are not homogeneous structures. Rather, particular sub-structures perform fairly specific functions. Just like the diversity of operations needed to maintain a community, various brain functions are simultaneously localized and interreliant. In a healthy brain, the net result is what would be regarded as a well-balanced person. However, such is often not the case for a person who has suffered severe and localized brain injury.

Fig. 3.6. Like other parts of the body, brain areas change in size depending on how they're exercised.

With use, areas become larger, and the neurons within them become more densely clustered and more complexly interconnected.

With lack of use, areas shrink and their neurons die more quickly.

Such damage rarely gives rise to generalized impairments. Rather, localized injury tends to diminish some capacities while enhancing others, depending on a complex array of conditions (e.g., where the damage is, its cause, the age of the victim, etc.). The resultant deficits are easily explained, since abilities are usually associated with fairly specific areas of the brain. A corresponding enhancement of ability, though, is somewhat surprising, and seems to be linked to a sudden release of resources in the brain. As one region no longer requires such resources, a nearby region can exploit them. Such localized damage can give rise to a range of enhanced capacities, one that is as broad as the range of possible disabilities. A sensory capacity or other physical function might be impaired or enhanced, mathematical abilities might be devastated while verbal abilities are improved, and so on.

Of course, there is more to giftedness than an extraordinary capacity — which is to say, one must be careful not to reduce giftedness to unitary traits or singular causes. For exceptionalities to be manifested, there must be motivation to exploit abilities. In fact, motivation is often sufficient to parlay otherwise typical abilities into extraordinary performances. (On this issue, it is interesting to note how often genius is linked to obsessions, compulsions, paranoias, and manic-depressive illnesses. Recent studies of artists and writers put the rate at about 10 times that of the rest of the population.)

Many qualifications to the discussion are necessary here. First, it must be reemphasized that giftedness in one area does not necessarily imply a deficit in another. Such is most often the case, but is hardly a universal. Second, it is not always the case that exceptionalities are narrow and specific. On the contrary, abilities in one domain often support abilities in another. Third, while the rate of occurrence is certainly more pronounced, one should not assume a link between genius and localized brain damage. A more appropriate reading of the details presented above is that, in the case of giftedness, personal profiles tend to be marked by more than one extreme, but the origins of those extremes in personality and ability can rarely be reduced to singular causes or straightforward correlations.

Rather, what must be borne in mind is that the spec-

Hunting Gifts?

There are many popular accounts, most of them revolving around either mathematical or musical prowess, of exceptionally talented persons.

The recent Hollywood movie, *Good Will Hunting*, is typical of this genre: A young man with a bad attitude but able to solve the most sophisticated logical problems appears on the scene at MIT.

In actuality, instances of such exceptional giftedness, erupting full-blown without years of concentrated study and focused practice, are simply unheard of. Across domains — writing, chess, music, etc. — the top professionals tend to share two qualities: They began early in life, and they engage in intense solitary practice for more than 20 hours each week. (In contrast, most professionals practice less than 10 hours each week. Most of this practice is either highly repetitive, drillwork sorts of exercise or direct copying, imitation, or examination of others' works.)

This is no less true of those who are seen to demonstrate prodigious mathematical talent. In fact, it has even been shown that idiot savants, those distinguished for their calculating, prime-number-identifying, date-determining, and other number-crunching abilities, also involve themselves in extensive practice. In a nutshell, the evidence suggests that exceptionality is much more about dedicated and sustained effort (even obsession) than it is about innate ability.

trum of exceptionalities is broad and derives from a range of origins, including the extrapersonal. Such a realization highlights the inadequacy of a statistics-based conception of normality. Social and biological conditions are simply too varied and too dynamic for there to be any useful and stable category of "normal."

However, the opposite to such *normalist* notions — the *relativist* stance that all difference is equally valid and valuable — is no more appealing. Relativism might be considered the opposite of normalism. As a theoretical stance, it posits that knowledge and values are relative to a person's nature and situation. As an ideological stance, relativism asserts that all difference must be at least tolerated, and preferably embraced.

But an uncritical and wholesale, relativistic embrace of difference is no better than the desire to flatten exceptionalities into normal abilities. Simply put, not all difference is good. Decisions around what is and is not acceptable are constantly being made and enforced. Every society has implemented structures to control or contain those differences that are seen as deviances.

Formal education seems to be caught up in the unending debate that arises between the poles of normalism and relativism. At the same time, public schools are for the most part ill-equipped to address either set of worries. Clearly, no teacher could possibly be expected to be aware of and to tailor instruction *relative* to the specific profiles of each learner in her or his classroom. Yet, gearing one's strategies to the fictional *normal* child will necessarily set the conditions for boredom and for frustration.

Once again, there seems to be a clear need for another way to think about difference.

Sources of Creativity

There is a coherent discourse that looks at difference differently — not as deviation, abnormality, or dysfunction, but as a necessary quality of life.

Recent developments in complexity theory have presented us with a startling challenge to popular conceptions of normality (and abnormality): Difference and diversity among sub-structures are critical to the vitality and viability of any complex form, whether talking about a brain, a person, a community, a species, or whatever.

Relative to one another, we are different. Formal education should foster our unique talents and gifts. Instruction should thus be mostly child-centered.

How, what, and when we teach is informed by what we know about the development of a **normal** child. Instruction should thus be mostly teacher-centered.

SHAKY COMMON GROUND
Persons are autonomous; ability is contained in the individual; intelligence is innate (natural) but subject to the constraining influences of context (nurtured).

Fig. 3.6. While offering conflicting prescriptions for schooling, relativists and normalists tend to have very similar beliefs about identity, ability, and other matters.

In other words, if every neuron or organ or person or culture were made to conform to statistically determined *average profiles*, the organism or organization would either be frozen in static patterns of action or would perish. Whether biological or social, the viability of complex dynamic forms is dependent on internal diversity. With regard to the differences among humans, then, complexity theory not only embraces diversity, but delights in it.

This shift in thinking amounts to a rejection of the deeply entrenched habit of interpreting *complex* phenomenon in terms of *complicated* ones, as was developed in Chapter 2. To recap, complicated objects (e.g., clocks) are mechanical and predictable; complex forms (e.g., humans) are ever-evolving phenomena that cannot be reduced to discrete parts. Rather, complex forms arise in the interactions of similarly dynamic forms (e.g., organs arise in the joint actions of cells), without the benefit of a controller or orchestrator. For such systems, it is simultaneously true to say that the overall behavior guides the actions of the parts *and* the actions of the parts cause the overall behavior.

This distinction between complicated (mechanical) and complex (organic) amounts to a devastating critique of the application of statistical methods to social and psychological phenomena. These methods were developed to examine complicated phenomena. As developed earlier, a major impetus for the emergence of statistics as a field was the need for a systematic means of assessing variations among manufactured objects — and, admittedly, statistical methods are powerful tools in the maintenance of standards. The situation for complex phenomena, though, is almost exactly the opposite. Rather than needing to minimize variation, a complex system actually *relies* on the differences among its components. Complexity theorists thus reject popular interpretations of "average" and "normal."

Why? Because novelty, creativity, change, learning — that is, evolutionary and cognitive events — can only arise when there are differences that enable and compel departure from established patterns. Underpinning this assertion is the recent realization that, contrary to previous belief, life is not about "maintaining balance." Almost the opposite, life occurs far from equilibrium. By way of illustration, the simple activity of walking requires one to deliberately put oneself off balance. That is, walking is a controlled fall, a matter of constant disequilibrium.

Fig. 3.7. In humans, genetic information is held in the form of 46 enormous molecules of DNA which have, in total, an information capacity of 10^{10} bits. If all this information were actually written out, it would fill a book of over a million pages.

As these immense molecules interact with their surroundings, the stage is set for a tremendous amount of variation among persons. An emerging sensibility is that this variety is not accidental, but critical to the ongoing viability of the species as it enables humanity to adapt to an incredible range of unpredictable contingencies.

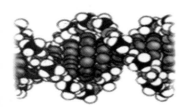

The point here is *not* that all variation is good. Clearly we would be foolish to embrace cancerous cells, psychotic murderers, hate propaganda, and so on. Nor is the point that the notion of normal is bad. In a complex and ever-changing world such as ours, it often seems that sanity is linked to our shared capacity to impose pattern and order, however contrived, on varied experiences. What is important is the realization that variation is necessary to creativity, which is in turn necessary to evolution. Creativity, like its consequences of evolution and cognition, is a process of diversification, of expanding the realm of the possible. For new possibilities to arise, we need there to be differences in opinion, in interest, in ability.

Nature or Nurture?

Are personal traits and capacities innate or acquired? Are growth and development controlled by information contained within genes, or is the external world mostly responsible for shaping who we are? Are abilities fixed at birth, or can we, for example, become smarter?

Such worries about the relative influences of nature and nurture have been around for centuries. Despite their prominence, though, few thinkers have championed either extreme. Rather, for the most part there has been a consensus that the environment must provide adequate conditions for the realization of one's pre-established potentials: Popular opinion is that nurture supports nature.

More recently, however, more complexified formulations have arisen, ones that highlight the poverty of the nature/nurture dichotomy. Research in psychology, neurology, and biology have demonstrated the complex interdependencies of genetics and experience — and, in particular, have shown that the dynamics at genetic and experiential levels aren't as different or as differentiable as once thought. In fact, the processes are so similar and intertwined that it doesn't really make sense to consider them as separate, let alone as opposed.

Consider, for example, the commonsense habits of talking about brains as biological (nature) and learning as experiential (nurture). Such a conception assumes a tidy line between nature and nurture. However, as it turns out, brains are constantly rebuilding themselves, evolving with the rest of the body as it moves through the world. New learnings do not simply enter a prefabricated brain; rather, learning actually involves transformations of brain structure. (In other words, brains aren't hardware and learning isn't a matter of software or storage. Such metaphors are problematic because learning changes both the "programming" *and* the "circuitry." That is, the brain is effectively rebuilt through experience. Subsequent experiences are handled by a different brain.)

As studies of the physical-and-mental differences between genetically identical twins have shown, essentially the same complex dynamics that are at work in the brain are also at play in the social realm. Twins' personalities, appearances, abilities, and so on can and do drift apart as each undergoes different experiences — and this drifting begins in the womb. Again, it makes little sense to separate nature and nurture in tracing such differences.

In brief, there is no genetic blueprint, there are no deterministic social forces. But it all matters. Even though development is not *determined by* such singular influences, it is utterly *dependent on* them.

So understood, creativity is not a trait that is specific to some and not to others. Rather, all living forms are inherently creative beings. Humans are particularly so, as they continuously demonstrate their flexibility, originality, and fluency. This is especially true early in life as young children engage in novel actions, shape new sentences, and otherwise demonstrate the play of existence. The problem with the conventional conception of normality, then, is that it works to discard unpredictability, messiness, and surprise through the pathologizing of difference. It forgets that, just as the only constant in life is change, so the only feature common to all living forms is difference.

Against this realization, it would appear that the school has traditionally offered little to support creativity, structured as it is around age-appropriate routines, standardized curricula, unified pacing, and so on. In the traditional classroom, little space tends to be left in the school day for random exploration, free initiative, uninterrupted and sustained concentration, narrowed focus, daydreams, diversions, or obsessions. Such *playful* activities are usually seen as contrary to the *work* of learning, rather than being embraced as vital to understanding, discovery, and insight. It is thus not surprising to hear that many of the most creative personalities in our society were frustrated by the school experiences — and have sought out or created situations that support creativity in their adult lives.

Complicated Ideas About Intelligence

These changes in thinking about the nature and the role of creativity are reflected in recent discussions of intelligence — a term for which there is surprisingly little agreement on definition.

Current debates on the nature of intelligence revolve around a range of issues, two of which have particular relevance for educators. The first has to do with the sorts of traits and capacities that are involved in intelligence. Closely related, the second has to do with whether those qualities are best thought of as individual traits or as cultural phenomena.

The purpose of this section is to survey some of the range of current opinion on these and related matters, with a view toward setting the stage for a more complexified exploration of intelligence.

What's being tested?

The following pair of items is reflective of the sorts of questions that are used to determine IQs.

QUESTIONS

1. Which of the four items pictured to the right (i.e., the hammer, the saw, the ax, or the block of wood) does not belong?
2. Which letter goes in the blank? T W Q , O T J , U Y ___

ANSWERS

1. The log. All the other items can be collected in the abstract category, "tool." [Depending on cultural background, age, and profession, many respondents select either the saw or the ax, reasoning that one could stand in for the other if necessary. Such persons are not reasoning logically (which requires abstraction categorization), but narratively (according to their day-to-day experiences). While critical for daily life, this manner of thinking can be a detriment in formal testing settings.]

2. Q. The second letter of each set is as many letters further in the alphabet as the third letter comes before the first letter.

COMMENTARY

A few of the problems with IQ test items are highlighted here. The first question points to the narrow sorts of logical processes that such tests tend to address — and, with that, the cultural, ageist, and other social biases implicit in testing. The second shows how such tests aim to measure one's ability to logically analyze overly contrived situations — in effect, to find the "trick."

To be fair, most intelligence tests are far broader than these examples might suggest, and cover such areas as vocabulary, comprehension, arithmetic, and short- and long-term memory.

Intelligence Quotient (IQ). Over the last century, discussions of intelligence have been greatly influenced — if not totally dominated — by the notion of Intelligence Quotient. By definition, an IQ is a ratio of mental age to chronological age, and it was originally proposed in an attempt to measure intellectual ability and to predict academic potential.

The idea of IQ arose as part of the movement toward statistical methods in the late 1800s. In spite of its youth, IQ has powerfully influenced conceptions of intelligence and potential. In particular, it has prompted intelligence to be seen less as a *quality* that is manifest in day-to-day life, and more as a *quantity* to be measured and ranked.

For the most part, IQ tests are structured around knowledge- and logic-based performance tasks (see inset box, above), ones that have been deliberately selected and refined so that the tests generate more-or-less normal distributions when administered to large numbers of persons. (In spite of a century of effort to engineer this quality, and

Fig. 3.8. An adult's brain accounts for about 5% of body weight, but uses about 20% of the body's energy. In other words, there's a lot of physical activity in the brain.

Interestingly, while awake, both the brain's energy consumption and its activity level are pretty much constant — whether concentrating on a difficult mental task or day-dreaming.

This fact highlights the relative smallness of consciousness. In terms of actual brain activity — including both conscious and nonconscious processes — it doesn't seem to matter how hard we *think* that our brains are working. They're simply always working.

despite many claims to success, IQ test-makers have not yet been successful in generating a truly normal distribution. Even so, the fact that normal distributions can be approximated has been used by test-makers to argue that a real, natural phenomenon is being measured.)

From the beginning, there have been challenges to the idea of an IQ. Some critiques focus on definition, arguing that intelligence is a more fluid, complex, and contextually sensitive phenomenon than tests can measure. Other critiques focus on implicit cultural biases, both in terms of the priority assigned to formal logical processes over other modes of reasoning and in terms of the specific cultural knowledge needed for some questions. (For example, North Americans have an advantage in responding to the following: For the group consisting of Barney Rubble, Betty Boop, Bugs Bunny, and Burt Bacharach, identify one quality that distinguishes each character from the others.) Historically, the cultural biases woven into IQ tests have had some troubling consequences. Two prominent examples from the early 20th Century arose in the screening of immigrants and in the identification of "officer material" from among army recruits. In both cases, based on test results, priority was given to upper middle class, English-speaking, Caucasians over other social classes, nationalities, and races.

Another historical event even more powerfully supports the assertion that IQ tests do little more than measure the imposed assumptions of their designers. Until the mid-1930s, the average IQ score for men was a few points higher than the average score for women. At a meeting of test designers, it was agreed that the tests should be analyzed for those items that contributed to this difference. The offending items were isolated and eliminated — and, as a result, women and men have since had similar average IQ scores. However, similar efforts to isolate and remove items that contribute to measured differences among racial, cultural, and social groups have not been undertaken, even though it would not be difficult to do so.

Other critiques of IQ tests are founded on the observation that a person's IQ score can vary dramatically with age, with even modest environmental changes, or through instruction in IQ-test sorts of questions. Further, several decades of research have demonstrated that, contrary to their announced purpose, even the most sophisticated IQ tests have little predictive value. At best, it appears that IQ scores can account for about 25% of the variation among students' school grades and roughly 10% of people's performances later in life, suggesting that there must be other, perhaps better, indicators of intelligence.

Indicators of Intelligence. The word "intelligence" derives from the Latin term for *discernment* — and, in terms of current usage, the ability to discern essential features of a situation is one of the few indicators of intelligence for which there is general agreement. Other suggested characteristics include memory, adaptation, wit, judgment, reason/logic, problem-solving, and understanding.

Other qualities are more contentious. Some parties have argued that versatility and the capacity to juggle several ideas at once are vital; others have proposed almost the opposite, that sustained concentration on a single focus is the hallmark of intelligence. Some have included creativity, wisdom, and morality as necessary aspects; others have argued that *capacities*, such as intelligence, should not be conflated with such *virtues*. Some have argued that intelligence derives from a broad knowledge base; others have countered that intelligence is a matter of processing power, not database. What is clear from such disagreements is that, contrary to assumption implicit in the notion of IQ, intelligence is not a unified phenomenon.

This realization has prompted some to develop lists of different sorts of intelligence (e.g., verbal, logical, social, musical, etc.) — an approach that is supported by neurological evidence which shows how such capacities seem to be specific to particular regions of the brain. Such a tack has helped to broaden conceptions of ability and potential, and has thus had some positive impact on educational practices. It has also supported a belief that persons with limited abilities in one domain will be compensated in another — a notion that often appeals to one's sense of fairness. In reality, apart from cases of specific neuronal damage, this doesn't happen much. People who score low on tests of one of these categories of intelligence usually do poorly on tests of other kinds.

As a final critique, the strategy of listing discrete sorts of intelligence has reinforced some deeply embedded and troublesome assumptions: that intelligence is innate, that ability is culturally independent, and so on.

Fig. 3.9. Different human capacities tend to be associated with highly localized parts of the brain — a discovery that has been used by some to argue for an array of different sorts of intelligences.

More recent research has shown that, regardless of the specific task it is working on, *all* of the brain is active. And so, even though it is clear that particular regions do specialize, it is just as clear that the brain is not modularized. This more complex understanding of brain activity helps to explain why, for example, art-based and physical activity can enhance abilities in other domains.

In brief, the notion of discrete intelligences seems to be an oversimplification of a more complex phenomenon.

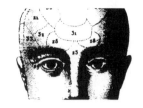

Fig. 3.10. Human communication relies on assumption, familiarity, pattern, expectation, and so on — all of which surpasses logical analysis. The respondant, above, for example, has assumed that the first person (a) is looking for his keys, (b) used them the evening before, (c) wants some help finding them, and (d) might have left them in a garment, although none of this was explicitly communicated.

Most human communication involves such "reading between the lines," a complex ability that is developed early on in life. It has proven to be an extremely difficult capacity for a computer to master, however.

Locations of intelligence. One contribution of theories of "multiple" or "varied" intelligences is a clear demonstration of the fact that any manifestation of intelligence is dependent on there being something to be intelligent about. That is, regardless of how one might understand intelligence, its products must be valued in at least one cultural context. Otherwise, particular abilities either will not be noticed or, if noticed, will likely be seen as pathological. (This point is demonstrated by recent proposals of two new sorts of intelligence: spiritual and naturalist. Persons demonstrating exceptionality in such categories might have been seen as fanatical or deluded only a few decades ago.)

However, despite a tacit agreement that all intelligence has a social dimension, it is overwhelmingly discussed as though it were an internal, brain-based capacity of the individual. This deeply inscribed belief is problematic, but not entirely wrong. Clearly, individuals do differ in their abilities to assess, to adjust to, and to manipulate their settings. What tends to be lacking in popular conceptions of intelligence, however, is an appreciation of the roles of learning, of access to information, of others, of specialization, and so on in the articulation of our abilities. As such, different lines of questioning are now emerging: Is intelligence really a quality of the individual, or is it more a matter of collective activity? Why are high school students able to understand ideas that were inaccessible to the geniuses of past generations? Are the limits of individual ability prespecified, or can we become more intelligent?

In other words, intelligence is coming to be understood as a dynamic and complex phenomenon, one that cannot be predetermined, measured, or localized.

Complexifying Intelligence

Such wonderings are prompted in large part by new understandings of learning, knowledge, perception, and identity. In particular, disciplines that have incorporated the insights of complexity theory have helped to demonstrate that brain and world are more deeply intertwined than was previously suspected — a notion that is often associated with the theories and research of Jean Piaget.

Piaget began with the assumption that the origins of intelligent behavior are in the baby's first actions in the world — actions that are both guided by and that give structure to perception. (See Chapter 1 for a discussion of the recursive nature of this relationship.) Such activity, Piaget suggested, eventually lends structure to thought and language. Each "stage" in one's growth is, in effect, an elaborated version of what has come before. The development of language, for example, greatly enables the individual's abilities to notice relationships and to make connections. Such elaborations set the stage for more flexible, encompassing, generalized abilities — that is, they enable more intelligent activity. In effect, Piaget suggested that intelligence is neither an innate capacity nor an acquired ability: Intelligence, rather, is a biological-and-cultural evolutionary event through which one's repertoire of possibilities becomes more diverse and more complex.

Other conceptual developments in recent decades have supported even more dramatic rethinkings of what intelligence might be.

Artificial Intelligence (AI). One of the more surprising sources of new insights into intelligence in recent years has been research into artificial intelligence. A domain that has been given to over-optimistic forecasts for decades, with confident predictions for the creation of electronic minds that would far surpass flesh-based intellects, difficulties encountered in AI research have helped to reveal some deep-seated cultural assumptions about intelligence.

Decades after hopeful first efforts, even the best of our "artificial intelligence" devices are decidedly unintelligent — able to perform spectacularly in narrow domains, but incapable of adapting to novelty or contingency in a way that would suggest they are thinking.

Why the apparent failure in AI projects? Part of the answer to this question can be found in two troublesome assumptions about the nature of intelligence.

The first has to do with what tends to be seen as intelligent behavior in humans, namely, extraordinary performance on the logic-based tasks that one finds on IQ tests and in mathematics texts. Very early on, AI researchers achieved great success in programming computers to outperform humans on such tasks, leading many to forecast that computers would soon be made to recognize faces and words. Most, however, doubted they could be made smart enough to prove theorems or to play chess. The opposite turns out to be the case. Computers have defeated

Fig. 3.11. Assisted by powerful new technologies, neurologists have started to gain insight into what makes some brains smarter than others.

There have been two prominent hypotheses: One is that the smart brain "runs hot" — that is, it has a good deal of energy to burn when faced with a mental task. The other is the opposite: the smart brain is cooly efficient.

It appears that each view is partly correct. The smart brain starts out by devoting considerable resources to a problem. However, once the discernments needed to understand the situation have been made, the smart brain quickly simplifies and routinizes the task, thus making efficient use of energy. That is, once an answer has been found, the smart brain slips into unthinking routine, freeing up concentration for new problems.

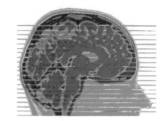

the best chess players and have created novel logical proofs. As for recognizing faces and words, however, computers lag behind the young of many species, demonstrating that evolution has solved many problems that are well beyond the most advanced products of human intelligence.

The second problematic assumption of AI researchers was that intelligence is a matter of having a powerful central processing device and a large store of data. This belief is clearly aligned with the popular assumption that the most intelligent people are the ones who process things quickly and who have good memories.

With regard to the first assumption, AI itself has demonstrated that the critical aspect of intelligent behavior is not what people learn to do in schools, but what children learn *before* arriving at the school's door. Simple everyday sensibilities and capabilities are what computers have been unable to handle. Such commonplace competencies as using language flexibly, distinguishing among objects, predicting outcomes, and interpreting indirect references are the sorts of things computers do not do well — mostly, it seems, because these are the sorts of things that depend on having a body that must constantly negotiate its way through diverse and complex situations.

This point helps to highlight the problem with the second assumption (that intelligence is a matter of centralized computational power). The one area of AI research that is now showing the most promise is a branch of robotics that does not rely on powerful central processors or preprogrammed stores of data. Instead, these new robots are equipped with several independent control systems that must "learn" to work together to achieve particular goals such as moving around a room or manipulating objects. This strategy of imitating the organization of complex forms (i.e., of smaller systems nested in larger systems) has met with considerable success in terms of creating machines that are flexible, adaptive, and able to generate new behaviors.

Although still falling well short of human intelligence, such successes in robot intelligence are aligned with the long-standing realization that the human brain is not a unified central processor. Neither is the brain a collectivity of specialized systems under central direction. Rather, it is now clear that the brain is more like a social collective in which each specialized subgrouping reacts to the others.

Fig. 3.12. When patterns such as the flocking of birds, the foraging of ants, or the functioning of brains are observed, it is often assumed that there are centralized causes.

Most often, however, there are no such controls. Rather, the observed patterns are *self-organized*. There are no leaders, nor is there any general plan inscribed in the heads of individuals. Instead, such collective activity emerges from a mass of local interactions as each participant responds to its nearest few neighbors.

This realization has prompted a dramatic shift in discussions of brain function and intelligence.

Thought and behavior arise from the co-action of many brain regions. (An upshot is that there is no unified self who exercises overall control. Rather, "self" is more an emergent consequence of such collective activity. This matter is taken up in Chapter 4.)

What does this say about intelligence?

Most importantly, intelligence arises in the complex interplay of brain regions, body, and environment. In effect, learning and intelligence are all about strengthening and diversifying relationships among things, from the level of synapses to the level of overt behaviors. Intelligence, in other words, is all about being able to rapidly initiate the next move in real-world situations, not simply about identifying the missing item in a logical sequence.

Intelligence, that is, is *not* a specific attribute or competency. Like consciousness and creativity, it is a global emergent property, one that is as dependent on what goes on *outside* of one's skin as what is happening *inside*.

Animal Intelligence

Few would question the assertion that humans are more intelligent than other species. But does it make sense to compare the intelligence of humans to, say, dogs, cats, dolphins, or monkeys?

On some levels, such comparisons do make sense: Other species seem to be able to adapt, to abstract, to reason, to plan, and to communicate. And, more important, interspecies comparisons have highlighted that all "intelligent" animals have a penchant for seemingly pointless, often repetitive, and usually energetic behaviors — that is, play. Dolphins, whales, octopuses, and primates, for example, all use play to expand their repertoires of experience and possible response. So understood, playful activity is essential to intelligent activity.

However, humans have managed to parlay sensory systems, bodily structures, and social tendencies that evolved on the African savanna into abilities that sometimes prompt us to forget our natural origins. It is language, more than any other of our technologies, that has afforded us a sort of transcendence over our circumstances.

Comparisons of ourselves to other species tend to ignore this critical factor. We have a language that enables us to analyze a much broader range of potential action and to weed out truly stupid ones before committing to them in an unforgiving world. Language enables fantasies and hopes (like flying to the moon) that can work to guide thinking in surprising ways. Beyond such anticipations, language allows us to share thoughts with one another and to live in worlds that no other species can access. Indeed, such complex constructs as consciousness and personal identity, seem to be largely dependent on a recursive use of language (that is, being able to identify ourselves).

In brief, superficial comparisons of humans to other species (on such bases as brain size, trainability, and so on) miss the essential point that our intelligence derives in large part from the fact that our brains are linked into a single cognitive system through language. Nonhuman minds are not dulled or lesser versions of human minds. They are qualitatively different.

Fig. 3.13. Imagine a dog, surrounded by cans of beans, winking at you.

This is an *easy* mental task.

Despite its simplicity, though, only humans are capable of such imaginings — thanks to our languaging abilities.

And it's not just that language makes it possible to think odd thoughts. Everything that has passed through your mind while reading this book is simply unavailable to non-language users. Language is the house of our intelligence.

Intelligent Artifacts. Every one of us can readily understand ideas that were beyond the grasp of the best minds of past generations. How is that possible?

Given that there hasn't been much time for biological evolution to enhance brain functioning, the answer would seem to have to do with cultural evolution — that is, with the possibility that we have structured the world in ways that support more sophisticated thought. There seems to be an ongoing process of *offloading* that makes it possible for individuals to draw on, build from, and add to "objects" of intelligence — objects that include tools, myths, cultural narratives, books, computers, and so on.

Anthropologists made this point long ago in reference to advances in technology. Historically, the invention of new tools often coincides with sudden cultural advances. The suggestion has been that a great deal of information is embedded in a well-designed artifact. That is, a useful tool is not only the product of intelligence, it bestows intelligence as it allows one to focus one's learning efforts on other details. Consider, for instance, the impact of the calculator on mathematics learning. Relieved of the burden of mastering procedures and memorizing facts, young learners are now able to focus their attentions on a much broader range of mathematical situations than before.

Such artifacts have a certain snowball effect as simple external props and practices help us to think better, enabling the creation of more complex forms. In effect, a powerful feedback loop is set up that can allow for exponential increases in our abilities — as is being demonstrated in the current "electronic revolution." While dramatic, the current revolution is not without historic precedent.

Languaging. In terms of the enabling of human intelligence, by far the most powerful technology available to us is language. With language, human brains have been equipped with habits, methods, associations, and information — in effect, mind-tools — that draw from the experiences of millions of other lives and that have been honed over thousands of generations. The technology of language underpins the human ability to come together in grander cognitive systems, ones whose capacities vastly surpass the abilities of individuals.

Such a claim may seem exaggerated. But consider how novelists and poets have demonstrated that, thanks to the incredible flexibility of linguistic systems, there is no limit to the persons and events that can be created and experienced. Or as is demonstrated in every high school course, teachers can guide learners through problems and paradoxes that mystified the human race for generations. In effect, language enables a sort of common mind, an intelligence that is vastly more than what can be embodied by any individual.

Language is more than a system of words. It is a network of associations that extend across time and space. Language might be characterized as an evolving form that constantly modifies and reorganizes itself through the continuing interactions of humans as they negotiate the world, giving rise to a collective corpus whose reach far exceeds any individual intelligence.

The power of language to support intelligent action goes beyond the ways it stretches across minds and time. Language enables humans to do something that no other species can: to ask "What if ... ?" Humans can experiment

---

Encouraging Thoughts

Want to think more clearly? Then eat, drink, be merry, and vary your activities!

Eat: The brain requires ten times more glucose and oxygen for its size than any other organ — which means that proper nourishment is vital to its function. It also means that, in this age of performance-enhancing substances, one of the best "smart drugs" is already present in a healthy diet.

Drink: Like the rest of the body, the brain must be well hydrated. Even modest reductions in fluid levels can prompt fatigue, distractibility, and irritability. A glass of water is sometimes more important to learning than the most carefully crafted classroom event.

Be Merry: The same neurochemicals that are released during events of emotional arousal prompt the brain to make lasting records of events. We simply remember better when there is an emotional impact. Contrary to the folk belief that emotion is opposed to rationality, they have been demonstrated to be necessary to one another.

Vary Activities: Regular, sustained, and strenuous exercise is vital to mental and physical health. Exercise prompts the brain to release extra endorphins ("feel good" chemicals), it improves the functioning of all organs, it boosts oxygen levels in the brain as it increases blood flow, and it speeds the removal of toxins. In brief, exercise can make people happier, less anxious, less depressed, and more intelligent.

As well, regular exercise can be one aspect of one's varied routines— or "distractions," as they are sometimes called. History is rife with tales of how many of humankind's greatest insights did not happen during moments of focused concentration but when minds were otherwise occupied — with getting on buses, during dreams, while chatting with friends, and so on.

with possible plans of action before committing to them. Language enables forethought, anticipation, planning, strategizing. (To be fair to other species, there is ample evidence that humans are not alone in the abilities to plan and anticipate. However, it is just as clear that our language greatly amplifies such abilities.) In other words, language frees us from the confines of the immediate present.

Language embodies another quality that also amplifies intelligence: the possibility of varied associations and conclusions. As we have all experienced, much of human interaction seems to revolve around trying to make sense of differences in perception and interpretation. While sometimes frustrating, such differences can be the sources of tremendous creativity as humans must work to make sense of one another, in the process opening up new possibilities for thinking. Such negotiations also contribute to the ongoing evolution of our language.

In brief, then, language is a natural reservoir of variation, a sea of possibilities. As such, language is not just a way to express intelligence, but a principal source.

Developmentalism

One more topic needs to be addressed in this brief survey of the issues and opinions that are prominent in current discussions of difference and ability: human development, or, more precisely, *developmentalism*.

Developmentalism is a term that refers to any attempt to lay out a sequence of stages through which a person is expected to progress on the route from birth to death. A number of developmental hierarchies have been proposed over the last century and, as might be anticipated, such structures have been interpreted and taken up in some very different ways.

The issue of developmentalism is addressed here because of the pervasive use of such theories to inform classroom practice and educational policy. In particular, this section aims to raise issues around the ways that many of such theories have been interpreted in terms of "normal" development — and, hence, have been used to defend the practice of teaching the same thing in the same way at the same time to a group of people who might have nothing in common except the year of their birth.

Developmentalist theories and frameworks are gen-

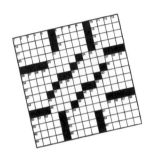

Fig. 3.14. Do intellectual abilities decline because of age?

No. A few rather ambitious, long-term studies have shown that intellectual abilities can be maintained, but it depends on how people keep their brains busy.

Eighty-year-olds who have made a habit of such activities as playing bridge, doing crosswords, and building jigsaw puzzles, tend to score as well as they ever did on tests of mental acuity. In contrast, those who never made a habit of activities that demand mental effort tend to show significant declines in intellectual abilities as they age. They also appear to be much more susceptible to the effects of degenerative brain diseases.

erally founded on some fairly reliable observations. Young children, for example, are generally more playful, more easily distracted, and more captivated by repetition than older children and adults. Moreover, young children tend to be more readily able to learn new competencies (e.g., riding a bike, playing the piano) than adults.

In terms of language development, a common observation is that babies babble every sound of every language. Over the first year of life, the range of vocalizations narrows to reflect the local language. The abilities to detect and generate sounds that are not commonly heard is lost by early adolescence. (Because of this loss, persons who learn a new language after adolescence are rarely able to speak it without an obvious accent.) At the same time that this pruning occurs, the child is learning new words at a rate of about two per waking hour, a capacity that is also greatly diminished by early adolescence. (It's not all bad news. What seems to be a loss in the capacity to learn language is counterbalanced by a dramatic increase in reasoning abilities.)

Such observations clearly support the notion that humans move through fairly precise stages — shifting, for instance, from concrete manipulation of objects to more abstract operations. As much evidence as there is for this assertion, however, it tends to be accompanied by the troublesome assumption that developmental stages are controlled by pre-programmed, internal mechanisms.

Coupled to the forementioned observations, the assumption of innate unfolding underpins one of the most prominent features of educational discourse in the 20th Century: a collection of linear and/or hierarchical sequences and taxonomies that are generally presented in terms of staircases, pyramids, and other vertical progressions. (See the inset box on pages 130–131.) Such images reflect a belief in direct movements toward universal, inevitable, identifiable, and desirable endpoints — an imagery that, as developed in Chapter 2, is now being replaced by more unruly, recursive alternatives.

Such alternatives have been made necessary by mounting evidence for the assertion that developmental "stages" are not so much a matter of "natural unfoldings" as they are necessary shifts in cognitive strategy that emerge from an accumulated weight of experience. This suggestion is supported by the fact that the brain simply doesn't change

Bloom's Taxomony of Question Types

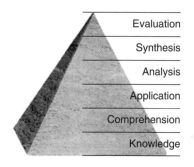

Fig. 3.15. Among educationists, "Bloom's Taxonomy" is perhaps the most prominent classification scheme. First published in the 1950s, the scheme is used to sort questions according to their level of sophistication and frequency. The simplest and most common questions are at the bottom; the rarest and most complicated are at the the top.

The associated pyramidal image is meant to suggest that one must build to higher level questions. That vertical and accumulative framework has supported the practices of lesson planning that begin with many repetitive exercises and that move toward one or two more involved questions at the end.

Although useful for examining the tasks that we set for children, there are two key problems with such taxonomizing:

First, it suggests that the sophistication of a query is inherent in the question — as opposed to being determined by the answerer. (A "synthesis" question for one student may be a "knowledge" question for another.) What matters most is not what is asked, but how it is answered. Hence, the model has limited practical value when it comes to preparing lists of questions for actual learners.

Second, the model assumes that mastery occurs through processes of *repetition* — as opposed to treating the development of understanding as a matter of *recursion*. Derived from "recur," a recursion is not a repetition, but a "looping back," an "elaboration" — one that can quickly give rise to surprising complexity.

An alternative image for such classifications is developed on the next page.

much as a person's thinking strategies, social behaviors, moral judgments, questioning styles, and so on shift from one developmental level to another. In the first few years of life, for example, the child is occupied with learning what to attend to. As those discernments are learned, the brain becomes more occupied with making associations among them (and, hence, there is a sharp rise in language ability alongside a marked reduction in one's capacities to discern sounds and other sensory details). So conceived, different stages likely arise from knowing too much, not from sudden triggerings of innate mechanisms at preprogrammed ages. We do seem to move through discrete stages, but these progressions have to do with replacing one interpretive strategy with another, more encompassing strategy. The linear images associated with developmental stage theories are thus coming to be replaced with more flexible and fluid alternatives.

Further evidence for this idea has come from studies of persons in other cultural settings. Given that different cultures sometimes employ dramatically different interpretive strategies, it follows that their citizens would likely move through different stages (or, at least, progress at different paces). Such indeed seems to be the case. In fact, we need not step ouside our own society for such evidence: It appears, for example, that the pace of development in young children varies dramatically from one family to the next, as it is linked to a complex mix of linguistic heritage, social context, experiential diversity, communicative practice, and interpretive assistance from adults.

Unfortunately, much of schooling practice is founded on the normalist assumption that developmental stages are innate and universal. This naïve notion has supported curriculum initiatives that assume individuals should be capable of learning the same sorts of ideas at about the same time through the same sorts of teaching methods — or, in other words, initiatives that assume that experience has little to do with what one is capable of learning.

A more informed approach to teaching would take into account diversities of experience and, hence, ranges of interpretive strategies. One important teaching emphasis in this regard is the opportunity for common experiences for all the members of a learning community. Such activities as reading the same story or playing with the same manipulative materials could serve this purpose.

Developing Images

Developmentalist models, which rest on the premise that all humans move through consistent and identifiable "stages" along the path to full achievement, have been prominent in discussions of formal education in recent decades.

Overwhelmingly, these theories have been interpreted in terms of linear progressions from incompleteness (i.e., childhood) to wholeness (i.e., adulthood). (Although some authors intended this sort of start-to-finish image, it should be emphasized that most had something more fluid and complex in mind.)

Unfortunately, perhaps in part because simple images of ladders and staircases fit with the linearized structures that were already in place in schools, educationists have been among the worst interpreters of these theories. It is thus that images of simple vertical structures predominate in the educational literature — and those images support such highly problematic principles as:

- developmental progressions are the same for everyone;
- there are definite and discernible endpoints to these progressions;
- stages of development are discrete and non-overlapping;
- as one enters a new stage, it replaces the previous stage.

Research has demonstrated clearly and consistently that these and other assumptions are wrong.

Part of the problem is with the fact that some of the original research for these models was with very specific cultural subgroups (e.g., male undergraduate students, or children of well educated, upper class professionals). But a more significant difficulty seems to be the assumption of linearity.

It has become clear, for instance, that developmental levels do not *replace* one another. Rather, a particular stage is better thought of as an *elaboration* of preceding stages — all of which are still available to the individual. For instance, it is commonly thought that most adults in a modern and Western society are usually thinking at "formal operations" level. That means that they are able to use fairly sophisticated abstract reasoning skills to make sense of situations. However, most such adults would find it easier to learn a new mathematical concept *concretely* and *sensorially* through physical manipulation of physical materials than *formally* from an abstract explanation. In other words, it's not that Western adults operate at a formal level; it's that they're *capable* of operating at a formal level. They have a broader spectrum of strategies and responses to draw from as they move through diverse experiences. There are no linearities or hierarchies when it comes to thought and development, merely increasingly varied ways of responding to different situations.

The key point here is that "development" is not about progressing to a prespecified (adult) endpoint. Rather, it is about flexible and appropriate adaptation to the immediate situation. That is, *development isn't about the future, it's about the present*, as conditioned by past experience and biological predisposition.

Recent thinking thus suggests somewhat different images might be more appropriate to describe development, and one possibility is a cyclist moving over a varied terrain. Depending on the demands of the moment, the cyclist will shift gears — in effect, selecting the most appropriate manner of dealing with a particular landscape. Similarly, we readily "shift" from one mode of

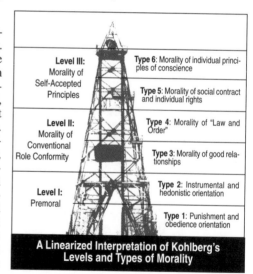

Level III: Morality of Self-Accepted Principles	Type 6: Morality of individual principles of conscience
	Type 5: Morality of social contract and individual rights
Level II: Morality of Conventional Role Conformity	Type 4: Morality of "Law and Order"
	Type 3: Morality of good relationships
Level I: Premoral	Type 2: Instrumental and hedonistic orientation
	Type 1: Punishment and obedience orientation

A Linearized Interpretation of Kohlberg's Levels and Types of Morality

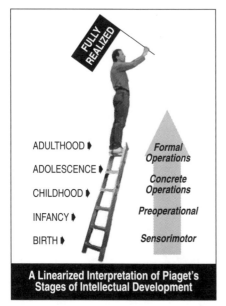

A Linearized Interpretation of Piaget's Stages of Intellectual Development

ADULTHOOD ▶   *Formal Operations*

ADOLESCENCE ▶

CHILDHOOD ▶   *Concrete Operations*

INFANCY ▶   *Preoperational*

BIRTH ▶   *Sensorimotor*

FULLY REALIZED

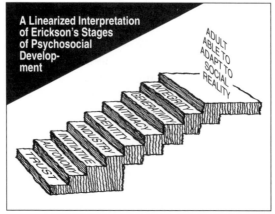

A Linearized Interpretation of Erickson's Stages of Psychosocial Development

ADULT ABLE TO ADAPT TO SOCIAL REALITY

INTEGRITY / GENERATIVITY / INTIMACY / IDENTITY / INDUSTRY / INITIATIVE / AUTONOMY / TRUST

thinking/acting to another in response to new or difficult situations. A cyclist with only one gear would be at a distinct disadvantage. But a cyclist who can switch between lower gears (simpler strategies) and higher gears (more sophisticated, farther reaching strategies) would be able to deal with much more varied circumstances.

This image is supported by findings in neurology which indicate that the brain prefers to operate at the most familiar, habitual, and efficient (i.e., nonconscious and automatic) level that it can. This preference for efficiency would explain why it sometimes

appears that we progress through distinct levels or stages: As more encompassing and efficient strategies arise, the brain gives them priority over previous strategies ... until, of course, situations arise that are so unfamiliar that earlier strategies (i.e., "lower gears") are called for.

The suggestion here is that, as one's experiences are broadened, in effect, one develops "new gears" — that is, strategies that are more encompassing and flexible. This manner of recursive elaboration, reminiscent of the growth of a fractal image (see pp. 70–71), seems to be a much more powerful way to interpret development.

And it has an immediate and vital educational implication: Development should not be thought of as a linear progress or as some sort of accumulation. Rather, it might be better considered as a process of recursive elaboration, moving to ever more sophisticated ways of interpreting experience. So understood, the most critical aspect of the teacher's role is not provision of information, but participation with learners in the development of strategies to interpret that information.

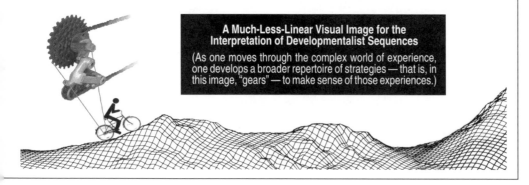

A Much-Less-Linear Visual Image for the Interpretation of Developmentalist Sequences

(As one moves through the complex world of experience, one develops a broader repertoire of strategies — that is, in this image, "gears" — to make sense of those experiences.)

Discerning Abilities

For at least the past century, most of schooling practice
has been framed by the assumption that there are universal and determinable norms for all aspects of human activity. This assumption has supported widespread efforts
to identify and to measure various qualities, which in turn
has supported a "culture of classification."

When *normal* is defined, so is *abnormal*. And when the
construction of *normal* is seen as desirable, variation becomes something to be minimized, ameliorated, remedied,
remediated, overcome.

That sensibility is changing. It is giving way to the notion that difference is not only inevitable, but necessary
for existence and creativity. This understanding has helped
to highlight the poverty of those popular debates and initiatives that rely on the assumption of normality, along
with the associated attitude toward diversity. In the process, profound and troubling questions have been raised
about traditional educational practices.

The importance of these transitions cannot be understated. Such popular worries as "Should we try to accommodate difference in the regular classroom?" or "What is
normal for this age group?" are rendered problematic as
new questions arise: "What sorts of learning events might
draw on the rich diversity that is always present among
learners?"; "How might we structure tasks that learners
can adapt to their own talents and interests?"; and so on.

These sorts of teaching issues are examined in the re-
maining sections of this chapter. Those sections look at how
a focus on the development of learners' abilities to discern
can help the teacher discern abilities and possibilites for
learning.

"You can make a whole by adding one half to one fourth to one eighth to one sixteenth to one thirty-second to one sixty-fourth .... Well, you just keep doing that forever."

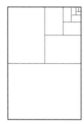

Kim's picture, showing how a process of assembling successive halves will lead to a whole unit. (More formally, this insight might be expressed as:

$\frac{1}{2} + \frac{1}{4} + \frac{1}{8} + \frac{1}{16} + \frac{1}{32} + \frac{1}{64} + ... = 1$)

This was part of Kim's explanation of a picture she had drawn in response to my (Brent's) prompt, What are some of the ways you can use your Fraction Kits to cover a whole page?

This event occurred about 10 days into our unit on fractions in Kim's Grade 3 mathematics class. I'd noticed Kim's interest in the process of successive halving right from the start of the unit — which began, as all my units in mathematics begin, with a few activities intended to provide learners with some shared experiences that could be interpreted mathematically. In this case, the starting place for our explorations of the patterns and relationships underlying fraction concepts was a series of paper-folding tasks.

I had first used such paper-folding activities several years earlier, and had found them to be effective tools to use when structuring units of study on fractions. In particular, paper-folding has served as a means to tap into my students' prior experiences with and knowledge of the topic.

When I began teaching mathematics, I often found it frustrating to structure tasks that drew on the diversities of understanding that were already represented in my classroom. I knew, for example, that my students' had all had rich and extensive experiences of cutting, subdividing, assembling, sharing, and so on. I was also aware that they arrived with at least a preliminary knowledge of fraction notation. As well, most came with good, although sometimes fragmented, understandings of various relationships among fractional amounts (e.g., 4 quarters makes a whole, a half is more than a third). The problem was that these experiences and insights were simply too diverse. I couldn't draw on them in ways that would be meaningful and useful to everyone.

A shared activity solved the problem. The common experience of folding gave us something we could all talk about, in the process highlighting what was already understood and what needed to be studied.

In this grade 3 classroom, we had spent the entire first session of our unit on an exploration of half-folds. With piles of scrap paper in the middle of each group's table, I asked students to fold pages in half in as many different ways as they could imagine. As might be expected, the first two folds that were made by every group were lengthwise and widthwise. These were followed by folds along diagonals and folds made by matching up opposite corners. But then there was a pause as groups wondered about other possibilities.

"Do the halves have to be the same size?" several students asked, opening the door to a brief exchange around the mathematical definition of one half and the less rigid interpretations of one half that often come up in day-to-day life. Even though the notion of bigger and smaller halves was familiar to everyone there seemed to be no difficulty appreciating that mathematics would not allow for such variations. Only equal parts were permitted when working with fractions.

That comment prompted a worry: Is a half that is made by folding a piece of paper lengthwise the same as a half that is made by folding it widthwise?

Everyone seemed to agree that they must be the same size. Wanting them to think more in terms of formal justification of such claims, I asked, "Pretend that you have a friend who thinks that the squarish half [i.e., folded widthwise] was larger than the longish half [i.e., folded lengthwise]. How would you prove to him or her that the two pieces were the same size?"

It took only a few minutes of discussion among themselves before Kim's group offered, "You could cut the halves in half. Both kinds of half can be made out of two half halves." That is, both a half-cut made lengthwise and a half-cut made widthwise can be shown to cover the same area as two identical fourths — an argument that most everyone agreed would convince an uninformed friend.

A **"proof"** that one sort of half is the same size as another sort of half: Combining the folds produces fourths. Each half piece can be made from two identical fourths.

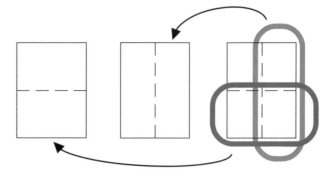

With this demonstrated insight, I felt that the class was ready to examine more complicated folds. To start the next day's class I asked, "What would happen if I folded two times to make fourths ... and then folded again?

What I had expected was that everyone would answer, "You'll get eighths," thus setting the stage for my planned lesson on combinations of folds. What actually happened was that, although a handful of students were willing to argue that three half folds in a row would generate eighths, the majority of students who were willing to put forward their opinions felt that the product would be sixths.

I was surprised by this response, but I wasn't dismayed by it. It did, after all, show that these children were thinking in terms of patterns and relationships. One fold generated two pieces, two folds led to four pieces. It seems quite reasonable to expect that three folds would result in six pieces, four would generate eight, and so on.

A quick experiment to check the hypothesis demonstrated that a different pattern was at work, though. It wasn't that each successive half fold increased the total number of sections by two, but that each such fold doubled the number of pieces.

Kim was among the most vocal in expressing her surprise at this result, but seemed to resolve the issue to her satisfaction by the end of the day. Her journal entry for that class included a comment about the event, noting that "every part gets folded" — that is, that the number of sections doubles when a new half-fold is made. Alongside she drew a series of diagrams, showing a sequence of folded pages (which very much resembled the diagram of the "Fraction Kits," presented on page 137).

Perceiving some potential for the added development of the concept at hand, I pressed the issue a bit further. How many pieces would there be if we made another half-fold? If we did it a fifth time? What if we did it ten times?

I set the students to work on these tasks — and the second surprise of the lesson occurred. I expected everyone to continue the doubling pattern that I thought I'd just highlighted. But, to my seeing, only a few students took this tack. Everyone else began to fold and unfold, count and recount, assigning one another the tasks of determining the totals for four or five or ten folds.

It took only a few minutes for frustration to set in. The pieces of paper began to refuse the creases and the folded sections became too numerous to count accurately. In the hope of assisting students in their efforts, I drew a chart on the board. Although my initial intention was simply to provide a means to collect the emerging responses, I realized that this recording tool could also be used as a generative device as I was drawing it. That is, the chart proved useful in helping learners notice and extend the pattern that was at work here.

Number of half-folds	Number of sections
0	1
1	2
2	4
3	8
4	16
5	32
6	64
7	128
8	256
9	512
10	1024
⋮	⋮

The **filled-in chart** showing the relationship between the number of folds and the number of parts.

The pace at which the number of pieces increased was surprising to many. Even after a quick discussion of the logic behind the doubling pattern (and a double-check on the calculations), a few students announced their doubt. Given that the paper refused to cooperate beyond six or seven folds, a pair of skeptics (Kim was one of them) took out pencil and ruler and began to draw in the folds rather than actually making new creases. Though less-than-perfectly divided, a page covered with lines that marked out 1024 "sort of" equal parts was soon ready for display. In the meantime, others in the class experimented with extending the pattern with larger pieces of paper.

Happy with the thinking that I saw happening, I prepared a few questions that I thought might help to extend the investigations: What would happen if we did third-folds instead of half-folds? How many half-folds would it take until you were in the millionths range?

The first question didn't take. The second one, however, generated a great deal of interest, and the balance of that class was spent in folding, cutting, drawing, and shading efforts, all aimed at isolating "about one millionth" of a sheet of newspaper (which turns out to be slightly smaller than 1 mm x 1 mm) and about one millionth of one panel of the chalkboard.

The math lessons over the next few days were used to explore different folds (mostly thirds) and combinations of folds, as students examined which fractional amounts could and could not be easily produced.

What we were doing over these lessons was observing regularities, studying number patterns, learning about primes and composites, representing fractional amounts, making equivalent fractions, and practicing basic operations (mostly multiplication). Few, if any, of the students actually saw things in terms of formal concept development, however, with more than one asking some variation of, When are we going to have to do math again?

The query was repeated a few times during the lesson in which Fraction Kits were introduced, about a week into the unit. Consisting of red wholes, orange halves, yellow fourths, green eighths, and blue sixteenths — all made from neon-colored paper — these kits were intended to support the development of addition concepts by allowing students to compare and combine different-sized pieces more readily.

Kim was a bit disappointed when she opened her envelope. "There aren't any purple pieces in here," she protested.

I responded pragmatically: "There are only five different kinds of pieces, so I only used five colors. I was done before I got to the purple paper."

"You could add a different kind of piece," Kim offered.

"I think that would just get too confusing," I answered, not wanting to expand the kits before we'd had a chance to examine some of the relationships that they were intended to illustrate.

Kim acquiesced. Or, so I thought. We were well into an orienting activity of identifying some of the relationships among the pieces (framed in terms of "trading" certain parts for other parts) when Kim came up to me and asked if it would be all right if she were to make her own purple thirty-seconds. I agreed, and promised a sheet of neon purple if she reminded me at the end of the school day. She didn't forget.

In the next few lessons, we continued to explore the relationships among the pieces, focusing mainly around questions that asked students to find different ways of assembling a particular amount (e.g., What are some of the ways you can cover one fourth of a page?), of comparing amounts (e.g., Which is more, 3/4 or 13/16?), and of combining pieces (e.g., What do you get if you put together 2/4 and 1/16 and 1/8?). In every instance, I started the explorations with a few sample questions and then, upon a brief discussion of how they might be answered, invited students to make up their own questions.

It was these sorts of activities that led up to the "What are some of the ways you can use your Fraction Kits to cover a whole page?" task.

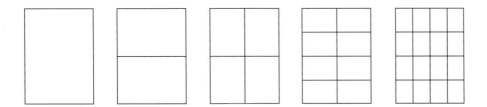

The **Fraction Kit**, consisting of wholes, halves, fourths, eighths, and sixteenths.

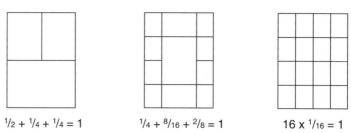

$1/2 + 1/4 + 1/4 = 1$ $1/4 + 8/16 + 2/8 = 1$ $16 \times 1/16 = 1$

Some other ways of covering a whole page using the Fraction Kits.

And, given the details about the unit that have been recounted here, it's not at all surprising that Kim would have given the response that was presented at the start of this chapter (that is, the product of an endless process of successive halving).

What may be surprising, though, is that she was the only one in the class of 25 who suggested the possibility. Her own groupmates, in fact, were only mildly interested in her drawing. As did most of their classmates, they chose to approach the task by reorganizing and trading pieces, making what appeared to be more or less random arrangements of pieces that covered a whole page. (A few examples are illustrated.) On my prompt, they also wrote addition and multiplication statements to describe and record what they'd done.

Other students didn't use the kits at all, choosing instead to list addition statements (e.g., $1/2 + 1/2 = 1$; $3/4 + 2/8 = 1$). One learner, Alex, began this way, but quickly realized there was a more efficient strategy for recording these combinations. In fact, he realized that he could make use of a table that was not only faster, but that could be used to generate *every* possible combination of pieces.

Two students working with Alex followed his lead in using the chart, but in very different ways. Jake, who couldn't quite follow what Alex was doing, made a chart in which he listed all the combinations in which the numerators and denominators were equal, proudly reporting to me that he knew "everything about one" after filling in the numbers along a diagonal. Tory, who also had trouble following Alex's logic, used the chart as Alex had set it up, but in a less systematic way (less as a generative tool and more as a recording tool).

Prompted by these events, I wondered what might happen if this strategy were introduced to the rest of the class. After calling for their attention, I presented my version of Alex's idea, being careful to represent the chart only as a recording tool. (As Jake's and Tory's responses had demonstrated, Alex's more abstract use to the charts to generate all possible combinations was not an easy jump to make.) I had in mind the hope that students' use of the charts might support more sophisticated understandings of the relationships among fractional amounts.

The idea was taken up in earnest by every group. A sort of friendly competition quickly emerged as a set of students posed for themselves the challenge of generating a longer list than Alex's. Unhappy with the challenge, Alex soon convinced them that he had already generated the complete list — until a member of the second group, Lynn, suggested that it might be possible to use subtraction as well. (The topic of negative numbers had not been formally addressed, and in fact was several years away in this jurisdiction's mathematics curriculum.) Several new possibilities were quickly generated before Lynn added, "Hey, we can use parts of pieces too!" — noting, for example, that a combination of 3 fourth-pieces and a half of a half-piece covered the whole page.

Over the course of this 50-minute block, then, these 8- and 9-year-olds were adding, subtracting, multiplying, and dividing fractions, although my original intention with this activity was only that they have a little practice with some basic additive relationships.

As their teacher, I was quite excited about these events. Not only were these students demonstrating sound understandings of fraction concepts, they were showing that their understandings extended beyond the conceptual constraints of the kits. As such, the kits had served their purpose well. They'd provided a starting place, a location to develop a set of shared experiences that enabled learners to talk about and to extend their understandings of fractions.

Our fractions units lasted 1 more week, culminating in a "Fraction

1	1/2	1/4	1/8	1/16
1				
	2			
	1	2		
	1	1	2	
	1	1	1	2
	1	1		4
	1		4	
	1		3	1
	1		2	4
	1		1	6
	1			8
		4		
		3	2	
		3	1	2
		3		4
		2	4	
		2	3	2
		2	2	4
		2	1	6
		(2)		8
		1	6	
		1	5	2
		1	4	4
		1	3	6
		1	2	8
		1	1	10
		1		12
			8	
			7	2
			6	4
			5	6
			4	8
			3	10
			2	12
			1	14
				16

Alex's Chart (Each row represents a different possibility. For example, in the circled row, the combination of 2/4 + 8/16 is recorded.)

1	1/2	1/4	1/8	1/16
1				
	2			
		4		
			8	
				16

Jake's Chart

1	1/2	1/4	1/8	1/16
1				
	2			
		4		
	1	2		
		2		8
	1	1	1	2
		3	1	2

Part of Tory's Chart

1	1/2	1/4	1/8	1/16
1				
	2			
		4		
		3	-2	
2	-2			
2	-1	-2		
	1/2	3		

Some Entries in the Chart from Lynn's Group

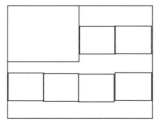

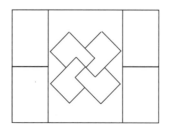

Sofi's Flag (Her question was, How much of the background is still showing?)

Finn's Flag (His question was, How big is the combined piece in the middle?)

Flags" activity. Working from the kits, students were invited to create flag-like arrangements and then to pose questions based on those flags for themselves, their classmates, and their parents. A few examples have been re-presented here, but it's impossible to provide much of a sense of the richness, diversity, and conceptual sophistication of the work done by the students.

Perhaps a better sense might be conveyed through one parent's comment upon observing the posters that the children had made of their flags, their questions, and (hidden under a flap of paper) their responses: "I have no idea how to answer most of these. How did you teach the kids to do this?"

"You had to be here," I answered.

3C   Minding Occasions

Section A of this chapter was focused on the relationship between diversity and ability. A key assertion in that section was that difference and specialization are necessary to creativity and intelligence. Traditional schooling structures, however, are often aimed not at flexibility of tasks, variation of interests, and ranges of abilities, but at homogeneity and homogenization.

In Section B, an event of teaching fractions was recounted. That episode was intended to illustrate some of the ways that a flexible and adaptable learning activity can give rise to insights that exceed *normal* understandings.

In this section, the teacher's role in these sorts of learning occasions is examined. The main emphases are on the sorts of attitudes and habits that might be useful to the teacher who wishes to participate in the flow of classroom activity in ways that open up surprising opportunities while being attentive to curricular expectations. Particular emphasis is placed on matters of difference and diversity — regarded here as sites for possibility rather than deviations from normality.

Point 1 • ADAPTING OCCASIONS

Learners are different from one another. Classroom events can be structured to embrace this diversity.

As developed in the first section of this chapter, the notion of the "normal child" has infused much of educational practice over the past century. Bolstering a trend that began some time earlier, the idea that persons with diverse histories, interests, and abilities could be expected to learn the same things in the same ways at the same time supported a pervasive move toward grouping children primarily (and sometimes exclusively) on the basis of age. The resulting classroom emphases were appropriately dubbed "teacher-centered," highlighting the assumption that the teacher was most responsible for the learning that occurred.

The movement toward "student-centered classrooms" rose to prominence a few decades ago, alongside a growing unease around the consequences of rigidly standardized classrooms, curricula, instructional methods, and evaluations. This movement, however, has also proven highly problematic, as it seems to require teachers to monitor and structure learning programs for many heterogeneous individuals rather than for a single homogeneous classroom. This emphasis places an extraordinary demand on the teacher.

How, then, might a teacher think about her or his role if neither teacher-centered nor student-centered classrooms are tenable?

A way to address this apparent dilemma is to devise classroom activities that allow learners to adjust the difficulty and otherwise modify tasks to suit their own learning needs without compromising the intentions of the activity. Several good examples of tasks that allow this sort of learner participation are described in the previous section. One specific instance is the incident in which the teacher invited everyone to examine and make use of Alex's charts. In terms of the subject matter, the teacher's intention was to prompt students to compare, relate, and add fractions — and a quick glance at some of the charts generated reveals that this intention was realized. A further analysis, though, highlights that many different things were actually happening, according to interest, ability, and perhaps even accident. What is quite apparent is that learners were able to adjust the task. Everyone was working at

Unfolding Paths

It's interesting to watch an ant move about in an unfamiliar terrain. Its path is never straight. Rather, its movement seems aimless and erratic ...

... aimless and erratic, that is, until the ant comes across some desirable object. Its path back to its nest is somewhat more direct that its original ramblings as it retraces its own scented trail. As other ants follow its lead to the prize, the bends and loops in the original path quickly smooth until an almost perfectly straight path is marked out.

This sort of event is a powerful analogy for the ways that knowledge is generated, that learning happens, and that, correspondingly, teaching should be structured. Very often, the original route to particular insights is indirect and overly complicated. As insights become more familiar, one's memories of the complex paths that led to them are often "straightened" — a habit which is both beneficial and problematic. On the upside, more direct routes can save a great deal of time and energy when it comes to helping others to see the importance of particular ideas. On the downside, the obscuring of such paths to insight may contribute to oversimplifications that hide the complex, explorative activities that are often necessary for learners as they make sense of the world. The question that must always be asked when considering anticipated learning trajectories is, What sorts of experiences are likely necessary for a learner to make sense of this notion?

a level appropriate to their backgrounds and abilities. Everyone was learning — but not everyone was learning the same thing or in the same way.

In other words, in this setting, the teacher was able to structure a single task (as is the case in teacher-centered classrooms) that allowed for highly individualized learning (as is hoped to be the case in student-centered classrooms). However, most of the complex work of adapting activities was entrusted to the learners themselves.

As a sidenote, it bears mentioning that learners were able to go well beyond curricular expectations — that is, most far surpassed what is considered *normal* at this age. These learners demonstrated themselves able to handle very sophisticated notions, largely because they had a stake in interpreting, adapting, and posing tasks for themselves. Moreover, within this structure, the teacher had to provide neither enrichment activities to advanced learners nor remedial work for learners who were experiencing difficulty.

There is an important caveat here: A quality necessary to the success of such classroom structures is the teacher's own knowledge of the subject matter. *Both* the ability to create flexible tasks *and* the capacity to follow student leads clearly depend on fairly broad and flexible understandings of the concepts at hand. If, for instance, the teacher had conceived of addition of fractions strictly in terms of rules and right answers, he would hardly have been able to perceive the value of such playful activity — let alone undertake a path whose endpoints were not (and could not) be prespecified.

●   **Connecting Thoughts**   ●

A number of specific teaching events are described in the teaching event, "Organizing Shapes" (Chapter 3B). Choose one, and make some conjectures about the teacher's intended aims and structures.

Were these intentions reflected in learners' activities? How did learners adjust the tasks to suit their own interests and understandings? What are some of the qualities of the classroom task that helped or hindered students' abilities to modify it?

Point 2 • RESPONDING OCCASIONS

Although there are obvious directive aspects to teaching, a more vital element of the role is flexible response. That is, teaching is a matter of *occasioning*.

As many experienced teachers will attest, there are vast differences between *wonderful lesson ideas* and *wonderful lessons*. The best teaching plans can fall flat if the teacher is unable to maintain an environment that supports learners' engagements with subject matter and with one another.

A key quality of such settings is a flexible responsiveness to events that unfold in a classroom — a responsiveness that is faithful to the stated learning aims, but that understands that all complex engagements involve adjustment, compromise, experiment, error, detour, and surprise. That is, teaching is largely a matter of *occasioning*. The term *occasioning* refers to the way things and events "fall together" in complex and unexpected ways. The notion arises from the realization that learning is always *dependent on* but can never be fully *determined by* teaching. The study of fractions, described in Part B of this chapter, provides an illustration of this idea, as the teacher's actions co-emerged with the learners' actions. (It might be useful to contrast this teaching event with your own recollections of the learning of fraction concepts — which was, more than likely, more rigidly organized and disjointed.)

The suggestion that a teacher cannot *cause* a student to learn anything in particular is now understood to be almost a truism. What is learned is always a complex matter of historical circumstance, immediate context, and anticipated activity. This realization has transformed conceptions of teaching. In particular, it makes it impossible to think of teaching in terms of the mastery of such technocratic competencies as lesson planning, classroom management, and outcome evaluation. What is vital in the pedagogical relationship is a responsive attunement to learners.

Another way of making this point is to say that teaching is more like a conversation than a monologue. The participants in a conversation are open to one another's contributions and suggestions. The conversation flows in a way that is not really controlled by anyone, but which is generally purposeful and focused. Drawing an analogy between teaching and a conversation, then, highlights the inevitable range of activity and interpretation that will arise when a roomful of diverse persons is invited to think about the same topic. In contrast, a monologue is preplanned and minimally responsive to its audience.

The notions of *occasioning* and *conversations*, as applied to teaching, might be characterized as moments of maintaining balance between order and chaos. As developed in the previous chapter, the teacher needs to impose order (constraints) on learning activities, but those constraints need to be ones that are allow for diversity of activity (liberate). In the fractions activities, for example, the teacher was able to strike a balance between overly prescriptive tasks (e.g., specifying which pieces to use, rather than examining ranges of possibilities) and overly open tasks (e.g., allowing free exploration, rather than orienting explorations with focused questions). In establishing this space between rigid structure and "anything goes," the teacher opened the door to unexpected possibilities while ensuring that learners would have ample opportunity to examine the concepts at hand.

Performing Occasions

Anne liked to have her Grade 4 and 5 students read novels chosen by their group, meeting for conversations about questions that arose during their reading. After they finished the novels, the groups were asked to share their book with the rest of the class. (Anne had prepared the students to make such decisions by teaching them many of the alternatives for responding to literature.) Sometimes the entire group would do the same activity while other times they would divide up into twos or threes to offer several interpretations of the story.

What Anne remembers best from those activities were two boys who were confident only when involved in "macho" activities, the most prominent being hockey. "After reading *Fantastic Mr. Fox*," she said, "the two boys decided that they would do a puppet play as their interpretation of the story. They built a trifold screen for their puppet theatre and decapitated one of their Cabbage Patch dolls for a puppet body. Then they worked all Saturday creating a nylon stocking head for the farmer and sewing a puppet fox from a sock, including creating a Velcro detachable tail."

The performance was very well received by their fellow classmates, including hysterical laughter when the fox's tail came off. Afterwards, everyone had incredible curiosity about how the production had been done. The students had not seen a trifold screen before, nor had they thought about sewing their own puppets. "After that," Anne said, "a whole variety of different puppet plays appeared and a community of performers where ideas were exchanged and developed was created." Two boys, who had been shy in front of their friends found a new way of relating in the class and to their peers. And the students were learning from each other far more quickly than if Anne had tried to direct and structure their responses more specifically.

Occasioning can only occur, however, if the teacher genuinely has the capacity to be surprised. That is, the teacher needs to be attentive to events in a way that enables him or her to see more than what he or she expects to see. For instance, a person who sees Fraction Kits only as a means of illustrating concepts would be less likely to notice the range of ideas represented in learner actions. Nor would such a teacher be able to stray far from the rigid security of a preplanned lesson.

A teacher who has adopted and practiced a more attentive attitude, in contrast, would be more likely to follow leads that present themselves. Such a teacher would probably be better able to structure settings that enable learners to adapt activities to their own interests and understandings.

   Connecting Thoughts

The teaching described in Chapter 3B, "Organizing Shapes" was sometimes very directive and sometimes much less so.

Working with the same teaching episode that you chose for the last question, highlight how some of the learner actions influenced subsequent teacher actions.

Point 3 • PLAYING OCCASIONS

The key element in any learning and teaching occasion is *play*.

Virtually every principle developed in this text could be construed as some variation of the idea that play is *the* key element in any event of learning.

The understanding of *play* that underpins this statement is a broad one. In popular terms, play tends to be regarded as the opposite of work, and so it is often associated with distraction, purposelessness, and disorder. Play, that is, is generally regarded as what we do when serious responsibilities are fulfilled.

However, a careful look at the many ways that the word *play* is used suggests that this understanding is not just narrow, but wrong. Considered across such usages as "stage play," "word play," "child's play," "play in under-

Directing Occasions

Preservice English teachers crowd into the multimedia lab, each choosing a computer station for their experimentation with a new CD-ROM. The CD contains a director's clip from a production of Shakespeare's play, *As You Like It.* Also available are outtakes, interviews with the director about why various shots were chosen above others, as well as information about how the particular shots have framed important symbols, moods, or plot development of the play. The students have the opportunity to watch the director's clip from the production and listen to the interview. They then can choose from a variety of angles, lighting choices, and dialogue to edit their own scene. Working with these choices, students can make decisions as if they were directors or film editors, realizing how their particular choices frame certain details that condition the interpretation of the story.

The students thoroughly enjoy playing with the possibilities, realizing as they do so, that there are many decisions that shape a filmed production of a Shakespearean play. They also begin to see that their own history with Shakespearean plays influences some of their decision making. What had seemed a transparent process to them before, became more complex and meaningful.

standing," and so on, it is evident that the opposite of play is not *work*, but *rigidity* or *motionlessness*. In this way, a key quality of all living forms is play — and, conversely, a likely indicator of an inert form is a lack of play. With such broadened appreciations of the importance of play in life, it's not surprising to note that playfulness is rapidly coming to be seen as a necessary element in the workplace, especially where creativity and problem solving are expected of workers. In contrast, careers that are defined by fixed and narrow responsibilities (i.e., ones that are *not* playful) are increasingly being seen as undesirable and "dead end."

The emergent understanding, across almost all segments of culture and society, is that some element of play is essential to all events of creativity and learning. Once again, learning is never a simple matter of acquiring information or skills. It always involves a change in conceptual structures, however minor, through which the learner adapts actions and interpretations to new circumstances.

In this context, play is *the possibility of movement*. So understood, *ideas* can be playful (i.e., they can be interpreted differently) just as a child's physical explorations of the world are playful. Such an attitude toward the necessity and inevitability of play contributes to a very different conception of errors. If, for instance, knowledge is seen in terms of fixed notions that learners must acquire, then errors are things to be avoided. They must be flagged, corrected, and sometimes even punished.

If, however, there is an appreciation of the play of knowledge, errors can serve as interesting locations for exploration. In the Fraction Kits class, for example, Jake's claim that he knew "everything about 1" is clearly wrong. His chart indicates, in fact, that he knows very little. But zeroing in on the error as something to be "fixed" or remediated would not likely have had the same educational impact as exploring the possible play in this insight.

This is not to say that all errors should be embraced. Clearly not. The point is simply that the production of knowledge — personal and collective — proceeds in fits and starts; it gets caught in blind alleys and it stumbles onto surprising insights. In a phrase, learning is playful.

Teaching must be able to get caught up in the play of learning. Although it would have taken the same amount of classtime and just as much teacher effort, a "textbook" fractions unit that focused on fragmented concepts in rigid sequence, each with a page of repetitive exercises, would simply not have had the same effect as the more playful Fractions Kit unit.

●   **Connecting Thoughts**   ●

A number of playful moments are presented in Chapter 3B, "Organizing Shapes." Select one incident and point out how it was (and was not) playful — considered in terms of spaces for bodily engagement, for variations in interpretation, for diversity in activity, for flexibility in teacher response, and so on.

Point 4 • PLANNING OCCASIONS

Teaching plans ahead, but in a way that enables it to select from possibilities as it goes along.

Learning is about interpreting and elaborating on experience. More specifically, learning relies on the continuous repetition of simple patterns of noticing and processes of analyzing as one moves through life. Such repetitions are sometimes conscious and sometimes nonconscious, sometimes deliberate and sometimes accidental. But all are necessary. All new insights, from the most mundane act of noticing to the grandest of epiphanies are made possible only through the slow and steady incorporation of small experiences into one's life.

The upshot? There are no shortcuts in learning.

Traditionally, however, much of formal schooling has been founded on a belief in shortcuts — shortcuts that in many cases completely bypass any efforts to structure meaningful experiences. Fractions, for instance, still tend to be taught purely on the symbolic level as a sequence of disjointed and fragmented ideas. If any potentially meaningful interpretations are offered, they are presented as illustrations, not as starting places for understanding.

The opposite is true of the Fraction Kits unit. There the teacher began his planning by identifying experiences that the mathematical concepts might be used to interpret. Those formal concepts were all addressed in the unit, but they were only used as means of reporting, recording, and interpreting what was being noticed as learners played within the various activities. The teacher gave little formal instruction on such topics as addition of fractions. Yet, by the unit's end, every learner in this classroom was able to work with fractions at a level that is expected of children who have been in school for twice as long.

How did this happen?

A large part of the answer lies in the specific qualities of the activities. The opening task of folding paper, for example, embodies the concept of fraction multiplication: A half of a half is a fourth, a half of a fourth is an eighth, and so on. Students began by folding and cutting, all within a setting that allowed for discussion, for adjustment of the task, and for error. As a common repertoire of experiences

Improvising Occasions

In recent years, improvisational theatre (or "Theatre Sports") has become quite popular. Participants in these activities are given unexpected prompts, circumstances, and/or tasks and, from those beginnings, are expected to create coherent scenes that incorporate all of the suggested elements — immediately.

For instance, a pair of actors might be told that they're stranded on a desert island with a famous person. The audience is then asked to call out names of celebrities to add to the complexity of the situation — and so the fellow castaway could be anyone from Bart Simpson to Cleopatra.

Clearly, the structure of the ensuing act is unpredictable. Even so, that structure inevitably has a certain familiarity, given that actors must rely on well rehearsed patterns of exchange and association. Good teaching has a similarly improvisational structure. The teacher must be practiced and prepared, but flexible and attentive to the unfolding situation.

unfolded, the teacher began to point to specific happenings and to provide means of interpreting those happenings — such as, for example, understanding the product of a sequence of folds in terms of fraction multiplication.

Learners were not provided with a set of formal rules in advance. And, it bears emphasizing, it was important that the teacher didn't even attempt to equip students with abstract concepts prior to the activities. An instructional sequence which begins with the concept and which then moves to "real life" examples often has quite a different impact. If intended-to-be-meaningful experiences follow abstract concepts, they might serve only as illustrations rather than as bases for or moments of interpretation.

At first hearing, it might sound like hairs are being split here. But consider the difference between the way you learned your first language as a child and the way that a second language is often taught in school. As a child, your teachers (parents, siblings, friends, etc.) did not attempt to teach vocabulary and grammar first. Rather, as you experienced various parts of the world, they followed your lead and offered words and phrases to interpret those experiences. With this strategy, you were able to become proficient in a language (or maybe two or three languages) with amazing rapidity.

The traditional approach to teaching a new language in schools has been in the opposite direction: It generally starts with an attempt to front-load vocabulary and grammar with little opportunity to connect that information to the dynamic events of engaging with others around whatever matters at the moment of interaction. Persons with years of this sort of instruction in a second language are often unable to engage in the simplest of conversations.

The point is not so much that such persons were badly taught. Rather, the point is that the teaching tried to take a shortcut. It tried to plan the entire route in advance, and closed the doors to rich possibilities in the process. It didn't allow itself any moments to interpret — to play with new words, new phrasings: to follow learners' leads.

Connecting Thoughts

The critical question for a teacher is not, How can I best explain this concept?, but, What sorts of experiences might this concept be used to interpret? How did the teacher in Chapter 3B respond to this latter question in his planning?

Point 5 • VARYING OCCASIONS

The teacher's attitude toward the diversity that is represented among learners is a vital quality in effective classroom teaching.

There is a long history of thinking of teaching in terms of control of learners and of learning outcomes. An unfortunate consequence of this habit is that many of the relationships that are represented in the classroom tend to be cast in managerial terms.

An appreciation of the complexities of human engagements should prompt a somewhat different attitude, one that is more concerned with learning engagements and community building — or, phrased somewhat differently, both with the individual and with the communities that unfold from and that are enfolded in those individuals.

A remarkable insight of recent studies of community dynamics is that one of the critical qualities of any healthy social body is that its members be provided with opportunities to *specialize*, to pursue their own particular interests, talents, and obsessions. That is, robust community arises out of diversity and specialization, not from homogeneity. Attempts to structure communities around narrow conceptions of normality, imposed rules, and assigned roles rarely give rise to long-lasting collectives. In contrast, the most stable communities are the ones that allow the most play among their members.

Of course, we shouldn't idealize here. All regimes and ideologies are fraught with their own particular inequities and injustices. The simple point, though, is that the most generative, creative, and stable communities are the ones in which the members are able to balance the pursuit of their individual interests with the necessary constraints and compromises of cohabitation. When this insight is contrasted with the structure of the traditional classroom — in which learners are treated as more-or-less homogeneous — it should hardly be surprising that control and management arise as key worries. Such communities cannot sustain themselves. They *have to be* controlled.

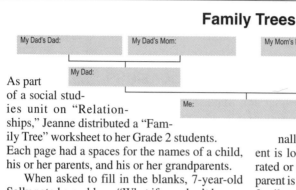

Family Trees

As part of a social studies unit on "Relationships," Jeanne distributed a "Family Tree" worksheet to her Grade 2 students. Each page had a spaces for the names of a child, his or her parents, and his or her grandparents.

When asked to fill in the blanks, 7-year-old Sally noted a problem: "What if you don't have a dad?" she asked.

"Of course you have a dad," Jeanne responded. "Everyone has a dad."

"But what if you don't?" Sally persisted.

"Well, what were you, born in a jar?!" was Jeanne's final response.

Sally pressed the matter no further, but took the sheet home for some assistance from her parents. In the process of asking for help, she relayed her teacher's assertion that "everyone has a dad."

Her parents, a lesbian couple, were upset by the incident and made immediate arrangements to meet with Jeanne. When they gathered in the classroom the next day, Jeanne acknowledged her "slip of the tongue," explaining that she had no direct information on the home lives and varied family structures of the children she taught. She apologized to Sally and to her parents, but confessed that she didn't know what to do. Now more attuned to some of the considerable diversity among families, and more aware of the potential emotional and political charges when some sort of norm (i.e., the intact nuclear family) is assumed in this diverse context, Jeanne was at a loss.

Together, Jeanne and Sally's parents decided to consult an acquaintance, Sarah, a long-time social activist who also taught in a teacher education program. After hearing of the incident, Sarah decided to use it to structure a discussion in a class of 85 preservice teachers.

"How would you deal with this in your classrooms?" she asked, prompting animated discussions of the issues and exclusions implicit in the Family Tree exercise and, later, of alternative ways to structure this sort of activity. Among the variety of family arrangements that were not considered in the exercise as originally conceived were those in which a parent is lost, a child is adopted, parents are separated or divorced (and, perhaps, re-partnered), a parent is in jail, parents are same-sex, the extended family cares for the children, and/or fewer or more than two parents are involved.

Asked how they might handle the topic in their own classrooms, the teacher candidates brainstormed such ideas a the use of webs, networks, root systems, circles embedded in larger circles, and so on — in brief, images and metaphors that made more explicit use of organic and fractal-like notions.

These suggestions were reported back to Jeanne, who began work immediately on a "family web" idea that she introduced to her class a few days later. Beginning with their own name in the middle of a page, children were asked to write the names of the main caregivers in their lives in the next layer of the web. At that point, they were asked to take it home, along with an explanatory note, for assistance in identifying the next layer(s) of caregivers.

As might be expected, the final products amply illustrated the diversity of family structures. As she reviewed these webs, it was clear to Jeanne that the learning intentions of the original exercise were not just achieved, but greatly surpassed. The exercise had given them much to talk about in class, and the ensuing discussions demonstrated that the children had learned a great deal about families and relationships.

For Jeanne, this study of the diversity of families began to affect other aspects of her teaching. She found herself much more aware of how classroom reading materials, popular media, mathematics word problems, and so on often assumed the standard of a nuclear family. The error of that assumption was a recurring topic of discussion in most subject areas as the year unfolded.

Now consider the Fraction Kits unit. Although it was certainly the case that learners' attentions had to be refocused regularly, "control" was much less a worry here than in many classrooms. Learners were able to participate in the definition of tasks; they were involved in interpreting events rather than being told how to interpret things; they were permitted to pursue divergent lines of thought. In fact, even when learners seemed to stray off task, they were usually playing with the Fraction Kits in one way or another. In brief, the teacher embraced the individuality of the learners and, in the process, set the conditions for a healthy, self-sustaining community within which "management" was more a matter of conscientious participation than detached efforts to control.

This point should not be read as an imperative for sudden change in classroom routines. On the contrary, children who are familiar with fairly inflexible structures may not readily embrace more playful contexts. Humans are creatures of habit, complex products of their histories, and a sudden change in expectations and structures may prove highly problematic — potentially accentuating rather than diminishing the need for managerial actions.

The issue here is, then, not that rigid structures be abandoned. It is, to adapt an adage, that effective changes are more about evolution than revolution. Innovations such as reorganizing classroom space, instituting rituals that encourage discussion and debate, incorporating activities that allow more choice and specialization, and so on might be enough to open new possibilities for embracing variety.

The point: A teacher who wishes to make *learning* a bigger concern than *control* would do well to interrogate personal beliefs around the nature and role of diversity.

●   **Connecting Thoughts**   ●

In preparing the accounts of teaching that are presented in this book, we (the authors) made a deliberate attempt to avoid the language of business (e.g., management, quality control, etc.). It might be a useful exercise to review some of the Parts B and take note of some of the ways that interactive and relational dynamics are described. (We actually did this ourselves with an early draft of the manuscript.)

Chapter 4

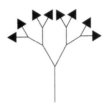

Learning and Teaching Forms

Derived from the Latin, *forma*, shape, **form** refers to the characters of events, objects, and other phenomena — of tables, running, trees, waterfalls, language, and so on.

Forms are about identifications — which are complex, two-way processes. The statement, "I can identify" suggests both an outward act of discernment and an inward act of self-description — acts that are simultaneous and inseparable. One's self is formed amid one's identifications of/with forms.

The forms associated with *formal* education include objects (novels, chalk, pencils, etc.) and practices (sitting in desks, singing the anthem, memorizing number facts, etc.). In developing relationships to such objects and practices, students are both *learning form* and *coming to form*. They are being *informed* and they are *conforming*, even as they participate in the *reform* of subject matters, culture, and identities.

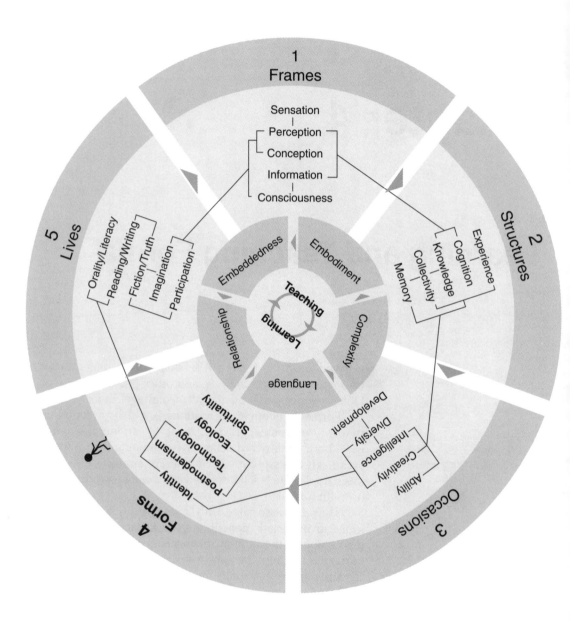

Self-concept and self-esteem are among the most prominent topics in current discussions of formal education. The assumption underlying these and related concerns is that a primary purpose of schooling is to nurture the individual — in particular, to support the development of personal senses of identity and agency.

A question that is not often raised within these discussions is, What is this *self*? That is, what is believed about identity, personality, individuality, subjectivity, and personhood? And, more pointedly, how are these beliefs enfolded in our efforts to educate?

Selfhood has been a major topic of philosophical inquiry for hundreds of years. Discussions have been organized by difficult questions: Does identity pre-exist experience? Or does experience make identity? Is identity constructed by language? Or does language arise in the need for human subjects to communicate? Are personality traits innate? Or are they learned? Or both? Does biology influence thinking and the process of identity-making? Does history? Does climate? Geography? Nutrition? Health? Do practices of narration and symbolic representation contribute to the making of human identities?

The arguments around these matters have been extensive and varied. This introduction to some of the major themes and issues that have arisen in discussions of selfhood, then, is little more than a brief overview. To bring some focus to breadth and the variety of opinion that has been expressed, this chapter is developed around explorations of the relationships between prevailing conceptions of human identity and predominant practices of schooling, particularly over the last few hundred years.

The discussion that follows is framed mainly by Western — that is, Anglo-American and European — histories and sensibilities. The intention here is not to exclude other worldviews and educational practices, but to focus on the happenings and mindsets that have contributed most to schooling practices in North America and Europe.

This discussion has been organized around four conceptual placeholders, each of which corresponds roughly

Fig. 4.1. Where, if anywhere, are the boundaries of *self*? Is there a border or a membrane that separates *me* from *not-me*? Is there some sort of shell that circumscribes one's identity? On what bases do we make such distinctions as self/other, private/public, individual/collective, human/natural?

to an historical period. The first three temporal markers are widely acknowledged as distinct eras: the premodern, the modern, and the postmodern. The final category, the ecological postmodern, differs in this regard. It is used here to point to an emerging sensibility, one framed by recent developments in ecological and complexity theories.

In subdividing the discussion this way, the intention is not to suggest that it is in any way possible to portray the complexities and subtleties of what it means to be human. The four conceptual placeholders, then, should not be regarded as fixed or distinct categories. In fact, within each are the traces of what has come before and the seeds of what follows. Although aspects of previous worldviews might be openly scorned and suppressed, they are never completely erased. Most often, changes in perspective are elaborations of specific aspects of previous sensibilities, rather than full-scale rejections, and careful study can reveal traces of past beliefs and practices that have become

---

A Moment in Learning to Teach

"They know that I'm afraid of them!" thinks Jamie, as she waits for the Grade 7s to settle into their seats for the first class of the morning. Although she has carefully prepared for this moment — attending university seminars on curriculum and pedagogy, spending many hours on lesson and unit planning, buying new "teacher clothes," and adopting a well-rehearsed "firm but friendly" demeanor — Jamie does not feel like a teacher. She feels out of place, out of sorts, disoriented, worried. Her breath catches in her throat, her heart pounds, her face is flushed. Jamie sees that the students are not settling as they should.

"Okay, I must tell them what I want them to do."

As Jamie opens her mouth to speak, however, only a croak emerges. She tries again. Another croak, this time louder. She feels her throat tighten — and then, suddenly, a surge of energy, a moment of memory, and a slightly shaky but

very assertive, "Okay class, we're ready to begin. Take your seats, settle down, and open your books to Chapter 2. I'm going to start by asking you a few questions about last night's readings."

To Jamie's relief, the class responds. The roar of chatter falls to a hush, then a hum, finally to the sound of students sitting and books opening. Within a moment almost all eyes are upon her, the teacher.

Jamie's initial panic is replaced by a new sureness. Her voice seems to come from somewhere else, her movements as if owned by another body, her responses like those borrowed from ghosts of teachers past. And yet, although strange, Jamie's experience of teaching this class is familiar. This is deeply satisfying to her. "Now I feel like a teacher!" she thinks. It is also puzzling. "When did I become this person who these students see as the teacher? And what will become of the person that I was before?"

What can we say about Jamie's initial terror — her inability to feel part of this situation — and her eventual success? How might different conceptions of self be used to interpret Jamie's experience?

Fig 4.2. What counted as knowledge in premodern times? All things were considered connected and influential to one another. Knowledge thus had to do with the ability to notice these correspondences and to be able to understand one's position within them. Learning how to farm, for example, was not about "taming" the land, but about paying attention to what was needed to encourage the land to produce well — including, of course, attenting to the spiritual and mystical forces that affected climate.

This sensibility is suggested by the pervasive presence of circles, spirals, and dancing motifs among early icons and symbols, highlighting notions of connectedness and recursivity.

sedimented in new paradigms. (A good example of this sort of sedimentation can be found in the traditions that have collected around the modern celebration of Christmas. Many current customs, such as tree decorating, gift giving, caroling, and feasting, are much more reflective of the rituals that were once used to mark the winter solstice than they are of Christian traditions.)

The four conceptions of personal identity presented here should thus be seen as linguistic conveniences that are useful for making sense of the ways that humans have organized their relations — to themselves, to other humans, to society, and to the more-than-human world. This heuristic is intended to help make sense of where and how the boundaries between the self and the not-self have been drawn, along with how such boundary-marking has been caught up in prevailing conceptions of biology, language, sociality, culture, and ecology. The four placeholders, then, are intended as interpretive lenses to highlight some features of varied conceptions of identity and to trace the evolutions of those conceptions.

In order to connect these discussions to practices of learning and teaching, the chapter is punctuated by a series of interpretations of an episode of one person's experiences of leaning to teach. The episode is presented in the box on the preceding page.

The Premodern: Self as Organic and Spiritual

The "premodern" era is an immense one, collecting together all of history prior to about the 17th Century.

It would make little sense to argue that a singular and coherent conception of self identity predominated across this vastness of time, not in the least because few societies maintained records of their theories and beliefs about identity — if direct discussions on the matter even took place. Much of what follows, then, is conjecture that is based on studies of narratives, epics, and other extant artifacts.

Despite the tremendous cultural variety that is represented in the premodern world, it does appear that most of its citizens held some similar assumptions about the nature of personal identity. In particular, for most of history humans seem to have understood themselves as inextricably entwined in the ecologies of the planet and the cosmos. Even through the Middle Ages, for example, the world was seen as an ecological whole, of which one was part. This world was not believed to be fully knowable, nor was there a desire to fully know it. In a word, the universe was believed to be enchanted: An integral part of being human was to participate in the ongoing project of making meaning out of happenings and experiences — as opposed to offering irrefutable explanations of events.

In most premodern cultures, the world was seen in terms of local boundaries and divine constitution. Humans tended to locate themselves as at the center of a universe which was understood to have come into being for some divine purpose and through some sort of spiritual intervention. The cosmos was not thought to be greatly affected — much less controlled — by humans. At the same time, the living earth was seen to demand human attention. Human interactions with the more-than-human world were thus organized by an ethic of care and responsibility.

Divinely constituted, the world was understood to have an inherent meaningfulness. Its deep significance, though, would only reveal itself to those who were attentive and responsive to natural events — or, more specifically, to those who were attuned to the spiritual forms that were believed to govern earthly effects. So framed, the advancement of knowledge was more a matter of divination and revelation than of derivation or discovery. Learning about the world was a matter of entering the Mind of a higher being. Knowledge was thus closely aligned with prayer, celebration, ritual, sacrifice, and other acts of reverence — practices that served to root collective and personal identities deeply in the earth.

The "mind" of the premodern subject, then, was likely not considered as distinct or as distinguishable from the human body. However, neither would mind have been seen as located *in* the physical body. Rather, Mind was something of which one was part. That is, Mind was considered as much about being caught up in the unfolding of the cosmos, with all its mystical, spiritual, and magical dimensions, as it was about personal efforts and interests. And so, although persons probably did develop senses of individuality and agency, these selves were likely not considered wholly within individuals' control or possession. An individual human was not understood to *have a mind*. Rather, together humans *participated in Mind*; they were part of the wholeness of being.

Fig. 4.3. The premodern sense of self was organized by relations to the spiritual and the organic. This is an example of a "participatory epistemology."

A participatory epistemology is a theory which asserts that aspects and objects of the world — animate and inanimate — participate with humans in the ongoing project of knowledge production. Knowledge about a tree, for example, entails insight into ways that the tree is woven into a grander relational web.

Though most often associated with premodern sensibilities, participatory epistemologies are re-emerging on the contemporary academic scene and are usually associated with a resurgence in interest in ecological and spiritual matters.

A Premodern Reading: *Attending to the Call*

How might premodern conceptions of identity be used to interpret Jamie's experience of teaching?

In some ways, this question doesn't make sense. Events of schooling in premodern times were not organized in the ways that they are today. Contemporary schooling is structured around beliefs that would be nonsensical to the premodern educator, including the assumptions that there are distinct subject areas and that the teacher is the one who is primarily responsible for creating the conditions to support learning. In contrast, disciplinary boundaries in premodern cultures, where they were drawn, were much more fluid and ambiguous. The mathematical was mixed with the mystical, science existed comfortably with theology, and so on.

Similarly, in premodern settings, the task of teaching was generally considered more in terms of *accompanying the learner* on a journey than in terms of *directing the learning*. (The word *teacher*, in fact, derives from a term meaning "to show.") As such, teaching was considered a *vocation* — literally, a (divine or spiritual) calling, a mindful participation in the social collective.

To become a teacher, then, was to heed the call. It is thus that teachers were often the priests, the mystics, the prophets, the shamans — those persons who, it was believed, had some special relationship with the more-than-human world. (Notably, *rabbi* and *doctor*, among a host of other titles, mean "teacher" in their original languages.) The teacher, from this perspective, is not merely a person who has learned a discipline or a set of pedagogical skills. Rather, the teacher is a person who lives where human culture meets the more-than-human world.

Becoming a teacher, then, is not principally a matter of personal decision. It is more a matter of being identified as someone who is able to assume the roles of cultural interpreter and spiritual mediator. Jamie's experience, then, would not be seen as a moment of personal triumph, but of attunement and fulfillment, a participation in a grander order. It is thus that, when Jamie stepped into the role that she had been fated to take on, there was a sudden harmony of action among teacher and students.

Put differently, in premodern conceptions, the self tended not to be seen as self-contained or well bounded. If a citizen of a premodern culture were asked for a self-description, the answer would likely be in terms of relations and responsibilities (e.g., parents and children, status in the community, vocation) rather than personal qualities (e.g., shy, modest, etc.). Questions of *who one was, what one knew,* and *what one did* were rarely, if ever, separated.

The more encompassing conception of Mind that is at play here contributed to very different attitudes about the nature and generation of knowledge. Attempts to understand an event such as the movement of the sun did not begin with efforts to establish an "objective distance" from the phenomenon. Rather, implicit in all knowledge and understanding of the universe was the notion that one's experiences were entwined in the object or event of study.

The human subject, in this view, was not something that is carefully and deliberately crafted by the individual, nor was it seen as the product of schooling and other cultural practices. Rather, one's sense of self was as much regulated by spiritual and organic forces as by human intentionality, human culture, and human thought.

In this way, matters of learning were always matters of ethical import. A similar sensibility is evident in many of the Eastern wisdom traditions which have long asserted that every event, no matter how small, affects every other aspect of existence. For the premodern person, then, something as seemingly insignificant as a shifting thought was important — because that thought was not simply about some aspect of the universe, it was part of the universe. As a thought changed, the universe changed. Learning was thus not about acquisition, but about transformation of who one was. It wouldn't have made sense to pry apart knowing, doing, and being.

The Modern: Self as Isolated and Fixed

Prior to the 17th Century, the Western world's efforts at inquiry were predominantly framed by the belief that humanity was in harmonious co-existence with the rest of the universe. This belief about the relationship between the human and the not-human underwent a dramatic change in Europe during the 17th and 18th Centuries in a period known as the Enlightenment.

During this time, a new emphasis arose in the quest for knowledge. The focus shifted away from uncovering the intertwinings of phenomena and toward delineating their differences. Research became more analytic.

Derived from a term meaning "to cut apart" or "to dismember," *analysis* and *analytic inquiry* are premised on the belief that phenomena are best studied in isolation — an emphasis that contributed to a sudden emergence of taxonomies and classification schemes. Where relationship was discussed in these schemes, it was overwhelmingly in terms of hierarchy, conflict, and conquest — as opposed to the emphases on co-implication and interdependency that were typical in premodern worldviews.

One result of this dramatic and sweeping embrace of analytic philosophies and analytic modes of inquiry was that the relationship between the perceiving subject and the perceived world — between the knower and the known — was rendered problematic. True to its emphasis on cut-

All claims to truth must be logically derived from self-evident, irrefutable premises. That is, to be valid, claims must be **rationally** defensible.

All claims must be useful in describing and predicting worldly phenomena. That is, to be valid, claims must be **empirically** demonstrable.

SHAKY COMMON GROUND

All phenomena are reducible to fundamental principles and particles. As these are discovered, we progress toward a complete understanding of the universe.

ting things apart, analytic inquiry sought to render all observation utterly objective and free of the errors that fallible human observers were bound to make.

The means to achieve this objectification arose from an uneasy alliance of *rationalist* and *empiricist* research methods. In brief, rationalism, which finds its formal roots in Plato's philosophies, is an activity of thought. It begins by identifying irrefutable truths and proceeds, via formal logic, to knit those axioms together into more elaborate assertions. These assertions are then used in efforts to explain and predict the world. (Mathematical proofs are often cited as good illustrations of the way that rationalist arguments are constructed.)

Empiricism, in contrast, is more concerned with physical demonstration. It begins with experimentation on and measurement of the world — and is only interested in those results that can be verified by precise repetition of experimental procedures. Through deliberate, controlled, and replicable manipulations of isolated aspects of the world, empiricism aims to derive fundamental laws to explain the operations of the universe. In a sense, empiricism is the opposite of rationalism, as it works to derive foundational notions by analyzing phenomena, as opposed to deducing phenomena from basic principles.

These attitudes toward research, though, are more alike than different. Both rely on the logical argument, both assume that complex phenomena are reducible to a small set of identifiable laws, and in both cases knowledge of a phenomenon is considered synonymous with the abilities to predict (and preferably control) the phenomenon. As well, both hearken back to an ancient debate, articulated by Democritus in the 5th Century BCE. He argued that the universe was composed of discrete particles that were too small to see, and these atoms — not the gods — were what controlled life. Although not popularly taken up at the time — and, in fact, not widely endorsed for 2000 years — Democritus had expressed the key difference between premodern and modern worldviews.

The notion that the universe is reducible to fundamental particles was readily aligned with the logical argument, since the latter assumes that all knowledge claims are reducible to their fundamental assumptions. For these intertwining assertions about existence and knowledge to be taken up in the 17th Century as *the* correct ways to make

Fig. 4.4. *Rationalism* and *empiricism* are often regarded as opposing mindsets.

The difference between them, however, is really a matter of degrees and emphases. Both, for example, are committed to a conception of *Truth* as traceable to fundamental elements, and both regard knowledge-gathering as a more-or-less steady progression toward a totalized understanding of reality.

sense of the universe, certain conditions were necessary. In particular, there needed to be an alliance between craft/ artisan knowledge and philosophical/scientific knowledge — an alliance that was made possible through Gutenberg's invention of the printing press. With the mass production of texts, artisans and craftpersons were able to publish details of their production methods. There was a sudden proliferation of knowledge that had previously been confined to guilds and passed along only through apprenticeships and oral narratives. Now widely accessible, this information provided scientists with the technical knowledge they needed to conduct some sophisticated experiments, thus setting the stage for the Scientific Revolution.

Intertwined with these developments was the rise of capitalism in Europe. The alliance of science and technology enabled increased productivity and improved armaments — which, in turn, contributed to European expansion and to exponential increases in capital. At the same time, the intellectual biases toward the organic and spiritual sensibilities that had persisted through the Middle Ages, began to break down. Supported by scientific, technical, and economic changes, worldviews took a sudden shift toward the mechanical. Specifically, the universe came to be seen in terms of the most advanced machine of the time, the mechanical clock. In short order, all physical forms, including the human body, came to be regarded as clock-like: logical, manipulable, ultimately knowable.

The co-evolution of the Industrial Revolution and modern science supported the emergence and eventual dominance of a new mentality: Humans came to see themselves as the sole purveyors and arbiters of knowledge. No longer could objects or other life forms in the world be seen as endowed with "mind," much less be considered as aspects of "Mind." Instead, mind was cast as a uniquely human quality, one that was particular to each individual and contained within the physical body. Two profound divisions were assumed here: The mind came to be seen as separate from the physical world, and it was thought to exist prior to and independent of human culture.

That is, whereas mind had previously been understood as woven into and through the organic and spiritual worlds, in the 17th and 18th Centuries, it came to be associated only with the individual thinking human. This shift contributed to a cascade of transformations, the most dra-

You are here.

Fig. 4.5. In modernist terms, *self* tends to be discussed as though it were a kernel of identity that springs forth, fully formed, at either the moment of conception or the moment of birth.

The pervasiveness of this conception of an encapsulated self is evident in the many novels and movies whose storylines involve the transplantation of an identity from one body into another (or into an animal, a machine, etc.). This sort of plot relies on the belief that identity is independent of body, brain, experience, knowledge, context, and so on.

matic of which was a new conception of the relationship between humanity and the rest of universe. Previously framed in terms of embeddedness and conscientious participation, the world came to be seen as something to be mastered, a resource to be owned, managed, and exploited. More locally, the self came to be seen as separate from others — evidenced in a pervasive shift in the way people described themselves. No longer framing identity in terms of interpersonal relationships and communal responsibilities, modern individuals began to characterize themselves in terms of internal, personal qualities.

The self thus came to be cast as a discrete and isolated phenomenon. Understandings of the role of the individual shifted away from the project of attuning oneself to the living world and toward the project of asserting one's assumed-to-be pregiven and unchanging identity. Practices devoted to self-awareness, self-fulfillment, self-concept, self-esteem, self-actualization, self-efficacy, and so on quickly arose. At the same time, "experience" ceased to be understood as integral to one's self — a shift that was tied to the new break between knower and known. Experience merely served as a means to acquire knowledge about a reality that was deemed separate from the individual.

A Modern Reading: *Achieving a Personal Goal*

What might modernist conception of self suggest about Jamie's experiences of learning to teach?

First, it would be assumed that the project of becoming a teacher is a developmental one. One's full achievement in a role occurs through a process of learning, an aspect of which is the deliberate acquisition of skills and knowledge. Jamie's initial fear, from this perspective, would be seen to arise from inexperience — and from the fact that she is caught between the roles of student and teacher. So conceived, her eventual success with the students on that day might be seen as a triumph over this ambiguous positioning through the successful projection of a teacher identity. From this perspective, becoming an effective teacher is a matter of acquiring and deploying a set of technical competencies — a process that is believed to have no effect on one's essential core identity. Though Jamie is now differently positioned in relation to her students, though she is engaging in activities she has never performed before, she is still the same character.

Modernist conceptions of self suggest that Jamie would be able to fully represent her experiences as a new teacher to herself and to others. Further, once represented, she would be able to critically interpret these personal narratives. Such abilities, although framed by her university courses and practicum experiences, would be seen as Jamie's personal achievement. Becoming an effective teacher, then, from a modernist perspective, is conditioned by social and cultural forms, but is, in the end, an example of how the individual mind can attain personal goals.

These modernist beliefs about the self were eventually aligned with prevailing religious (primarily Christian) doctrines on the nature of God and the imperfection of human subjects. In particular, the modern notion of mind was linked to the more ancient notion of soul, giving rise to a conception of personal identity as some sort of kernel that springs forth, fully formed, at the moment of birth (or, depending on one's perspective, at the moment of conception). This move contributed to further diminutions of the physical world and the biological body — both of which had to be suppressed and ignored for the purposes of achieving salvation of the mind / soul / self.

This conception of self remains predominant today. It is a self that is believed to exist within clear boundaries, one that can be completely and fully achieved through hard work and discipline, and one that can be fully known through practices of self-disclosure and self-representation. This modernist self, it is believed, can eventually say everything that there is to say about itself. It is a self of specific and predetermined limits or potentials. The achievement of such potentials, from the modern perspective, involves the development of one's understandings and skills through the internalization of external knowledge.

Correspondingly, modernist educational practices are oriented by the goal of providing individuals with the knowledge deemed necessary for reaching one's potential. Assumptions about the self as isolated and fixed are not only evident in prescribed curricula, however, They are also embodied in classroom arrangements and instructional strategies. Commonly, students are organized to suppress movement and interaction, enabling them, it is thought, to focus on the development of their minds by reducing the distractions of their own and others' bodies.

Modernist conceptions of identity do not assert that the self is static. However, there tends to be an assumption of some "essential" self, one that is unique to the individual and that remains constant across situations. This belief is evident in such phrases as "one's true self" and "the person you're meant to be." Popularly, this self is seen as autonomous (literally, living under its own laws), self-determining, and free to choose its own thoughts. This self is seen as able to master very different roles (which is sometimes described as "wearing different hats"). Although one's relationships, behaviors, and thoughts may vary

Fig. 4.6. In a modernist conception, identity is seen as multifaceted, but coherent, well bounded, and unchanging. In popular terms, the self is a "hat wearer." That is, as one moves from one setting to another, one selects the appropriate behaviors from one's repertoire of possibilities — but one's core identity remains constant regardless of the hat worn.

The prominence of this perspective among discussions of schooling is revealed in the habit of fragmenting the teacher's role. Among the many hats donned by the teacher are those of the leader, the scholar, the facilitator, the coach, the policeman, the director, the colleague, and the community member.

dramatically across such roles, one's identity is not seen to vary or to be context-sensitive. Rather, such roles are seen as aspects of a multifaceted, but unified person.

In brief, then, in modernist conceptions, the self is cast as isolated from other selves and insulated from the physical world. The self is thought to be innate and its potentialities prespecified, to be achieved through discipline and practice. This achievement, though, is subject to the oppressions and the vagaries of the social world. Selfhood must thus be claimed and exerted. As such, the "full realization" of one's self is dependent on expressions of independence and individuality. The highest achievement, from this modernist perspective, is to be a self-made person: independent, in touch with who you are.

Fig. 4.7. Postmodernism argues that modernism (and its vision of a unified and fully knowable universe) has collapsed. We live instead in a world of partial knowledge, local narratives, situated truths, shifting selves.

The postmodern world is endlessly contemporary, a constantly emerging hyper-reality of cyberspace, Disneyland, MTV, Barbie, and so on. Many of these cultural forms originated in the modernist project of modeling reality. However, the resulting simulations have given rise to a strange new reality.

There are no universal truths and no grand unifying themes in this postmodern world — apart, perhaps, from a rejection of modernist claims to reductive and totalizing truth.

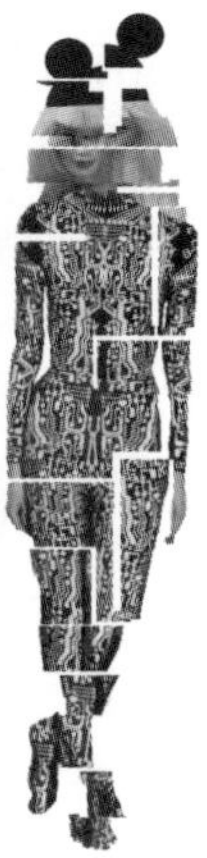

The Postmodern: Self as Fluid and Specified

The explicit aims of formal education that derive from modernist conceptions tend to be conflicted. On the one hand, the core self is seen as something to be nurtured, and so teachers are admonished to foster self-esteem and autonomy. On the other hand, the individual must fit into the giant machinery of society. As such, schooling has been deliberately designed to enable students to fulfill particular social functions. (The "Outcomes Based Education" movement is a good example of the sorts of educational structures that have been developed from this stance.) But is the self really in existence prior to language, experience, and education? Or might it be that who one becomes is the product of cultural influence and social interaction?

Experience suggests that senses of self, while seemingly coherent and ongoing, are always changing. One's childhood identity, for example, is usually markedly different from one's adult identity. As well, one's understanding of oneself often varies dramatically from the ways that one is viewed by others. These differences in perspective give rise to conflicting narratives of identity, which in turn contribute to the continuous updating of one's sense of self. Given such observations, it seems reasonable to suggest that personal identity does not pre-exist experience. Rather, identity seems to emerge from practices of identifying and being identified to, by, and with others.

Self, in this frame, can be considered a product of many experiences of identification with others in a dynamic so-

cial world. So conceived, the self is constantly emerging
from many intertwining and overlapping cultural narratives, and a number of prominent discourses over the past
century have highlighted aspects of these identifications.
Feminist theorists, for example, have shown how gender
is not merely organized by the individual's genitalia, but
is also shaped by cultural narratives about what constitutes the genders male and female. Their work has helped
to uncover the extent to which women in Western (and
other) societies have been oppressed by patriarchal discourses that are deeply inscribed with assumptions of male
superiority and privilege. Feminist scholars have also demonstrated how these dominant discourses have shaped
(and, in the process, come to be embedded in) differentiated practices of dress, social interaction and obligation,
and status among males and females.

Along similar lines, critical race theorists have shown
how race has in many respects been invented and deployed
by groups of persons (primarily Anglo-American and European Caucasians) to create and justify hierarchical distinctions among peoples — distinctions that privilege some
groups over others. Related studies by Marxist and other
critical theorists have focused on the ways in which ineq-
uitable distributions of material and intellectual resources
are maintained through exclusionary cultural (and, particularly, educational) practices. In another domain, researchers in gay and lesbian studies, along with queer theorists, have demonstrated how most societies have reduced
the polymorphous possibilities of sexuality among humans
to a narrow conception of heterosexuality, against which
all other experiences and expressions of sexuality are measured and judged. Together, these discourses have helped
to reveal the ways in which senses of self are continually
organized and shaped by many overlapping, intertwining, and often-conflicting cultural practices.

For the most part, these discourses have emerged as
critiques of modernist thought (and of the personal, social, and other practices that are born or modern, analytic
perspectives). As such, they all point to a broad change in
sensibility, one that has been called "postmodern."

Postmodernism is hardly a unified notion. The term,
in fact, has been subject to a wide range of interpretation.
Much of the variation in opinion around the idea of postmodernism arises from the fact that it is defined in terms

Fig. 4.8. *Semiotics* derives from
the ancient Greek term for
"interpretation of signs."
(Originally, the word was
probably used in reference to
the more ancient Semitic

of *what it isn't* rather than it terms of *what it is*, which opens up a vast range of interpretive possibilities. One point of general agreement, though is that the "postmodern" is a rejection of modernism, with its narratives of formal logic, objectified understandings, totalized knowledge, reductive assertions, and universal laws.

Particular to postmodern discourses is the understanding that one's knowledge about things and one's knowledge about self do not pre-exist one another. Rather, these are continually co-emergent phenomena. The act of identifying, it is suggested, is an act of differentiation: In recognizing a parent, for example, a child is distinguishing him- or herself from another person. One identifies the "me" and the "not-me" simultaneously — and, in these events of identification, one's sense of identity arises.

culture where the first alphabet — the one from which all modern Western alphabets have evolved — was invented.)

As a discipline, semiotics is interested in the ways that signs and symbols are incorporated into our existences.

This interest goes beyond a focus on alphabets, icons, and other obvious symbols. In fact, one might say that the motto of semiotics is, "Nothing is insignificant." Everything we notice is a potential site of interpretation.

With this emphasis on identifications, postmodern discourses have tended to focus on language use. Specifically, there has been an emphasis on the uniquely human ability to use words to refer to words, which is the quality that distinguishes mere communicative capacity from the powerfully recursive phenomenon of language. (Many species have been demonstrated to have sophisticated communication systems, but only humanity seems to have developed the self-referential and recursive use of words — that is, language.) Within language, humans have the capacity to create senses of personal identity and to theorize about that act of creation.

One's sense of self, it is suggested, unfolds continuously through the recursive and reiterative processes of representing and interpreting one's identity in relation to (and in distinction from) other forms — persons, objects, events, and so on. Postmodern discourses focus in particular on the ways that events of identification take place within *semiotic* systems — that is, within an array of signifying systems that include oral and written language, paintings, television, the internet, all forms of media advertising, songs, dances, gestures, gossip, and so on. Any system of representation and interpretation is a semiotic system. Conceptions of self that are aligned with postmodernism are developed around the belief that senses of personal identity emerge from and are embedded in the interrelations of these many semiotic systems and practices.

From a postmodern perspective, one's sense of self is always fluid and shifting. A sense of identity arises in the weave of what is remembered, what is represented from the present, and what is imagined for the future. The self, from this perspective, is not isolated and fixed. Rather, self is the product of communal relations and is thus always being produced. The self is fluid and contextual.

The suggestion that identities are in flux does not mean that they are fragmented and incoherent. What is rejected in postmodern conceptions of self is not the idea of a stable identity, but of a fixed identity. Postmodern discourses do not accept the modernist assumption that the self exists in some essential form that remains unchanged as it passes through experience. Instead, one's sense of personal identity is understood to emerge from one's involvements in signifying systems and practices — and, in some ways, to be contained in these systems and practices. The stories that one tells and is told, the objects that one cherishes and scorns, the activities that one supports and avoids — these are the sites of self identity / identification.

In other words, the semiotic systems that shape experience are important technologies for creating selves. Here, *technology* is used to refer to more than physical tools, especially those that have arisen since the Scientific and Industrial Revolutions. The word technology emerges from the ancient Greek *techne*, the original meaning of which was more toward "bringing forth" than "manufacturing." Various signifying systems and objects can be considered technologies of the self. Over centuries, humans have elaborated their linguistic technologies with the invention of written symbols, alphabets, printing presses, silent reading, mass communication, electronic information devices, and so on. For the most part, in fact, technology has been understood as these sorts of tools and machines, as opposed to the manner in which these artifacts and processes have been incorporated into human existences — that is, how they have literally become part of human bodies and culture and how, in the process, they have been used to help bring forth human identities. Postmodern conceptions of self have helped to show how such technologies are entwined in the practices used by humans to represent and negotiate cultural experience. In other words, all these technological elaborations of language are enfolded in every human subject's experience of self.

The word technology, then, refers to all developed procedures related to the making (or the bringing forth) of

Fig. 4.9. The term *technology* is usually used in reference to mechanical devices — and, in particular, to the most recent of human inventions.

The word originally referred to any means of enhancing human capabilities. In this sense, perhaps our most important technology is language.

Technologies, mechanical or otherwise, have a way of fading into the transparent backdrops of our lives. They come to be folded into our beings so seamlessly that some semioticians have suggested that we are all, quite literally, cyborgs.

individual and collective identities. Again, this definition does not refer only to manufactured tools and machines. Instead, it is intended to describe the ground of human existence — that is, the habits of acting that are embedded in routines, rituals, and ways of communicating experience. Any procedure or practice that influences thought and action is a technology of self-making.

Language appears to be the most important self-making technology. As a tool of consciousness, language greatly enables our limited capacities to gather ideas and to note relationships. Alphabetic writing, similarly, is another important tool, particularly as it enables us to record various details, interpretations, and narrative that contribute a certain stability to senses of personal and collective identity. (Written records are much more stable than their oral counterparts.) Other technologies are not so readily described as "tools," such as public schools, organized religions, legal systems, political parties, and so on. Nevertheless, such institutions form a large part of the backdrop against which the individual's sense of self comes to form.

A Postmodern Reading: *Acting the Part*

How might a postmodernist theory of selfhood be used to interpret Jamie's teaching experience?

Jamie's initial terror might be described as emerging from her remembered and currently lived experiences in the cultures of schooling — first as a student, then as a student teacher in the university classroom, and now as a beginning teacher with her own class of students. The signifying practices that have contributed to her present experience, then, include various narratives of experience about herself and about others. Jamie's sense of "identity," in this perspective, emerges not just from what she has directly experienced as a student and a teacher, but from varied popular narratives of what it means to be a teacher. Movies that depict the interactions of students and teachers, for example, are signifying systems that contribute as significantly to Jamie's sense of teacher identity as her own past experiences in school and university settings. At the same time, her experience is conditioned by the many representations of teachers that constitute her student teaching experience, including those conceptions of teachers that are assumed in popular media, in staffroom interactions, in cafeteria gossip, in formal textbooks, and so on.

Jamie's move from the terrified teacher to the confident one, then, might be described as a resituation. A collection of overlapping semiotic systems that organize her perception in one way has been rearranged into another.

This rearrangement, of course, has as much to do with the way in which "students" are created by signifying practices as with the way that "teachers" are created. As Jamie begins to renegotiate the category of "teacher," so too do her students. When what those students perceive in Jamie begins to approximate what they have come to understand as the teacher's voice, appearance, and manner of acting, they begin to offer responses that fit with Jamie's expectations. These historically effected signifying practices function to create the successful teaching event that Jamie eventually experiences.

In sum, in the postmodern view, the self is a linguistic construct, rendered coherent through a constantly revised web of narratives. These narratives are told mainly by the individual (enabling a sense of individuality and autonomy) in the process of interpreting his or her particular experiences. But the range of possible narratives is greatly limited by prevailing cultural sensibilities. That is, identity is largely specified by one's situation. To invoke a different metaphor, the colors on the palate from which one paints one's self are limited and pregiven.

Postmodern perspectives have helped to reveal the limitations of modernist conceptions of self. In particular, they have shown how senses of identity continuously emerge with the complex, overlapping discourses and technologies of culture. From this view, practices of schooling are seen as primary forces in shaping human identities. In contrast to the modernist premise that formal education should be oriented to helping individuals realize their preexistent potentials, postmodernism casts the self more as a product of the practices and the contents of schooling.

The Ecological Postmodern: Self as Complex and Situated

History demonstrates that the tools used to structure human experience eventually become invisible to their users. The idea that a book is a technology, for example, is foreign, even silly, to most citizens of a modern world — even moreso the suggestion that *language* is a technology.

This tendency for prior technological advances to fade into transparency occurs regardless of the relative impact of the tools on the ways that humans think about and act in the world. Like all forms that have grown familiar, they become part of the unnoticed backdrop of perception.

Part of the reason that technologies cease to be seen as such may be a long-standing habit of using the most recent innovations to interpret human experience. That is, technologies are often incorporated into metaphors which are subsequently taken literally. They become part of everyday commonsense, of the way things are, rather than figurative devices that can help to highlight some aspect of a phenomena. For example, in the 17th Century, René Descartes' described a "healthy man" as a "well-made clock" — a description that has not just influenced the way

Fig. 4.10. If, over the years, a ship were to be rebuilt board by board and sail by sail so that every part was gradually replaced, would it still be the same vessel? If not, at which point would we say that it was a different vessel?

What about the case of of a human whose body is constantly regenerating? The pancreas and the stomach lining, for example, actually replace themselves every 24 hours. Over 100,000 skin cells are replaced every minute. (The

humans think about themselves, but that has since oriented most of medical research. More recently, the inventions of hydraulics and internal combustion engines contributed to such notions of self-*motivation*, emotional *pressure*, mental *breakdown*, brain *power*, personal *drive*, and so on. All of these are metaphors, but they are rarely recognized as such. Currently, the computer figures prominently in thinking about thinking: Such notions as "mind as computer," "learning as inputting information," and "thought as processing" are taken literally in many situations.

Across such figurative associations between humans and human technologies, there is a persistent thematic: an assumption that humans are machines.

This modernist view of personhood has had specific and serious consequences. In the field of medicine, for example, it has supported a culture of specialization which has, to some degree, hindered the development of holistic medical practices. (Holistic practices are those that attend to the complex ways human bodily subsystems interact with one another and to the ways that, as subsystems themselves, human bodies interact with other human bodies and with their settings.) The same is true of other professions — including teaching, where most studies of pedagogy and learning are still focused on analyzing their components, rather than on examining complex intertwinings.

Of course, there have been tremendous intellectual gains achieved through the practice of fragmentation and specialization. However, there have been many tragic consequences. For example, despite the billions of dollars spent on research into heart disease and cancer, these afflictions persist — and, in fact, they are on the rise in many populations. Why? It is now theorized that the effects of specialized research and therapies have been overly focused on specific ailments, in absence of appreciations of how such ailments are conditioned by such social, cultural, and environmental factors as food, stress, and pollution.

Similar consequences of fragmented thinking have been noted by educators. A range of studies has demonstrated, for example, that students are often unable to make use of their classroom-based learning in their lives outside of schools. In fact, it seems that many students are not even able to generalize their learning from one course of study to another — or even from one topic to another in the same course. At least part of the problem here seems

dust in our homes consists mostly of bits of ourselves that have fallen off.) Every other part regenerates itself at its own pace. In essence, we are patterns in the stream of matter.

As well, one's experiences and the contexts of those experiences are in constant flux. "Self" and "situation" co-evolve — that is, they continuously affect one another.

In other words, identity is complex — dynamic, contingent, emergent, participatory.

Not all is flux, however. Through the continuous processes of transformation, the relatively stable patterns of our beings — as embodied in the stories we tell and are told, as preserved in the organizations of our bodies, and so on — enable us to maintain a coherent and ongoing senses of identity.

to be the long-standing practices of fragmenting topics into isolated concepts and teaching the resulting parts in prescribed sequences. The common hope that the learner will "pull it all together" is not always realized.

The tendency toward fragmentation and reduction — whether of a human body, a body of knowledge, or whatever — represents a failure to appreciate the difference between things that are *complicated* and phenomena that are *complex*. As developed in Chapter 2A, complicated systems are those that can be fully understood through a knowledge of their parts, such as clocks, car engines, and computers. Other phenomena, such as climates, the immune system, and societies, cannot be fully understood through examinations of their components, largely because their components are similarly alive or dynamic. As such, their behaviors cannot be fully predicted in the same way as, for example, the behavior of an automobile.

The boundaries of complex systems are much more ambiguous than those of complicated systems. It is not difficult, for example, to say where a refrigerator starts and stops. But one cannot say where an ecosystem or a society or a person begins and ends — simply because such systems are actively exchanging parts of themselves with their surroundings. Humans inhale and exhale, they eat and defecate, they shed and regenerate — and such processes expose the artificiality of such distinctions as "human versus natural" and "self versus other." To understand the identity of a complex system, one must look at its embeddedness and its intertwinings, not at its boundaries.

Fig. 4.11. The terms *environmentalism* and *ecology* don't mean the same thing.

Environmentalism is the study of what surrounds us — which,

With the recent realization of the profound differences between complicated and complex forms, a powerful new way of thinking about human identities has been presented. It has helped to highlight, for example, that events of self identification are not always about distinguishing an "I" from a "not-I." In fact, it may be that most events of self identification are about becoming part of a "we." Most of one's activities are framed by the groups and cliques with which one identifies, as are the opinions and perspectives that orient one's interpretations. For example, the most significant influence on a child's attitude about school work is not the home, the parents, or the teacher, but the peer group. Interestingly, the way a child adopts the prevailing opinions of a social group (e.g., regarding school work, fashion, habits, toys, etc.) is not generally a matter of giving into peer pressure. Most often, attitudinal change seems to be a fluid and nonconscious integration of sensibilities, assumed in much the same way that accents and mannerisms tend to be taken on (or lost).

This phenomenon has been commonly witnessed by parents and teachers who have observed children undergo dramatic changes in personality as they hook up with different groups. It has also been demonstrated in the highly problematic classroom practice of ability grouping. When groups of good students are separated from groups of less-able students, different group norms — that is different attitudes and different behaviors — usually emerge, giving rise to even larger gaps in ability.

Again, such transformations are not principally matters of deliberate conformation to established norms; there seems to be a more complex and organic process of collective identification at work. Unfortunately, though, research into identity has been overwhelmingly oriented by the modernist assumption that identity resides in the individual, and so there has been relatively little formal inquiry into how such group identifications occur.

by definition, assumes a separation between humanity and the natural world. It thus bespeaks a modernist sensibility.

Ecology is the study of relationships. It derives from the Greek *oikos*, household, and is used to draw attention to the intertwining webs of activity and meaning in which we find our selves. In many ways, the ecological movement recalls premodernist sensibilities.

It does appear, though, that people categorize themselves as an "us" at least as much as they categorize themselves as a "me," depending on where the spotlight is at the moment. Most of the time, they seem to float somewhere between the two, simultaneously, for example, able to represent group opinion while exercising personal choice. This tendency to identify both as an "us" and a "me" has been linked to the fact that humans are social creatures whose survival depends on the capacity to form cohesive collectives — a quality that may find its roots in biology. There is ample evidence that this is the case.

These ideas recall the premodern conception of Mind and challenge the modernist conception that identity is contained in a physical body. They also elaborate postmodern conceptions of self by embracing the idea that culture and sociality shape identity, and adding that there are also biological influences. In order to understand human identity, attention must be given to the complex ways that culture and biology become entwined in one's experiences.

These more complex views of self-making do not deny individual experiences of consciousness, experience, or subjectivity. Being a part of a complex cultural/biological system does not mean that humans are mindless automatons or inert cogs. Quite the contrary, in fact: An ecological postmodern view of existence *relies* on the uniqueness of individuals. In order for complex systems to remain viable, there must be diversity among the agents that comprise the system. Tremendous creativity and novelty have been shown to arise from such individuality, as expressed in the context of a larger system. (See Chapter 3A.)

This point is especially relevant to classroom contexts. In particular, it reveals the emptiness of the popular debate around whose interests, society's or the child's, should be served by schooling. The terms of this debate place the individual and the collective in conflict, and that conflict is oftentimes dramatically and tragically enacted in classrooms where the teacher (cast as a representative of society) is positioned at odds with the students (representing their own self interests). It is this mindset that gives rise to concerns over classroom management and control.

Although sometimes difficult in a cultural setting that is dominated by modernist (individualist) sensibilities, some teachers have demonstrated that a different way of thinking about the relationship between the individual and the collective can support very different classroom experiences. The key is to work with the human predisposition to identify with groups. For example, the use of some sort of shared project or goal as a basis for establishing a sense of collectivity might help to redefine the relationship between teacher and learners, as jointly engaged rather than in opposition. In the process, the teacher can sometimes greatly influence group norms, in a way that few other adults can (because few other adults deal with children in groups). In recent years, several prominent and powerful examples of this sort of shift in emphasis — that is, from a focus on the individual to a broadened sense of the individual-as-part-of-the-collective — have been presented in popularized accounts of some exceptional educators.

From this perspective, the experience of human identity is not something that precedes the individual's interactions with/in the world (a modernist conception), nor is it something that is imposed by prevailing cultural sensibilities (a postmodernist conception). Rather, identity emerges within complex systems — which include the subhuman, social collectives, and the more-than-human. Emergent identities also influence the context and systems in which experiences occur. In other words, there is a great

Fig. 4.12. In the modern scientific view, astrology and associated predictive practices are not highly regarded. As the argument usually goes, it makes little sense to attribute one's character and fate to events that occur millions, billions, and trillions of miles away.

But might such practices hint at an important insight that has been all but lost? Could there be something to a horoscope?

deal more going on in every moment than the experiencer can possibly attend to — much less describe or explain. Whether noted or not, though, there is a constant cascade of consequences to and possibilities for one's actions, and they can all affect one's identity.

This is an assertion that has been made by many working from postmodern perspectives on identity. However, an ecological postmodern sensibility also challenges some of the assumptions and assertions of postmodern views. In particular, an ecological postmodern view looks at language somewhat differently, less as not a transcendent phenomenon and more an element of human activity. With language, humans do vastly more than describe and interpret reality: They invent and transform reality, shaping the worlds in which they exist and the identities that they assume in those worlds.

Indeed, this point has been powerfully demonstrated over the past few centuries in some of the more troublesome consequences of humanity's language-based habit of thinking itself apart from and superior to the natural world. Such assumptions were relatively safe in the 17th Century, when they rose to prominence. When human populations were lower, the more-than-human world could absorb their impact. Rapid environmental change through the past decades, however, indicates that a dramatic rethinking of who and what we are is called for.

It is thus that an ecological postmodern sensibility expands on the sphere of interest represented in postmodern discourses. The latter tend to focus on the realms of human culture and sociality. Ecological postmodernism pushes the envelope to include what modernist and postmodernist discourses have tended to categorize as not-human: bodily subsystems, the biosphere, and so on. This shift in thinking has not been readily endorsed by many postmodern discourses, in large part because it opens the door to the suggestion that biology plays an important role in defining who we are — a notion that has been rejected by some more radical postmodern discourses. (Most often, this rejection of the biological is linked to the explicit goals of many discourses to demonstrate that social difference has no basis in genetics.) Despite their critiques, however, there is a dearth of evidence to support the assertion that one's identity has as much to do with biological constitution as it does with cultural circumstance. More

In this age of year-round conveniences, one might easily overlook the possible impact of the seasonal differences (in sunlight, diet, temperature, activity, and so on) on expectant mothers and on fetal development — and hence, on personalities. It may be that premodern citizens were simply noting the relationships between seasonal skies and behavior patterns.

broadly, there has been ample demonstration that the human organism is physiologically and intellectually entwined in the complex evolutions of the biosphere.

In summary, ecological postmodern perspectives on identity acknowledge the complex ways that senses of personal and collective identity are entangled in historical, cultural, biological, and more-than-human worlds. Like postmodern sensibilities, these ecological discourses acknowledge the importance of language and memory in the development of identities. But ecological discourses spread a wider net. Their interests are not bounded by the domain of human activity and interactivity. To understand human identity, they suggest, one must also consider how humanity is knitted into the web of life on the planet. Human identity does not merely reside in the stories that are told about it. In fact, most aspects of one's sense of self slip past such formulation. Identities in the complex interplays of experience, genetics, culture, and biology.

Fig. 4.13. Where do personalities come from?

Studies of similarities and differences among siblings (e.g., biological, adoptive, raised apart, raised together, etc.) have generated two consistent conclusions.

First, about half the variation in personalities among persons seems to have genetic roots and about half seems to arise from differences in socialization.

Second, the major social influences on one's opinions, preferences, habits, identifications, and so on are not one's parents, but one's peer groups. Children do most of their experimenting with identity in play groups, cliques, gangs, classrooms, and so on.

The self, then, is both the product of complex processes and a complex process that participates in its own making. The self arises amid established forms of knowledge as it participates in making new knowledge. The self is both invented and inventing, created and creating, product of learning and agent of learning.

Schooling practices, from an ecological postmodern perspective, begin with the realization that learning is not so much a deliberate act as it is an aspect of life. Every moment of existence, however familiar, calls for some manner of creative response. Every moment of life is a learning event, a creative participation in the complex choreography of existence.

Teaching, then, is all about effecting transformations. In encouraging particular sorts of understandings, the teacher is supporting the development of particular worldviews and modes of perception. The associated classroom experiences are biological-and-social events. On the sub-personal level, for example, they contribute to actual physical transformations in brain structure, as well as to other physiological changes. On the personal level, they frame how one sees and acts. On the interpersonal level, they influence collective dynamics as they affect how people think about and relate to one another. On supra-personal levels, they are enfolded in social and cultural patterns, which in turn impact on the grander systems.

An Ecological Postmodern Reading:
Establishing a Consensual Domain

How might an ecological postmodern perspective on self be used to interpret Jamie's learning-to-teach experience?

To help frame a response, if an ecological postmodern sensibility could be summed up in a few sentences, it might be, Everything matters, but we can be aware only a small part of what goes on around us. We can never know the full consequences of an action and, as such, we must participate mindfully in the unfolding of circumstances around us.

In terms of Jamie's story, then, this perspective would embrace many of the interpretations suggested by a postmodern sensibility. However, the scope of interest would exceed issues of explicit interpretation, cultural habit, and social circumstance. In particular, it would prompt attention toward ecological intertwinings and relational dynamics. That is, this perspective would look across levels of organization to try to understand the event in question.

Regarding relational dynamics, for example, it is clear that the roles of this classroom have tended to be explicitly defined in oppositional terms: The teacher is *not* a student. In fact, the teacher's role is to manage, to control, to oversee learners and their learning.

Such distinctions and definitions, however, are artificial. Teacher and students alike exist as a consensual unity, each specifying the domain of appropriate activity for the other. This is a profoundly cooperative event, although it is often interpreted in modernist terms of competition and conflict. (Indeed, this is how Jamie initially perceived things.)

An ecological postmodern perspective would thus urge that the classroom be seen as comprised of interacting and overlapping unities (i.e., teacher and students), as a unity in and of itself (with its own particular character and established patterns of actions), and as an aspect of grander collectives (e.g., a school, a community, an ecosystem, and so on).

In a similar manner, Jamie must

be regarded as a complex collective (of biological, historically effected, dynamic and interacting parts), as a coherent whole (i.e., she has an ongoing sense of her own identity and is perceived by her students as having one), and as an element of grander collectives. From an ecological postmodern perspective, it is not so much how she has established her identity that is most interesting. Rather, the important thing is how her complex identity participates in the project at hand — namely, the education of her students.

More broadly, a complex and situated theory of self also prompts attention to larger phenomenological, cultural, biological, and more-than-human matters. It would be of interest, for example, to know whether this event took place in a cold or warm climate, whether it was morning or afternoon, how active the students had been that day, and so on. The particulars of the students — their ages, their sexes, their levels of sexual and social development, their friendships and intimate contacts with others — would also be of interest, as all these details contribute to the character of the collective. Similarly, Jamie's physical appearance, her health, her age, her physiological responses to stressful situations, her sexuality, her gender, her dreams last night, her spiritual beliefs, and so on, all contribute to the unfolding situation.

The point here is *not* that all these sorts of details must be considered. It is that they all matter. Such a realization would shift one's efforts away from attempting to do "the right thing" and toward finding an appropriate pattern of acting in this setting. It is not a matter of exerting control — the dynamic complexity of the situation makes that impossible — but of being attentive to the effects of one actions.

Jamie, then, managed to establish a rhythm that fit in with the flow of those around her. She, in fact, noticed the sudden harmony of action. So situated, she found herself able to be more directive in structuring students' experiences in the classroom.

Inventing Subjects

To review, four ways that selfhood has been or might be conceptualized were described in this chapter.

In premodern times, the self was generally understood to be strongly influenced by the spiritual and the organic. The more-than-human world was understood to be enchanted, not something to be exploited and mastered. The premodern subject thus felt an obligation to be attuned to and guided by that world.

As the modern era emerged, conceptual divisions between the humanity and the biosphere and between mind and body arose. While prior beliefs in a divinely wrought and intricately spiritual world persisted to varying extents in modern settings, the prevailing conception of self shifted from a participant in to an observer of the universe. Modernist sensibilities gave rise to an isolated and fixed self, a self that believed a complete understanding of the cosmos was within the grasp of humanity. One needed only to uncover the basic laws that directed the universe.

Over the past half century, cross-disciplinary postmodern discourses have revealed the untenability of many modernist assumptions, focusing particularly on its narrow conception of language. Arguing that language is not a means of representing truth (as it was assumed to be in modernist discourses) but more a means of projecting a reality, postmodern discourses have suggested that the self is specified in the confluence of signifying systems and practices. This frame rejects the notion that identity is some fixed object or essence that is housed in the body. Rather, the self is seen as fluid and shifting. More specifically, one's identity is specified by one's involvements in culturally constructed and socially mediated forms of representation and habits of interpretation. The self of postmodernism, then, is not regarded as a vessel that contains knowledge, but as a permeable and malleable participant in knowledge-making. It is a self that both marks the world and that is marked by its worldly encounters.

As a further elaboration of postmodern sensibilities, ecological postmodern perspectives expand on the notion of "world" that is implicit in postmodern discourses. Rather than limiting the discussion to the social and cultural realms, ecological postmodern discourses take a view of the world that is reminiscent of that of premodern cul-

Fig. 4.14. Theories of identity or selfhood have always been implicit in teaching practices. This pair of images, for example, illustrate some dramatic changes in pedagogical approaches that occurred in the 17th Century.

In the image on the left, created early in the century by Van Ostade, the pedagogue is positioned among the learners who are engaged in a diversity of activities. It is clear that the learning that is occurring is not under the control of anyone in particular. Rather, each person influences every other person's

tures. Human identities, it is suggested, are as much biological as they are social events. Identities, in fact, come to form amid the intertwinings of many complex systems that span the human, the sub-human, and the more-than-human realms. Rejecting the modernist separation of mental from physical, the ecological postmodern perspective posits a more diffuse conception of identity. In addition to understanding the human sense of self as fluid and shifting, it sees identity as complex and situated, caught up in an ongoing choreography of existence.

activities in some manner. Boundaries are vague and shifting.

In the institutional setting on the right, painted later in the century (artist unknown), many of modernist sensibilities have been enacted. The teacher stands at the front, directing the activity from the edge of the classroom. Students are grouped according to age and are all focused on the same subject matter. Each individual faces the same direction, is working from his own textbook, and operates under the surveillance of the teacher.

To reiterate using a different metaphor — that of sound — premodern conceptions of identity tended to cast the self as part of an unfolding chorus, a participant in a universe that was sung into being. In modernist sensibilities, the focus shifted from the chorus to the individual voices — and, in fact, much of the modernist discourse is framed in terms of achieving and using one's voice as an expression of one's autonomy. Postmodern discourses exploded the illusion of autonomy, demonstrating that one's voice is mostly a matter of ventriloquation of collective sensibilities and dominant narratives. Ecological postmodern discourses, however, have restored a sense of agency to the individual, highlighting that one's participation matters: One's voice is more than an echo, it is an engagement that contributes to the unfolding of the universe in complex and unknowable ways.

That is, an ecological postmodern perspective on human identity recalls many of the sensibilities that were represented in premodern conceptions — an observation that highlights that none of these conceptions of identity can be tidily assigned to some historical period or to some cultural setting. To varying degrees, all four conceptions exist today — and have co-existed for quite some time.

Humans, then, have a diversity of strategies for thinking about existence — strategies that co-exist even while being in some ways contradictory. Owing to an array of historical contingencies, particular perspectives have risen to cultural dominance and have influenced political, economic, educational, and other systems. Even while a particular mindset may predominate, others can never be completely erased. To some degree, other possibilities — including ones that have not even been anticipated in this writing — continue to do their work, influencing the ways in which human senses of self develop and evolve.

Spirituality

In modern and Western settings, *spirituality* is usually defined in terms of disembodiment, of transcendence of the physical, and of denial of the worldly.

And, although this conventional sense of spirituality shares many assumptions with modern science, it also tends to be defined in contrast to a scientific sensibility. Spirituality is thought to be about faith; science is thought to be principally concerned with proof.

Because of this contrast, the topic of spirituality is rarely addressed by "serious" educational researchers. However, with the development of complex accounts of identity, the topic is starting to gain much broader attention — in part because these accounts cast us as part of a larger whole. There *is* a grander corpus, a higher unity according to these theories — and we are each part of it. Whether one chooses to think in terms of God, of a higher power, of One-ness, or whatever, there is now a legitimate basis — an *embodied* way — to address matters of spirituality.

For many, this is new. For others, it is more a remembering — a recalling that matters of the spirit are, literally, matters of breathing, of constant connection to and exchange with the rest of the world. According to historians and archeologists, the belief that humans exist in a web of relations that are not wholly developed by humans was and is fundamental to other cultures. Many North American Aboriginal peoples, for example, have long asserted the importance of this belief and, despite pressures to conform to modern Eurocentric attitudes, have continued to practice an ecological spirituality. For many North American Aboriginal cultures this has meant that the spirit world of animals, humans, and other non-human animate and inanimate forms intermingle throughout, in between, and over the courses of many human lifetimes.

Elements that are central to many of these orientations include a belief in the complex and necessary relationship between living and dying and a sense of the ethical responsibilities that humans have within the web of relationships. With the emergence of more ecological sensibilities, these forms of spirituality have recently come to be seen by others as crucial to the survival of the planet.

In the field of education, the modernist paradigm has dominated for at least a few centuries, and its influence is clear in the curricula, teaching methods, grading regimes, classroom arrangements, interpersonal relationships, and other structures that define the conventional school. However, as new insights into identity arise from such varied domains as biology, anthropology, philosophy, literary studies, curriculum theory, physics, and mathematics, schooling too is coming to be reinterpreted. In the process, while many of its inconsistencies are revealed, new possibilities for formal education are emerging. But these new possibilities cut to the core of commonsense beliefs about what schooling is for, what teaching does, and what learning is. More sophisticated appreciations of the nature of human identity prompt very different answers to the how's and why's of classroom practice.

As my (Dennis's) teacher education students file into class, they drop their bags in a pile in the middle of the room. Inside each bag is an old shoe of their own that I have asked them to bring. Before class begins, while students are visiting among themselves, I open all the bags and pile the individual shoes into a small shoe mountain. I have not yet explained why the shoes are necessary.

Once students are settled, I read aloud Mem Fox's children's book, *Wilfrid Gordon McDonald Partridge*. The main character in this book is a little boy named Wilfrid who learns from his parents that his good friend, 96 year old Miss Nancy, has "lost" her memory. Because Wilfrid does not understand what this means, he asks his parents and a few of the residents at the senior citizen's home where Miss Nancy resides about memory. They tell him different things: One of them suggests that memory is something you remember; another insists that it is something that is warm; one gentleman thinks it is something that is from long ago; two others believe it is something that makes you cry or laugh; another believes that it is something as precious as gold.

This research helps Wilfrid understand that having a memory is important, and this makes him concerned that Miss Nancy has lost hers. He decides to help by collecting things that are meaningful to him: a box of sea shells, a puppet, a medal given to him by his grandfather, a football, a fresh warm egg. He carries these objects to Miss Nancy and, one by one, hands them to her. As she and Wilfrid examine them, she begins to remember: She remembers the blue speckled bird's eggs that she found when she was a young girl in her aunt's garden. She remembers going to the beach. She recalls, with sadness, a big brother who went to war and never returned. She talks about a puppet she had shown to her sister. It seems that Miss Nancy's memory has been found.

"Now that you have heard the story, I want you to do some writing about it. Today, we'll practice doing some "timed writing." Timed writing is a way of collecting some thoughts you have without worrying, before writing, about what you're going to say. Today, we're going to do a five-minute timed writing that begins with your copying out the prompt: 'As I listened to the story, I was reminded of ....' It is important for you to remember that, with timed

writing, you are just to write! You begin with the prompt and then start writing. Don't stop! It's very important for you to suspend judgment. Don't try to censor or edit what appears on the page. Just write! You will not need to share what you write with me or with anyone else, so don't worry if some of the topics that come up are personal. This writing is for you only.

Remember, though, that although I want you to write continuously, you do not need to write quickly. It is also important to try to relax your body and to hold your pen or pencil loosely. In order to help limber up, let's all stand up and stretch. Put your pens and pencils down. Stand on your toes! Reach your fingers to the ceiling. Wiggle them! Now bend over and let your arms drop loosely to the floor. Feel the stretch in your back. Turn your head slowly from left to right. Stand up. Shake your arms and hands by your sides. Now, be seated, and let's get started!"

When I give the signal to begin, some students become immediately engaged, some seem to labor for a moment or two. Within several minutes, however, there is a collective concentration in the room. The breathing of the students becomes regular; shifting and shuffling have ceased; all hands are moving evenly over the page. As I watch and listen, it is clear to me that the act of continuous writing has helped the students develop focus.

I do not write while the students are writing. Although there is some literature which suggests that the teacher must model writing for the students, I find that while teaching I am not able to write. Instead, I survey the room to ensure that no one is "stuck." I notice that Darren has stopped writing and is looking anxious. I walk over to him and give him an encouraging look and make a gesture with my hands and eyes that is intended to suggest he should continue writing. He smiles and starts writing. I then notice that Helen's knuckles are white from grappling with her pen. Because I do not want her to be so physically tense, I walk over and touch her hand whispering, "Relax!" I also make a note to remind myself to discuss relaxation techniques with the students. While students engage in the practice of writing, I engage in the practice of teaching. Both require a focused attention to the subject matter.

"Time's up! Finish your sentence and put down your pens and pencils." (There's a short pause.) "Now, I'd like you to read over what you've just written and identify one idea that you find interesting and that you might be willing to share with others in a group of four or five. I do not want you to read what you have written to one another, just talk about some 'idea' that the writing announced for you. This may be some topic you wrote about, or it may be something about the process of doing the timed writing."

Students quickly become engaged in their groups. Discussion is animated and productive. As I walk around and "eavesdrop," I notice that students are not only relating personal associations they have made but, importantly, are trying to understand, conceptually, what these associations might mean. Madison suggests:

> "In my writing I described how I found an old letter written in the 1940s in a reference book that I borrowed from the library. I remember thinking how much more personal handwriting on paper is than a computer generated letter or an e-mail message. I know that I appreciate getting a handwritten note from someone more than one made on the computer. I think that it's because it's more personal and is more directly attached to the person who wrote it — just like the objects that Wilfrid found were personal and, because of this, were interesting to Miss Nancy."

As each group discusses what they learned through their personal responses and group discussion, I write words and phrases that represent their ideas on the blackboard:

> *trace, artifact, memory work, transitional object, archive, commonplace, transformation, narratives of self, subjects, subjectivity.*

As our class discussion progresses, it becomes clear that groups are coming to deeper awarenesses of the relationships among memory, cultural objects, acts of narration, and the ongoing development of human identities. The students are all very interested in how Wilfrid Gordon's objects become so personally interesting to Miss Nancy — especially since Wilfrid had not told Miss Nancy anything about his relationship to these objects.

As a teacher, I am satisfied that this introductory activity has achieved its purpose. In the first hour of this 3-hour class, I have created some conditions where my students and I can ask questions about the relationships between objects and memory, between a person's identity and the shared narratives of experience that occur when people get together to talk about things. I am now ready to ask students to begin examining the shoes that exist in the shoe mountain.

•

> "Okay, I think everyone's back from their break. Let's begin with the shoes! Now I'd like you to come up to the front, group by group, and I'd like each of you to select one shoe that is not your own. Now, it's really important that there be no talking at all during this selection process and even more important that none of you reveal to the others which shoe is yours."

Once everyone has selected a shoe, I ask that they examine it, paying close attention to the details of construction and the marks of wear. I ask that they not communicate with one another while conducting this examination. After approximately 5 minutes, I ask them to place the shoe on their table so that they can still see it and to begin a 10-minute flow writing that begins with the prompt: "This shoe is interesting to me because ...." I encourage them to focus on the shoe while they are writing, but not to feel limited by the shoe. Although they will begin by writing about the details of the shoe, it is likely that the various associations they make while writing will move them into a topic that is related to but not necessarily directly concerned with the shoe.

This writing activity is designed to help students pay attention to the particularity of the shoe that they have selected. It helps them to notice the marks of wear, the details of design, and the ways in which these provoke particular images and feelings for them. Most important, this activity is meant to support the development of some relationship with this strange object so that they are able to generate further writing about it. In deliberately trying to see past the familiarity of "shoes in general" to the particularity of the design and wear of *this shoe*, I am hoping that students come to see this shoe as having a particular history and a particular identity.

Tracking Ideas

I developed the "shoe" activity after a visit to the Van Gogh Museum in Amsterdam. Prior to my visit there, a friend suggested that I read the philosopher Martin Heidegger's essay, "The Origin of the Work of Art." In that essay, she suggested, is a discussion of Van Gogh's famous painting of old shoes.

As I stand in front of this painting at the museum, I think about Heidegger's words, particularly his description of the shoes of a peasant woman. As I examine the details of construction and the wear, I think about my own German and Polish ancestors — most of whom were farmers. I particularly remember my maternal grandmother who maintained a small farm in Germany during World War II without any assistance from a man. As I look at the painting, I listen to the audio commentary on the hand-held recorder provided by the museum. Surprising to me, it says that these shoes did not belong to a woman but, in fact, were shoes that Van Gogh had bought and worn himself. Although I am, in a sense, disappointed by this — since I preferred the associations I was able to make with Heidegger's explication of the origin of these shoes — I continue to find the shoe painting fascinating. For the rest of my visit to Amsterdam I pay attention to the shoes people are wearing, trying to "read" what these shoes might tell me about their wearers. On the flight home, I begin to think that trying to interpret old shoes might be an interesting way to help my teacher education students begin to think about the complex and necessary relationships among memory, personal identity, cultural objects, and ways in which knowledge and experience are represented. By the time the plane has landed I am very excited about the possibility of having my students bring old shoes to class to interpret.

As students are examining the shoes they have chosen, I notice that they handle them gingerly. Many students seem reluctant to touch the shoe and so they try to make as little contact with it as possible, keeping it on the table in front of them. Although I have suggested to the students that they try to use all their senses to understand the shoe, I notice that students are not smelling their shoes. There is, it seems, some deep understanding that although this is "just a shoe" it is also deeply and intimately connected to its own history — a history which, of course, includes its connection to its actual owner. Next, I ask the students to continue their examination of the shoe by asking two questions:

"What interesting place has this shoe been? and What event has this shoe participated in? Remember, you must not try to guess who in the class owns the shoe! Actually, you should probably resist thinking of any human attachment at all. Instead, think of the shoe itself as animate and in control of its own destiny. Try to make decisions about place and event that seem to suit the shoe. When you think you're ready, take ten minutes and write out the details of this place and event. Remember every detail is very very important. It's much more interesting to hear, for example, that the shoe has been in the Tiffany's on Fifth Avenue in New York City at dusk on Christmas amid a throng of busy shoppers than it is to hear that the shoe was out shopping for jewelry!"

As the students write I notice that they continue to pick up their shoes and examine them. They jot down notes. They stare out the window. Some are restless and anxious. Others appear relaxed and meditative. When some have not written after 5 minutes, I remind them that they must make some decisions and commit these to paper. Soon all students are writing intensely. Once again, the mood has shifted to a collective concentration that I notice and appreciate. As I watch the students work, it is apparent to me that the "shoes" are gathering their attentions and imaginations.

"Looks like you're all finished! Now, move back into your small groups. When you've done this go around the table and let others know the decisions you have made about your shoe!"

This provokes a great deal of animated discussion and laughter. As I move around the room, I notice that all students were very, very interested in hearing about the shoes. I continue to remind them that they must not reveal which shoe is theirs, even if it happens to be in the possession of someone in their group. Once it becomes evident that most groups have completed this task, I ask them, as a class, what it was like to describe and make decisions about someone else's shoe. I tell them I noticed that no one smelled the shoes in their possession. I wonder out loud why some were reluctant to hold the shoe for more than a few seconds. What's it like to do this activity? Many students are ready to respond. René suggests:

> "I know this sounds terrible, but once I got my shoe to my table (an old running shoe), I could hardly bear to touch it. I mean, there was dirt in the soles and I didn't know where it had been. The more I looked at it, the less I liked it."

Ray offers:

> "Because I was the last to choose, I had no choice at all and ended up with this shoe. (He holds up a black patent leather high heeled woman's shoe.) I felt really uncomfortable trying to describe and write about it. It felt, well, just too personal."

Jody explains:

> "I loved my shoe. (She holds up a well-worn brown leather men's sandal.) It looks like the kind of shoe that was really loved and that went on lots of vacations to nice places. The leather is soft and, I don't know, it just made me feel like going on a vacation myself!"

The conversation assures me that students are developing strong opinions about their shoes. They are definite in their statements. Although some do not find the activity pleasurable, they all seem to find it interesting. This suggests to me that I can continue with the next phase of this interpretive activity.

> "Now, find a partner and sit across the table from one another with the two shoes between you. Remind each other where each of the shoes has been and about the event the shoe has participated in. Your task is to create a short narrative that includes both sites and both events. It is likely that you will need to invent some transitional material that allows the two sites and events to become coherent. Once you have agreed upon your narrative, record the plot in point form. Each group will be invited to recite their plot to the class. Hurry! You only have 15 minutes to accomplish this task!"

Most students immediately begin to talk about which "event" and which "place" will happen first. There are many subjunctive constructions being used in their discussion — phrases that begin with "what if" and "might be." Although most groups seem to be progressing quickly — making decisions, jotting notes, rehearsing their narrative — one group seems to be frustrated. I join them to find out what they are doing. I learn that these students cannot think of a transition between the two places and the two events. I suggest that they do some switching — trading the original place and event so that a unique situation is created. This works and, very quickly, a new plot has been invented.

As I am helping the students get started, I am reminded that it is important to understand that this "inventing a relation" between unusually juxtaposed images and activities can be very difficult for many students, particularly if they are committed to creating something that closely resembles their own remembered experiences. I remind the entire class that these short narratives need not be at all representative of familiar experience. I suggest that they should feel free to be as outrageous as they feel they must be in order to complete the task.

Once it appears that students have completed this "inventing" activity, I ask all groups to take 2 minutes to summarize their narratives for the class. I tell them to be sure to mention both locations and both events. As they are recit-ing, I ensure that the shoes they used as prompts are visible to the class by holding one in each hand and walking around the room so that everyone can see them closely. In every case, the narratives are wonderfully rich, detailed, and imaginative. Most interesting to me is the complexity of the character that emerges for each shoe. Although I did not ask students to develop characters (only events and locations), the character development in these short narratives is astonishing. Students have created very definite and original personas. The fact that each shoe is owned by someone who is present seems to have disappeared from the students' consciousnesses during the writing practice sessions: A high heeled white lady's sandal participated in a wedding ceremony with a black patent leather loafer on a sailboat and then took off in a helicopter for a honeymoon on a battleship. A scuffed brown hiking boot went trekking down main street Toronto with a red satin slipper and, after becoming lost for several hours in the underground shopping malls, emerged to find themselves in the middle of a cornfield with cows milling about.

In our discussion following this activity, students are surprised at the way "characters" emerged from the events and the settings. Taylor explains her and her partner Joseph's experience:

"I have always wondered how writers come up with interesting characters. I thought that they conjured them up first and then created situations for them. Now I think that maybe that's not what happens at all! In Joseph's and my case, the persons who occupied the shoes did not really become clear until after we'd figured out what kind of situations the shoes were in and how these could occur in the places we chose for them. Then — whoosh — suddenly it became obvious who these people were! It's like they floated off the page and introduced themselves to us and said "Hey! We're here! This is how we want to be!"

Others in the class concur with Taylor, suggesting that this experience of having characters "float" off the page was both new and surprising to them. As we discuss how this happened, we begin to make connections to Wilfrid and Miss Nancy's experience, wondering particularly if the memories prompted by Wilfrid's objects are the "true" memories or if they are "invented." What are memories?, we wonder. Are they representations of the fullness of past experiences, or are they, like the characters emerging from the shoe narratives, inventions? How does the ability to represent memory in oral narratives (stories) change the past? How does what has occurred since the event become "collected" into new "versions" of old narratives? Most interesting for the students is a discussion of how written forms of stories (like personal memoirs and cultural histories) create an illusion that the past can be represented completely in a completely objective manner. Has the ability to read and write fundamentally changed the experience of memory and, if so, has it altered the way in which literate humans construct their senses of individual and collective identities? How do individual memories and narratives exist in relation to "collective" memories and narratives?

"What would happen, I wonder, if we continue to create interpretive links between the narratives that we've made? Let's try it! Each pair join up with another pair. Take the final narratives written by each group and create a revised story that contains all of the characters and as many of the already-existing elements as possible. You'll likely need to rearrange some elements and to invent new transitions. Because our class is going to end soon, I wonder if you could begin thinking about this today, knowing that we'll continue this in next week's class. I don't think we have to worry that we'll forget how to do this! In fact, it might be good to have some time to live with the narratives and characters you're developing. And, don't worry about the shoes! I'll keep them locked up in my closet until next week!"

The following week, I begin class by asking students to retrieve the shoes they chose in the previous class then to re-read, on their own, what they and their partners have already written. I then have them move into groups and give them one hour to finalize their joined narrative. I give no other directions. Because students had practice doing this work the previous week, I believe they will proceed without difficulty. Of course, this is not so. As I walk around the room, it is evident that most groups are having difficulty because they are resistant to altering what has already been written by the pairs. I realize that I must interrupt their attachments to what they have already produced.

"I can see that most of you are experiencing some difficulty accomplishing this task. I think that this week of living with what you have written has helped you to become very attached to them! Here's what we're going to do. I'd like you to trade the two narratives that you have, and the four shoes that you have, with another group. Don't worry, you'll get the shoes back! Once you've traded, read over the narratives you receive and try putting these together."

Almost immediately, everyone becomes animated, moving between examining the shoes and reading the already-written narratives aloud. The conversation quickly moves into the "inventing" stage with lots of excited "what if" and "how about" and "I know what we can do" comments. After about 30 minutes I ask them to stop writing and to present these new stories to the class. Again, I ensure that the shoes that sponsored this new writing are visible. This time, I ask the groups to remind the class about the original "plots" (written by the pairs the previous week) and then to recite their new story. The results are remarkable. In every case, the characters have become transformed, the plots rendered more complex. In the discussion that follows, students remark on this and, especially, how it was important for the new narrative to be written by different writers. We discuss how difficult it was to try to change what had already been "fixed" the previous week and how important it was to have an "interrupter."

"All right, we've done some very interesting work in the last two weeks. Now it's time to do some recollection. I know that it's been very interesting for you to write narratives about someone else's shoe and, in most cases, even more interesting to hear what others invented for your shoe. Let's conclude today by doing a ten-minute timed writing that begins with the prompt:

'Hearing the story about my shoe made me realize ....' Everybody ready? Okay, begin writing!"

The writing is intense and rapid. As students work, I walk around the room with a box and collect all the shoes. I arrange them in a long row in the front of the room.

At the 10-minute mark, I ask the students to stop writing. I ask them, table by table, to go to the front of the room, find their shoe, hold it up so that the class can see it, and return to their table, placing their shoe in front of them. This, of course, becomes extremely interesting for everyone and provokes a great deal of laughter, exclamations, and general chatter. I ask each to say a few words about why they selected their shoe and something about its actual history. Although this sharing generates a great deal of laughter, it also opens up a very interesting interpretive space. Some of the students, for example, comment on how they are amazed at how close the invented situations are to their memories of their shoes' histories. Even when the invented narrative and the remembered narratives are very different, both the writer and the shoe owner become complicit in developing new interpretations of the shoe. Even though Marla's white high heeled shoe had not been part of a wedding on a sailboat — but was, rather, worn to a high school graduation — the two stories now exist together and have become involved with one another. Marla explains:

> *"When I first heard the stories developing around my shoe I just thought I was amused at how wrong they were. Now, though, I don't think I'll ever be able to look at that shoe — or even to think about my graduation, for that matter — without remembering what was written about my shoe in this class. It's like my shoe now has a totally new life and so has my memory of my graduation!"*

Other students agree, although not always so positively. Peiris suggests that hearing the other narratives was not entirely positive for him:

> *"The sandal I brought is special to me because it's the one that I wore during my six months traveling through Europe. That shoe's had some very interesting experiences! Although I did find what the writers invented around my shoe interesting, I'm hoping that it won't interfere with my previous memories of this shoe, since I really liked them just the way they were!"*

These comments by Marla and Peiris are typical of the conversation we have about the shoe activity. The students are beginning to demonstrate a much deeper understanding of how their own senses of identity are developed through memory and narratives and, as well, how objects of the world (cultural objects) participate in the ongoing construction of identity. Because I think it is very important for teachers to understand these ideas, I continue to provoke the class with questions about what this suggests about teaching and curriculum: Does what we read in class matter to how people think about their personal and cultural identities? What does this activity suggest to you about teachers' selections of curriculum materials? What does it suggest about the various representation practices that are used in school?

In order to create a more fully integrated experience for the students, I conclude by re-reading *Wilfrid Gordon McDonald Partridge*. Following the reading, I ask students to prepare, for next class, a three- to four-page interpretive writing that explains what the shoe activity and our discussion of memory, narrative, and identity might suggest about the plot of this children's book. I require students to complete this final interpretive assignment because I believe it is very important for them to begin to interpret and resymbolize classroom experiences into an artifact of learning that is interesting and useful to them. As well, I believe it is important for them to understand and be able to articulate the relationship between the activities conducted in class and the particular theoretical beliefs that these activities are founded upon and that they are trying to demonstrate.

As I read their interpretive writings, I am impressed by the way in which they are able to describe what I have come to call "sedimented subjectivities" — that is, the complex way in which memory, cultural objects, narratives, and literacy practices contribute to the "layering" of human identity. I am most pleased that students do not see these layers as "fixed" like the layers of sedimentary rock but as layers that are continually being changed with time and experience. As new interpretations emerge, old memories change. What was known and what is known continually affect one another.

As a teacher, I am satisfied that these pedagogical structures have helped my students and me to experience how acts of learning are not merely "add ons" or "paths down a straight road" but, rather, how learning is all-at-once a reinterpreting of the past, the present, and the imagined. In trying to invent "subjects" to go with the old shoes, my students and I are, necessarily, inventing new "subjectivities" for ourselves and

for the owners of these shoes. The forms that are developed for teaching are always "organizing forms." Although this phrase is commonly understood by teachers as the practice of creating pedagogical conditions and structures for students, I continue to remind myself that, in doing such work, I am also creating forms that organize student perception, memory, and interpretation. Forms are not just made by humans, the forms that are made also function to organize what it means to be human. This, I think, is a lesson of pedagogy that I must continually remember and help my students to understand.

We concluded Section A of this chapter with the assertion that conceptions of personal identity — selves — are ongoing interpretations of relations with language, with others, and with the contexts of experience. Senses of self occur in complex linguistic, semiotic, biologic, and ecologic structures.

In Section B, a teaching activity using old shoes was described, with particular emphasis on the many ways that objects of the world can collect personal and collective experiences of identity.

In this section, we inquire into the relationship between the structures and practices of teaching and their effects on learners. Here we examine how teachers contribute to what learners know and who learners believe themselves to be. In other words, this section seeks to understand how curriculum organizes learning and how it contributes to the forming of human identity. As well, we look at how the structures of curriculum — schooling forms, we could say — shape human perception and learning.

Point 1 • ORGANIZING FORMS

Being involved in any curriculum form contributes to the ongoing production of the teacher's and learners' senses of personal and collective identity.

Few of us would use the term *inventor* to describe our life's work. This label is usually is reserved for those persons who seek to create ideas and objects that are unique. Yet, all humans are continually "inventing"; we are all caught up in a creative dance of invention and interpretation. The very act of maintaining a coherent sense of self is an act of invention. Learning to understand new experiences in relation to remembered and predicted experiences is a form of creativity. Maintaining social relations with others requires ongoing interpretation.

What, then, is the task of formal education? And, more specifically, what is the work of the teacher? How can formal education improve learners' abilities to be inventive and creative?

All invented products emerge from human interaction with existing knowledge and objects. This may be why practices of invention and inspiration are often associated with mysticism and magic, since it can sometimes seem

that alchemical or spiritual processes must be contributing to inventive transformations. How can it be, for example, that new melodies continue to be written? Is there not
some finite number of melodic possibilities? How does the
musician invent a new melody? Does it come, fully formed,
into the mind of the musician, or is it more a matter of
accident, emerging during playful moments of improvi-
sation? Does this sort of invention require basic skills, or
can anyone write music?

As developed in Chapter 3A, inventiveness is not
merely a matter of innate ability. Nor is does it arise in just
a combination of genetics and learning. One's immediate
circumstances also matter. Persons who have come to be
regarded as extraordinarily gifted at invention are inevitably immersed in situations that support creative processes. Reflecting upon the shoe activity from the last section can help us to identify some of these conditions:

First, inventors work with simple forms and objects
that they know very well. Inventions do not emerge from
elaborate processes but from ongoing involvements with
familiar objects and simple practices of interruption, juxtaposition, and resymbolization. It is from multiple interactions of simpler forms, as discussed in Chapters 2 and 3,
that all complex forms emerge. To illustrate using the learning activity, although the students were unfamiliar with
the particular shoes that they selected, they were all very
familiar with the idea of "shoes." Locating writing practices at the intersection of these strange and familiar associations became a generative site, not unlike the places of
creation inhabited by poets, songwriters, architects, and
others.

Second, invention requires deliberate practices of discernment and interpretation. In spite of participants' familiarity with "shoeness," their detailed examinations
helped them to discern the particularity of the shoes they
were studying. Unmediated or unfocused visual examination is not sufficient for the kind of detailed interpretation that was necessary in this sort of activity. The task of
having to craft a viable historical narrative around the shoe
created the condition necessary for students to notice small
qualities of wear and detail that were previously unseen.

Third, the invention of unique characters associated
with the shoes required that students' everyday habits of
mind and practice be deliberately interrupted with very

specific and structured practices. Simply having a strange shoe in their possession was not an adequate condition for the invention of new characters. Before such invention could be accomplished, students had to be directed to imagine events and geographical locations. In the deliberate juxtaposition of a cultural object and personal knowledge, students began to integrate their perceptions of the shoe with their memories, giving rise to new narrative possibilities.

Fourth, distinctions between personal and collective knowledge must be blurred. Creative activity aways has a social dimension — and, in fact, often requires deliberate collaboration. On their own, students were able to generate interesting and unique details about their shoes, but the opportunity to share these details and to integrate these personal narratives with others gave rise to intricate and interesting plots and characters.

In brief, the various activities around the old shoes functioned to organize learners' and the teacher's perceptions. As a liberating constraint, these practices asked each

---

Learning Dancing

In her movie *The Tango Lesson*, producer, actor, director, and screenplay writer Sally Potter narrates and interprets the complex ways in which her learning to dance came to be entwined with personal relationships, with thinking, and with habits of perception.

On the literal level, the movie traces how she, as a filmmaker interested in learning to dance the tango, eventually wrote, produced, and starred in a film about her experience of learning to tango. On the figurative level, the film shares a central theme of this book: All learning becomes part of a complex ecological dance.

Of Latin-American origins, the tango is characterized by its long gliding steps and sudden pauses. The tango is also known as an expressive dance of passion, where participants attempt to communicate deep emotion to one another and to an audience.

Like all dances, this one has a particular form — one that is specific and identifiable, but one that also allows for considerable original expression. There are as many ways to dance the tango as there are persons to dance it.

In the film, Sally Potter is able to show how learning to dance the tango does not simply mean adding a new skill to one's bank of knowledge. Like all learning, mastering the tango means becoming involved in a whole set of interpersonal and intertextual relations that are new to the learner. These involvements alter the geography of the learner's past, present, and imagined experience. As Potter learns to tango, she also learns to perceive, to remember, and to imagine in new ways.

Learning, then, is not making *deposits* in one's *data bank*. It is more like mixing a new ingredient into the *soup* of perception and cognition. As new experiences are added, the flavor and texture of the soup change. It is never possible to extract an experience once it has occurred. Even if allowed to slip from consciousness, its effects remain.

student to negotiate a relationship with an object that was both familiar and strange. The activities of noticing, juxtaposing, and interpreting required that students invent transitions between past personal experiences and new in-class events. Together, these memories and activities functioned as a generative structure — a form — that prompted new appreciations of the roles of objects as mediators of human memory and experience.

Like all curriculum objects, the shoes served as a focus for interpretation. Like all learning experiences, this one functioned to alter what students remembered, what they noticed, and how they interpreted. The act of using shoes to organize perception, then, affected memories and understanding — not just of shoes, but of identities. That is, the shoe activity did more than organize learning. It affected each learner's sense of self.

 Connecting Thoughts

Select one of the other teaching episodes presented in this book (or recall a learning event in your own life) and try to identify some of the elements that came together in the experience. What was familiar? What was unfamiliar? How were these elements juxtaposed and interpreted? What was learned?

Point 2 • INVENTING FORMS

Fostering creativity in students requires that particular conditions and practices be organized by the teacher.

What do these principles of invention, as demonstrated in the shoe activity and as elaborated in the previous point, suggest for teachers?

To begin, inventive pedagogies must include interruptions to the familiar. Students will be most inventive when they are engaged in tasks that ask them to think freshly about forms that they already know very well.

This assertion is consistently supported in the biographies of creative persons: While exotic objects and unusual practices have their places (in particular, as interrupters of things that have become overly familiar), creativity is mostly a matter of rethinking the everyday and the often-used. In the teaching episode, for example, it was important to interrupt familiarity by asking students to examine someone else's shoes. Trying to describe and invent details for an object with an ambiguous personal attachment served to disrupt students' thoughts (or lack of thoughts) about an ordinary, commonplace object. The familiar was rendered strange.

To be inventive, a person has to be able to focus attentions on specific aspects of an experience — which, in turn, means that other aspects, such as the medium of interpretation, have to be well enough mastered that the creative moment is not hindered by mechanical concerns. For a task like the shoe activity to work in a Grade 1 classroom, for example, the teacher would likely have to focus less on writing and more on verbal description, picture-drawing, oral recording, or other activities — while, of course, working to develop writing skills and techniques that might enhance future creative projects.

It follows that teachers who are structuring inventive pedagogies must be skilled with the forms that are used. This does not necessarily mean that teachers must have demonstrated extraordinary levels of accomplishment. It does mean, however, that teachers need to know the intricacies of the form and how these elements might be communicated to students. Great teachers of writing or mathematics or dance need not be great authors, mathematicians, or performers. They must, however, be persons who have a deep interest in and involvement with the form they are teaching. For students both to learn the skills associated with a form and to begin to improvise these techniques into unique products requires the help of a teacher who has a well developed relationship to the form being used. Otherwise there is a risk that the form will be reduced to mere mechanics — to rules, procedures, and exercises aimed at proficiency rather than creative possibility.

For teacher and learner alike, deep understandings of the forms used for invention require sustained engagements with those forms. Persons who are known for their inventive genius are generally those who have "lived with" particular ideas for many years, often to the point of obsession. In contrast, schooling often seems to be centrally concerned with breadth of exposure rather than depth of understanding. With limited classroom time and long lists of required content, teachers and learners often can do little more than *tour through* a subject area, with little opportunity to *dwell* — to reread a book, to live with an idea, to ruminate, and so on.

If pedagogy is to be inventive rather than merely reproductive, students must have the opportunity to develop intimate and deep relationships with particular forms and content. Within these sorts of more intimate engagement,

---

Using and Evaluating Portfolios

In recent years, portfolios have become an increasingly popular means for students to develop and display their work. Most often, portfolios are used as "collecting places" for various artifacts (such as products of art class, transcripts of musical composition, pieces of writing, etc.). These *archival portfolios* become important gathering locations, serving as both a resource for and a trace of the many stages of activity that are necessary to creative work.

Following their use in various artistic communities, these archival portfolios are eventually used to create a *display portfolio*, a showcase of the best or most representative work. Sometimes items are arranged chronologically, highlighting the evolution of the artist's thinking. At other times, items are organized according to motif, theme, or genre. A writer, for example, might have a section of poetry, another of short stories, and so on.

An archival portfolio can be a generative location for learning. In assembling various artifacts to represent their interests, learners can begin to develop a sense of how these objects might affect their understandings and their habits of perception. A Grade 12 class studying the Holocaust, for example, might be encouraged to create an archival portfolio that contains the following:

- summaries and personal responses to testimonies of Holocaust survivors;
- summaries and responses to literary fictions;
- information gleaned from the study of other historical documents;
- critical reflections of in-class discussion;
- photographs and other images;
- notes for and rough drafts of expository, poetic, or literary prose.

Transforming the archival portfolio into a display portfolio is a process of critical interpretation. In the above example, as the students study the Holocaust and collect various representations of their study, they should be encouraged to engage in ongoing interpretation of the relationships among various artifacts. What, for example, might they say about their responses to reading Jane Yolen's novel *The Devil's Advocate* and Anne  Michaels' novel *Fugitive Pieces* (a fictionalized account based on her study of the Holocaust)? What might students say if challenged to justify the reading of literary fiction as a way to understand one of the 20th Century's most horrifying events? And so on.

The two sorts of portfolios should receive different sorts of feedback. The archival portfolio is primarily a location for *assessment* of student progress. Derived from the Latin, *assidere*, to sit beside, assessment is focused more on ongoing response and direction. In the example of the Holocaust study, the teacher might emphasize interpretive writing skills — perhaps focusing on how to discern strong writing from weak, how students are constructing arguments, and so on.

The display portfolio is a more formal presentation of one's thought and, as such, is more a location for *evaluation*. From the Latin, *valere*, to be worth something, the process of evaluation is less concerned with formative feedback and more focused on summative comments on the student's achievement.

breadth need not be seen in opposition to depth. Rather, deep understandings, developed in the study of specific forms, can often enable a person to appreciate a broadened range of experiences. The shoe activity, for example, required a prolonged and sustained engagement. Although it might seem that attending to shoes could fulfill only a few, very minor curriculum aims, the depth of engagement and the many activities associated in that classroom event became a generous location for learning about many aspects of language, culture, and identity. In fact, *most* of the goals of the formal curriculum were addressed in one way or another.

 Connecting Thoughts

Identify some form that you're passionate about — a subject area, a skill, an activity, whatever.

How is that form knitted into your life? How is it useful for interpreting other aspects of your experience?

If you were asked to teach that form to others, what would be some of your main emphases?

Point 3 • COPYING FORMS

Copying already existing forms is an important way to improve one's knowledge and skill.

Research into language acquisition has shown that the key process in infants' learning to speak is the opportunity to mimic more advanced language users within meaningful social situations. Even though few adults are formally educated in matters of language acquisition, they usually understand the need for infants to copy sounds and phrases. Adult caregivers of infants will typically repeat words over and over, correcting mispronunciations and incorrect usages by offering correct forms for repetition.

Copying and repetition are valuable and important techniques in the development of complex competencies. However, the manners of copying associated with first language learning differ dramatically from the sorts of repetitive tasks that are common to many schooling settings —

such as rote memorization, drillwork, and timed exercises. The latter sorts tend to be aimed at narrow technical skills, rather than the flexible and complex competencies associated with language use. Moreover, they are often decontextualized, in contrast to the rich and varied settings in which language is usually learned.

The recognition of the differences between these two sorts of copying practices have prompted some recent and dramatic changes in educational practice. School-based second language instruction, for example, has seen a shift away from repetition of phrases, memorization of word lists, and completion of page after page of exercises. Current instruction places more emphasis on mimicking sounds and phrases within a more flexible, evolving situation. Rather than aiming at correct answers, this manner of instruction is concerned mostly with the ability to "think" in the new language by using what has been learned in familiar, yet unpredictable and creative ways.

These copying practices are not unique to language learning. Many music teachers begin their sessions by performing that week's musical piece — not so much to demonstrate what can be achieved through dedicated practice (although this might be one reason), but to invite the student into the "mind" of the musician. The same is true of many sorts of performance, including athletic activities. (See the inset box on page 203.)

Copying practices have long been popular among painters and their students. European masters of the 17th and 18th Centuries, for example, had their students copy paintings that they had already made. (Note: *master* originally meant *teacher*.) Once students achieved a certain proficiency, they were given the task of completing paintings that the master had already begun.

Apprentice chess masters also use copying practices. Working from transcripts of completed games, apprentices "replay" every move — sometimes several times over. Each replaying can take many, many hours as the apprentice works to "get into the mind" of the original players. At times, the same sequences of moves have to be repeated dozens of times before achieving any significant insight into the master's mind.

"Getting inside the mind of a master" has been espoused by many professional writers. A common writing practice for beginners is to select passages from their favorite authors and to copy them over and over. Through this repetition, the novice will gradually come to notice particular details of writing, including the "rhythm" of the writer's thinking. Those who have engaged in such practices often report that "traces" of form from the other writers sometimes "appear" in their own work. Oftentimes, stylistic elements become so transparently incorporated into that writer's way of thinking that the copying, while

Shadowing

Rita, a former Olympic medalist, now coaches young downhill skiers. Each year, a number of initiates attend a 2-week training camp where she and other professional ski instructors help them to improve their skills and, at the same time, work to identify those who seem to have extraordinary abilities. Although there are many exercises Rita uses with her students, her favorite is "shadowing."

Working with two or three students, Rita begins her lesson at the top of the ski slope by reminding her students that, in order to improve their skiing, they need to integrate their movement with their environment. Working from the knowledge that perception and consciousness lag slightly behind action, Rita knows that her students' improvement is linked to their ability to "let go" — that is, to understand that they cannot consciously choose every action. Rather, they have to learn to flow with the landscape, allowing their bodies to make the appropriate moves as they plummet down the hill.

Her instructions are simple, yet specific:

"Line up behind me. I'm going to ski down the hill and you are all to follow. You must keep your eyes on me at all times. Don't be distracted by one another or by anything around you. You must trust that the path that I am taking is safe. If you concentrate on me, following every corner I take, you will be safe. When we get one third down the hill, I will stop. When I do, I want the person directly behind me to go to the back of the line. I will stop two more times so

that each of you will have an opportunity to ski directly behind me. Remember, you are to concentrate on me. That doesn't mean that I want you to try to predict what I'm going to do. Just watch me and ski."

Rita and her students ski together like this for 1 hour. After each run, she and her students discuss their learning. Although it occurs at a different time for each student, by the end of the hour all of them comment that they have had an "aha" experience where they suddenly felt a change in their skiing. Mark explains:

"During the first run I had difficulty concentrating on Rita. My eyes continued to shift from her to the ground or to the trees. I was tense most of the time. By the second run, I felt more relaxed and began to get a feel for the way that Rita was skiing. I felt my own style begin to change a little. In the middle of the third run, I found myself daydreaming, while still watching Rita and was surprised to notice that my body was positioned very differently than it usually is: I was moving more quickly with much less effort. My center of gravity seemed to have shifted. It was an amazing feeling: It was like my mind was skiing in someone else's body."

Mark's experience of feeling as though his mind had shifted to someone else's body is one that all humans have at some point or another. In being asked to "mimic" exactly what his teacher was doing, Mark was being invited into Rita's complex patterns of movement and thought.

obvious to others, is not at all apparent to the author.

Providing students with opportunities to copy already existing forms and processes is an excellent strategy for helping them to "get inside the mind of an expert." In teacher education, these copying practices are used a great deal, but have seldom been acknowledged as crucial to professional development. In order to help beginning teachers understand how a master teacher thinks about pedagogy, it is important to first invite them into the forms that are the immediate products of this thinking. For example, rather than simply explaining to a beginning teacher how to introduce multiplication of fractions to a Grade 3 class, or offering a theoretical account as to why one might teach fractions in a particular way, an experienced teacher might ask the student teacher to observe and to make detailed notes during a lesson. Then, after opportunity to question and discuss these observations, the novice teacher might be asked to copy the lesson with another class — bearing in mind that this process of copying should not be considered a simple replication, but a creative event. The idea isn't to duplicate what was done, but to participate in a particular way of thinking.

 Connecting Thoughts

Repetition is a common and a vital classroom activity — especially in the development of such competencies as forming letters with a pencil, learning to serve a volleyball, learning how to read a map, and so on. Identify a few such instances and discuss how teaching might be structured so that learners' activities would be more than simple matters of replication.

Point 4 • REPRESENTING FORMS

Teachers must be critically aware of how forms used to represent knowledge affect student learning.

One of the popularly noted aims of conventional schooling is to prepare students for a future world by teaching them what is "true" (that is, what is held to be true at the moment of teaching). This aim has supported practices of assessment and evaluation that are almost entirely focused on the student's ability to represent already-existing knowledge. This occurs in spite of the often-heard claim that the processes of learning are as important as its products. As a result, for example, although students may be encouraged to learn about a novel by musing about circumstances and events that aren't explicitly developed in the text, in the end the teacher would evaluate their learning, not on what *might have* happened but on what *did* happen.

Strategies for representing knowledge are never neutral. Choosing one word over another in a written composition, an illustration, a chart, or a mathematical formula creates a unit of representation that shapes perception in particular ways. Because perception is intimately linked to thinking processes and ways in which thinking is represented, formal education must be critically aware of how the content of learning works to organize the interpreted world of the student.

Comprehension of any linguistic form depends on an understanding of how words and ideas differ from one another. It is not so significant, for example, that an infant can call out "mama," but that she can differentiate the word "mama" from "cat" and can assign each to the appropriate form. Language, then, and all forms of representation, depend on the learned abilities to distinguish between and among aspects of complex representational forms. And even though the processes and practices of differentiation tend to fade into transparency as the language-user grows more competent, they remain extremely influential to understandings and identities.

Consider, for example, the many ways in which the words "man" and "woman" have been understood. It may seem that these words exist to make a simple distinction between males and females. However, feminist theorists have shown how these terms are tied to a long history of women's subjugation to men. The many ways in which women's identities are narratively and visually depicted is intimately connected to these histories. In the last several decades, research has clearly shown that the ways in which men and women are represented strongly influence what people believe. Part of the work of the educator, then, is to help students interpret these representations of gender and, in the process, interrupt associated stereotypes.

Drawing Conclusions

Martha had been teaching young children for more than 20 years. In her recent graduate work, she studied the effects of patriarchy and the many ways in which various feminist movements, theories, and practices have influenced thinking about female/male relations. Although she was horrified to learn how women continued to be the victims of patriarchy and misogyny, she was convinced that the children in her Grade 3 classroom were more enlightened than previous generations. When she announced this during one of her graduate seminars, a number of other teachers in the class suggested that she might be wrong.

Determined to test her hypothesis, the following week Martha developed an assignment that she hoped would prove that her young students were more enlightened than her colleagues believed. During her combined science/mathematics class, she asked the 14 girls and 10 boys to draw pictures of scientists and mathematicians. Other than providing advice about technique, she gave no instruction on how students might represent these characters.

When the drawings came in, Martha was confused. Most of the students — girls and boys alike — had depicted scientists in stereotypical ways: white-coated, balding men with small moustaches in front of a lab table covered with beakers and test tubes. This was disheartening to Martha, not only because few women were represented but because of the way "scientist" and cartoon versions of scientists had been collapsed. It seemed that students were more influenced by the images of scientists that they saw on television than by the ones presented in school materials.

However, Martha was also delighted to notice that 12 of the girls and 6 of the boys drew women to represent mathematicians. She was so pleased with these data that she presented the pictures to her graduate seminar that night.

Martha's enthusiasm was short lived, however. One of her colleagues, Roberta, noticed immediately that almost all of the mathematicians seemed to be standing in front of blackboards in rooms that resembled classrooms. Upon closer scrutiny, it appeared that the vast majority of the representations of mathematicians were really images of female elementary school teachers in the process of leading their students through repetitive drillwork!

Martha was disheartened. Not only was it obvious that her students did not really understand what "mathematician" meant, they seemed to believe that elementary school teachers were female, even though there were a significant number of male teachers in her school. It seemed that her young students continued to believe that science research was done by men and elementary school teaching was done by women. Hoping that her students would, at the very least, value science research and teaching equally, the next day Martha asked her students what they thought the more difficult and important job might be: teaching Grade 3 or doing scientific research in a lab. To her disappointment, her students were unanimous in suggesting that science research was far more difficult and important than teaching Grade 3. Clearly, as a teacher interested in issues of gender and social equity, she has a great deal of work to do with these students!

● **Connecting Thoughts**

Locate two textbooks or curriculum documents for your subject area — one that is current and one that is as old as possible. Compare the ways that aims, explanations, activities, and exercises are presented. How might differences in presentation contribute to students' conceptions of the subject matter and the nature of the discipline?

Point 5 • IDENTIFYING FORMS

Teachers and teacher educators can do a great deal to support teacher candidates' ongoing self interpretations.

One's identity is always evolving, but one's sense of self tends to be fairly stable. There are times, though, that compel rather dramatic changes to one's identifications and, hence, to one's identity. Moving to a new city, switching careers, losing a friend, or becoming ill are among the events that can heighten one's awareness of the transitory nature of who one is. For most, becoming a teacher would also fall into this category.

Among the most demanding aspects of learning to teach is the requirement to work across two different — and sometimes opposed — communities: the host school and the university. What usually makes things difficult is that these two profoundly different institutions are not as overtly distinct from one another as most contexts tend to be. By way of contrast, it's relatively easy to keep track of how one is positioned in a department store or during a family dinner or at a wedding. The social and cultural markers are obvious. But the differences between being a student on a university campus and being a student-teacher in a public school are usually much more subtle.

Even though these settings are often assumed complementary, there are radical differences that arise from historical, social, political, educational, and structural circumstances. At the risk of oversimplification, the explicit purpose of the modern university is to push out the boundaries of knowledge — which often involves direct challenges to popular assumption and tradition. The modern school, in comparison, is most often seen as a place to convey what is already known — to maintain rather than to interrupt.

Unfortunately, if and when the roles of these institutions are explicitly identified in the context of a teacher education program, it is usually in terms of the highly problematic separation of "theory" (the university's forte) and "practice" (the school's contribution) — as though, somehow, one's interpretations of the world could be pried apart from one's actions in the world. This troublesome distinction is often supported by a lack — or absence — of direct communication between professor and host teacher.

Small wonder, then, that teacher candidates might feel conflicted as they negotiate their roles. Given their already demanding responsibilities, the added task of having to

---

Integrating Experiences

Celia had been a teacher and a teacher educator for many years. Like many university-based professors, she struggled with what teacher candidates reported as a dissonance between what she expected of them in her courses and what was asked of them in the classroom. She was especially concerned that she had very little contact with the teachers who were working directly with her students.

In an effort to create some interpretive link among her students' on-campus and in-school experiences, Celia undertook to work with university and school administrators to design a cohort-based teacher education program that involved the staffs of two schools, 30 teacher candidates, and herself.

Celia arranged to teach parts of the teacher candidates' required coursework in an empty classroom in one of the schools. She also offered an optional course that was scheduled to meet every other Tuesday evening. This course was open both to pre-service teachers in the cohort and to interested classroom teachers. In addition, Celia created several opportunities for classroom teachers to come to campus to teach classes and to participate in panel discus-sions on subjects of interest to her pre-service teachers.

While in the schools, Celia did not overly busy herself with the task of evaluating her students. Instead, she tried to become involved with the culture of the school. She looked for opportunities to co-teach with host teachers and with student teachers. She spent time in the staffroom socializing with members of the school community. She engaged in many spontaneous "hallway chats" with teachers and teacher candidates about matters that were of interest and importance to them.

In creating these structures for integration, Celia was able to assist her students with the ongoing projects of negotiating and interpreting their experiences. At the same time, she learned from and contributed to the thinking of the classroom teachers.

Perhaps the most significant outcome of this work was the tremendous reduction in anxiety among those involved in teacher education. Teacher candidates were less worried about the presence of their professor because it was no longer linked strictly with performance evaluations. Host teachers, similarly, saw Celia more as a source of interesting information and ideas than as a potential critic of their practices. In brief, it was obvious to all that they were engaged in the shared work of bettering the experiences of children through a less conflicted teacher education.

function as the interpretive bridge between the university and the school can be very problematic. In particular, it can prompt and help to perpetuate we-versus-they mentalities: professor versus teacher; ivory tower versus mind factory; teacher candidate versus everyone.

The challenge for those responsible for teacher education programs is to invent and continuously revise structures that support greater awarenesses of their shared project of teacher education.

That this project is shared, though, does not mean that everyone must agree on everything, nor that everyone should be making similar contributions. (As developed in Chapter 3, diversity of opinion and action can give rise to much more interesting and robust possibilities.) But it does mean that there has to be some agreement on the nature of the shared work, and one useful way of framing that project is in terms of identity formation. Host teacher and university professor are both supporting the development of teaching identities. As such, they share responsibilities for providing structures within which teacher candidates can interpret and interrogate what it means to live a life that includes teaching.

There are many possibilities for such structures. One successful example is described in the inset box. Another much different approach might be the creation of a small research project around an issue of shared interest to teacher candidates, host teachers, and university faculty. Not only would such a project present these parties with opportunities to participate in joint work, the fact that they would have to gather together to discuss topics and processes would afford everyone opportunities to be explicit about their interests, their worries, and their areas of expertise. In the process, there would be opportunity to highlight both the differentiated natures of their roles and the fact that these differences can indeed be complementary.

 Connecting Thoughts

Regardless of the thoughtfulness of the persons involved, there are inevitably problems with any structure created for teacher education. What are some that you've experienced, and how might they be addressed in the short and / or long term?

Chapter 5

Learning and Teaching Lives

Until quite recently, academics have avoided direct definitions of the word *life*. Rather, for the most part, life was discussed indirectly, usually in terms of essential qualities. If, for example, a form could move, was able to participate in reproducing itself, and was involved in the transformation of chemical products, then it was probably alive.

Unfortunately, there were holes in these lists of criteria. No matter how carefully they were presented, they omitted some forms that were in fact living. And, almost as often, they admitted inanimate objects of one sort or another.

The situation started to change a few decades ago, with a realization that living systems are not organized in the same way as non-living systems. The latter have readily definable architectures. If they are capable of motion, then their actions can be described in straightforward, cause-and-effect terms.

Not so with living systems. Their organizations are messier, less easily bounded; their actions refuse simple logical analyses and predictions. A living form is a complex body, one that emerges from the interactions of other forms, one that participates in an ongoing structural dance with similar forms, and one that, in the process, can contribute to the rise of more complex forms. Life, then, is not a matter of equilibrium, but the presence of disequilibrium. Life is an ever-expanding sphere of unpredictable possibilities.

In many ways, this "definition" represents a return to the historical roots of the word *life*. The original word also meant *body* — that is, life was not seen as some strange force that animated a physical form. It was, rather, coterminous with the dynamic possibilities of a body.

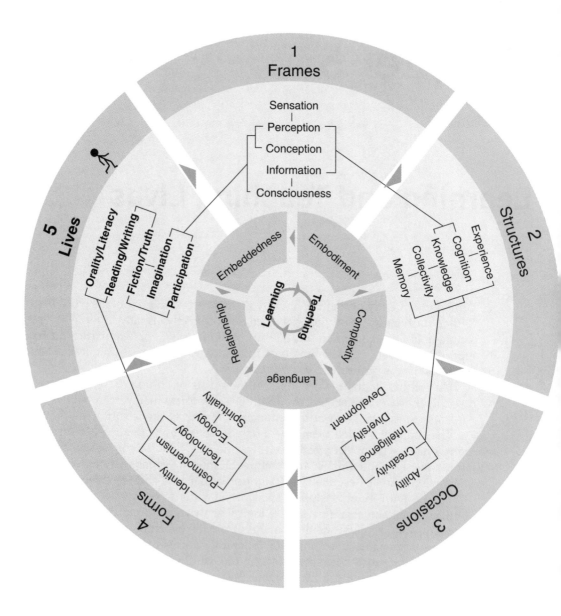

5A　Reading Bodies

Few would debate the suggestion that formal schooling is aimed at the development and promotion of literacy. Despite the relative consensus around this theme, however, there have been surprisingly few discussions about what it means to be literate and, conversely, how the capacities and habits of mind associated with literacy help to shape the world. Such are our present themes.

In recent decades, the notion of literacy has been elaborated from the traditional "3 Rs" of reading, 'riting, and 'rithmetic to include artistic, scientific, electronic, social, and other competencies. What has remained fairly constant is the core focus on the ability to interpret and manipulate symbols. As such, our uses of the words *literate* and *read* in this chapter are in reference not just to the capacities associated with making sense of the printed text, but with a broadened category of competencies and discourses that have to do with the use of symbols.

Fig. 5.1. The word *read* derives from the Latin *rede*, stomach of the cow. While perhaps not the most appealing image, it brings to mind such associations as digesting ideas, chewing over suggestions, ruminating, and regurgitation. In the process, this historical root highlights an early insight: Like all aspects of language use, reading and other literacies involve far more than decoding symbols. They are acts of reconstitution and profound transformation.

In some ways, this chapter might be seen as a honing of the many issues around language that have been raised in previous chapters. As already discussed, for example, the ability to use language is an extraordinary one. Language is an interpretation practice that structures human consciousness and activity. Not only has language enabled humans to communicate about immediate wants, desires, and experiences, it has made it possible to work with others to develop hypotheses and to test theories about the world — all without having to commit to particular plans of action.

As developed earlier, language is more than a symbol-based system of communication. Unlike the communicative strategies of other species, human language can be used to analyze human language, creating a recursive loop that has set the stage for philosophical, scientific, and other modes of inquiry. Understood in this way, language is more than a technology for communication.

Such sweeping statements about language always require some qualification, in large part because language functions differently in different settings. There are, for example, significant variations between predominantly oral cultures, wherein most communication occurs as face-to-face interactions, and more print-dependent contexts like our own. The invention of writing systems has profoundly altered the ways in which humans interact with language, with one another, and with the more-than-human parts of the world.

To elaborate, human understanding is greatly influenced by the conceptual tools that are available to it. Across cultures and over thousands of years, many verbal and written strategies have emerged. In fact, there is now an extensive literature developed around the histories of various traditions, focused in particular on the transitions experienced by those cultures that have shifted from mainly oral to mainly literate practices. Within this body of knowledge, there is general agreement that the incorporation of writing and print technologies into a society prompts significant changes in the processes of cognition and the experience of consciousness. In brief, literate practices have not merely changed what humans know, they have transformed how humans think and act.

It is important to note, though, that no clear division can be made between oral or literate practices or sensibilities. Similarly, it cannot be said that some cultures are oral and some are literate. No matter how steeped in literacy a society might be, oral practices of exchange and interpretation remain. Conversely, in societies (past and present) that might be considered oral, there tend to be pictographic and other representation practices. Moreover, whether reliant on formal systems of writing and representation or not, it is impossible for a society in today's world to shield itself from the effects of literate practices.

The Breath of Language

Like all higher order life forms on this planet, humans depend on oxygen for survival. As a continuous event, breathing might be considered our most intimate connection to our contexts. With each breath, the human subject participates in the ceaseless exchange of matter with and between every other living being. Breathing, then, is a form of interconnection, a reciprocal relationship between each living being and its setting.

What is understood as oral language is intimately connected to breathing. Speech is breath with sounds — or,

Fig. 5.2. *Literate* derives from the Latin *litteratus*, learned — or, more precisely, acquainted with *littera*, the letters of the alphabet.

That original meaning is quite telling. It highlights an early realization that the written word was a powerful technology. A simple knowledge of the alphabet was enough to separate the learned from the unlearned.

The term has, of course, come to imply far more since it was first used, now referring more broadly to any discipline or body of knowledge that relies on formal symbol systems.

more poetically, shaped breath. These sounds are normally formed during exhalation, meaning that language, like the breath in which it occurs, is sent out into the world of experience. There it intermingles with other sounds, those from the human and the more-than-human world.

As shaped breath, language begins as an oral phenomenon. Although we could never know with certainty, it has often been suggested that languaging began with the mimicking of sounds heard in the non-human world. As this line of thought goes, such acts of imitation proved useful in attempts to communicate (perhaps, for example, to warn of impending danger). In the process, imitated sounds might have begun to represent the animals or events that made those sounds, and that might have been the starting place of word creation. As vocabularies grew, and as brains evolved to cope with the physical and social demands which emerged with the capacity to shape breath, human communities gradually developed the abilities to make and to modify sounds in ways that we would now recognize as speech.

Inventing Authors and Readers

What does it mean to become a reader? Because we, the "authors" are speaking directly to you, the "reader," the usually invisible relationship between the printed text and the persons who made the text is somewhat more available for interpretation. As you read these words (and remember the material in the book that you have already read), you are engaged in the process of developing senses of the authors' identities. This act of *inventing authors* occurs each time any text is read, although the particularities of this experience vary with the type of text, the purposes for reading, and the contexts of engagement.

Just as readers must invent authors, writers need to invent readers. Of course, we could not know precisely who might end up perusing this book, and so, in order for our communication to be reasonably lucid and coherent, we needed to spend considerable time imagining identities for prospective readers — which is to say, you. To do this, we thought about the possible purposes and conditions of your reading and about the sorts of experiences and interests you might have that we could try to draw on as we attempted to develop various ideas.

This text, then, is intended to function as a commonplace for acts of representation, interpretation, and imagination. Although it is unlikely that we, the authors, and you, the readers, will ever meet face-to-face, we are able to form complex intersubjective relationships that are mediated by the alphabetic and pictographic representation systems employed in this text. This is one small way that literacy practices contribute to senses of identity. Inventing authors and readers are acts that don't make much sense within oral cultures, where almost all communication is face-to-face. In those settings, such matters as intended meanings and the identity of the speaker are more obviously contextual and fluid.

Curiously, however, although we can imagine these sorts of plausible accounts of the emergence of language, we are incapable of answering what seems to be an easier question: What might it have been like to live in a mostly oral world? As persons completely socialized into literate practices, it is impossible to set aside the habits of reasoning and interpretation that go along with the written word. We can make some guesses, though, about how the phenomenon of language might be understood in a setting where there is no formal, written mode of representing that language.

A first conjecture has to do with the concept of *word*. We literates have a habit of referring to words as though they were discrete objects — a tendency that arises from the way that writing makes it possible to represent sounds on paper and in other visual (versus auditory) forms.

It should be borne in mind, though, that what we come to recognize as words first exist to us as sounds. That is, early stages of language learning are not so much efforts at communication as they are intersections of sound, activity, context, need, and desire. As such, it is unlikely that very young children would understand language as a collection of independent objects called *words*. Rather, language is more likely approached as a global phenomenon, much as music might be heard by someone with no formal background in notations or performance. What matters most in early stages of music appreciation is not the identification of individual notes, but an attendance to the relationships among the notes (that is, melodies and harmonies). In a similar way, the early stages of language acquisition are not so much about the mastery of individual words as they are about developing a sense of the rhythms and structures of communication.

Fig. 5.3. Particular sensibilities about the linearity of existence, the tangibility of language, and the objectivity of knowledge tend to predominate in literate societies. Such sensibilities are supported by beliefs that words are discrete containers of meaning and that communication is a matter of forming chains of these containers.

In turn, these habits of thinking are supported by the apparently independent

In an oral culture, then, words are not understood as objects that contain information or that are used to represent aspects of the world. The notion of *word*, in fact, might not make sense at all. A more appropriate concept might be *utterance*, which implies both an utterer and a hearer. Utterances are not discrete entities. Rather, they exist only in the uttering. Moreover, an utterance is something with a rather strange power: It can be used to call something to mind that is not immediately present.

So understood, language — that is, a system of utterances — is never neutral. It has the power to invoke, to summon. Language use in oral cultures might be more consciously poetic — aware of the figurative and evocative nature of naming things. Such a conscious awareness would help to explain the prominence in oral cultures of matters of spirit (literally, breath or wind) and things spiritual. Since spoken language is shaped breath, speaking would necessarily be understood as a spiritual event. One would thus have to be careful about what one says.

A second conjecture has to do with the context of language. In situations structured by literacy, there is often a sense that word meanings are independent of settings. Thanks in large part to dictionaries and other texts devoted to the standardization of word usage, one might get the impression that language learning is mostly about mastery of fixed definitions and stable associations.

What is in some ways lost in this conception of language is a sense of the very particular patterns of domestic life, social conditions, and cultural situations in which language learning occurs. Language acquisition is not entirely about naming things, nor about mastering a vocabulary and a grammar. It is also a matter of learning about rhythms, patterns of intonation, modes of engagement, and so on that are specific to geographic locations, subcultures, and families.

existence of words that are printed on a page.

These habits of thought have come to be knitted through the language, and are so pervasive that a person raised in a literate society would almost certainly hold a very different world view from a member of an oral culture — whether or not he or she has learned to read.

This specificity would be much more apparent in an oral culture, where the notion of *language* only makes sense in the context of persons speaking to one another (or to themselves). There would be much less concern for standardized definitions because intended meanings are negotiated in face-to-face interactions. An immediate upshot is that languages that are not associated with written representations are much more fluid than those of literate cultures — which is to say, oral languages evolve much more quickly than written ones. This is likely true both in terms of the creation of new vocabularies and in terms of changes to meanings and pronunciations of established terms.

A third conjecture has to do with strategies for organizing knowledge and for remembering. We literates have many means at our disposal for off-loading demands on memory: We make lists, we publish dictionaries and encyclopedias, most of which are organized alphabetically, and so on — all of which make it possible to access great stores of information with relatively small demands on personal memory.

In an oral setting, methods for remembering are necessarily quite different. Strategies would include rhymes, rhythms, and repetitions, as exemplified in ancient epics. In particular, redundancy and consistency are qualities that facilitate the learning and maintenance of historical narratives. As well, frequent rites and rituals that involve chanting and recitation are key to collective remembering.

That means, of course, that the patterns of interaction in oral settings are frequent and intense. Somewhat in contrast to literate traditions, repetition would be common and strongly encouraged. Without it, important matters might be forgotten. One might also expect tight communal bonds, as well as rather specific senses of personal roles within a community. That is, persons would have to specialize, arising from the need to distribute knowledge across and among different individuals. Within such social structures, the relationships among what one knows, what one does, and who one is would be much more apparent as one's concept of personal identity would be framed mostly in terms of one's social role.

A very different sense of subjectivity or self is suggested in this formulation. As careful examinations of some cultural groups that are relatively uninfluenced by the literate world have shown, citizens of oral societies tend to describe themselves in terms of their relationships to others — whereas we literates are more apt to provide lists of personal qualities. That is, members of literate cultures seem to be much more prone to inward self-descriptions, thinking of ourselves as autonomous, individual, and self-contained. A citizen of an oral culture is more apt to look outward at interpersonal responsibilities and interdependencies.

A fourth conjecture, which arises from a joint consideration of the previous suggestions, is that citizens of oral cultures would likely prefer different modes of reasoning over those that are predominant in literate settings. As (we hope) is demonstrated by this sort of text, the goal of most written communication is clarity. Because the author cannot be present to elaborate on intended meanings, he or she usually tries to be lucid and unambiguous so that the reader can follow the lines of argumentation. A key element in this project is a linear mode of exposition, carefully moving from one idea to the next logically connected idea.

Fig. 5.4. The earliest symbolic representations of thought — that is, the earliest literacies —

Analyses of some of the earliest written texts reveal that such linear argumentation was not the preferred mode at the historical moment in which some cultures made the transition from oral to literate traditions. Such works as Herodotus's *The Histories* (c. 450 BCE), for instance, consist of what to us might seem a strange mix of conjecture, myth, gossip, personal opinion, and historical detail. These early texts are often very difficult to follow — difficult, at least, to those who have come to expect a coherent strand of thought to be carried from the start to the end of any piece of writing.

Instead, these texts sometimes more resemble the structure of a conversation or of personal thought, as they move from one topic to the next and take up varied manners of expression. As with oral communications, they tend to be less concerned with the demands and restrictions of logical exposition. This should not be surprising: Many early writings are likely transcriptions of actual face-to-face accounts. Since those accounts occurred in situations where the listener could interrogate the speaker's intended meanings, the authors were perhaps not centrally concerned with clear and unambiguous explication. What mattered more was a compelling narrative.

were probably iconic (e.g., rock paintings, statuettes) and/or numeric (e.g., using tokens and, later, tally marks drawn on the ground or carved into bones).

Some such artifacts have been dated back tens of thousands of years. Some claims go back more than 50,000 years.

In contrast, alphabetic writing seems to be no more than 4,000 or 5,000 years old.

Breathless Language

Of the many thousands of languages spoken over the course of human history, only about a hundred have been committed to writing — and, of those, only a handful have developed their own symbolic systems. Most grapholects, such as written English, borrow heavily or entirely on earlier alphabets (e.g., Latin and Greek), which themselves borrowed from still earlier systems (e.g., Semitic).

In any case, once contrived, a grapholect can be used to connect persons across great distances and over time. Writing is a gathering location for memory, history and culture.

With the capacity to span geographic and temporal spaces, one of the immediate impacts of the written word is a slowing of the evolution of language. Writing, however, does not stop the evolution of language. One need only compare the vocabulary and grammar of a modern text to those of a Shakespearean play. Or, perhaps more cogently, a comparison of a new text on electronic technologies to one from the early 1980s reveals both surprising stability and dramatic change, especially in terminology.

Language co-evolves with every other element of a culture. As new events unfold and past events are reinterpreted, language serves as a gathering place for emerging sensibilities — and these can "collect" without necessarily provoking the conscious attention of all speakers. Consider, for instance, the word *woman*. Decades of political and academic work, focused on the subtle and not-so-subtle structures that have contributed to the subjugation of women, have helped to prompt shifts in meaning of this common term. As is powerfully evidenced by, for example, the contrast in the roles of women in *Star Trek* episodes from the 1960s and *Star Trek* episodes from the 1990s, what is intended and understood by the word *woman* has changed (and continues to change) dramatically. The same is true to varying extents of the words *black*, *gay*, *poor*, and so on.

Language, then, is not an innocent and transparent medium that might be used to represent objects, ideas, or actions. Rather, the webs of relations that are knitted into a language as it evolves contribute to habits of perception and interpretation. Language bears the trace of the many ways in which humans are relationally involved with one another, with their histories, and with their contexts. In effect, our shared language structures our common sense — that is, it shapes what we think to be "true" and trustworthy as it orients our attentions toward what we believe is worth worrying about at any particular point in time.

The suggestion that "languages evolve" implies more than gradual shifts in word meanings, pronunciations, and vocabularies as speakers accommodate to changing circumstances. In fact, there are often much more deliberate elements at play in the evolution of languages. In particular, a key influence in literate societies is the dictionary, whose role in affecting the development of a language cannot be understated.

English, for example, is overflowing with words and word forms that have been adopted and adapted from many, many other tongues, English is often seen as one of the most open and flexible languages. It may be less accommodating than is commonly believed, however. For instance, even though most English speakers live outside

Fig. 5.5. An assumption that is often made in tales of time travel is that it would be relatively unproblematic to communicate with citizens of a different era. But there's a problem with that assumption.

Languages — even written ones — probably change too quickly for it to work. In fact, as evidenced by the experiences of persons who move to different countries, languages can change dramatically in only a few decades. Such persons often find their visits to their homelands more and more difficult as time passes — not because they've forgotten the language, but because phrasings, associations, vocabularies, pronunciations, not to mention worldviews, continuously drift.

Europe and North America, the overwhelming majority of definitions and examples in the premier authority on the language, *The Oxford English Dictionary*, are drawn from England and the United States.

This is not a subtle point. Bearing in mind that one's language exerts the most profound influence on what one can and cannot think, what this means is that most of the world's English speakers continue to be subject to a particular, somewhat insidious sort of cultural imperialism.

Colonizing Languages

In her writing, novelist Toni Morrison has attempted to foreground the subjugating power relations that are woven into language. In particular, she has worked to unravel the tyranny of language by using it in new ways.

THE MASTER'S TOOLBOX

Rationalism
Empiricism

In both her fiction and her more explicitly theoretical writings, Morrison has highlighted the importance of challenging the "whiteness" of the literary imagination by creating texts in English that situate both White and Black readers in new ways. By positioning the reader in textual structures that are both familiar and strange, Morrison hopes to challenge racist notions that are so deeply woven into the familiar uses of the language that they are difficult to notice and even harder to extricate.

In effect, Morrison is providing an example of the difficulty of, to borrow from Audre Lorde, using the master's tools to dismantle the master's house. If theorists limit themselves to modernist terms of debate (i.e., the rational argument and the empirical demonstration), they are already in some ways accepting the conclusions that arise from that

THE MASTER'S HOUSE

Modern Science
Eurocentrism
Patriarchy
Industrialism
Formal Mathematics
Imperialism
Capitalism
Analytic Philosophy

Foundationism
Reductionism

mode of thinking.

Getting past the confines of these dominant rhetorical structures has been a challenge for persons and cultures with histories of subjugation. In a number of post-colonial nations around the world (such as Zimbabwe and Zambia), there are innovative efforts to use English in new ways. Although there are those who insist that the only way to escape the ongoing colonizing effects of English is to stop using it entirely, others believe that such wholesale abandonment is neither desirable nor possible in countries with a long history of English-speaking. Even though the subjugating influences of English have become apparent, it is tangled in many generations of experience. Hence, somewhat paradoxically, the elimination of English also entails the erasure of some degree of personal, familial, and societal history.

There is no satisfying solution. However, two overlapping tactics in this project have been to blend vernacular language forms with Standard English and to create and present hybrid art forms (including dance, music, poetry, and theatre).

In brief, language both liberates and subjugates. In literate societies, both these qualities are amplified. At the same time that writing enables the accumulation of ideas through various efforts at standardization it places tighter boundaries on what is thinkable.

There are profound consequences for schooling here. In particular, there are problems with the tendency to justify instruction in reading, writing, and other literacies mainly (and sometimes exclusively) in terms of the access these skills allow to informational and intellectual resources. As just developed, this popular rationale ignores an inevitable subjugation of thought that goes along with literacy. It also ignores the fact that various "stakeholders" have deliberately worked to limit access to knowledge. That is, although it might seem that the technologies of the written alphabet, the printing press, and electronic communications *should* make for an equitable distribution of what is known, it is clear that such is not the case.

Historically, one of the key strategies to ensure that mass access to knowledge is not permitted was to use an entirely different language for academic and scientific pursuits. Such was the role of "Learned Latin." No longer really spoken, Latin was primarily a written language when it was taken up, accessible only to those who could afford an expensive, upper class education.

In addition to contributing to a deeper entrenchment of social class structures, the academic use of Learned Latin seems to have also contributed to an array of cultural transitions, including the Scientific and Industrial Revolutions, capitalism, urbanization, and colonial expansion. As a largely abstract written language, divorced from references to daily domestic relationships and responsibilities, Learned Latin served as an ideal means to develop and advance those theories and ideologies that privileged a separation of abstract thought from everyday action, context, and obligation.

Of course, through the 20th Century, Learned Latin has been almost completely abandoned by academic communities. As its use has waned, however, new strategies of exclusion have emerged. Persons who wish to attain membership to particular discourse communities, for example, are expected to use specific vocabularies. In fact, virtually all scholarly disciplines are disparaging of the use of "plain language" or of efforts to "popularize" ideas.

Fig. 5.6. The word *grammar* refers to the organizing structures of language, and it tends to be interpreted in terms of established rules.

Its earlier uses, however, suggest that it derives from somewhat richer notions. The Middle English *grammarye*, for example, was used in reference to occult and magical lore. And a now obsolete Scottish word, *glamor*, meant "spell-casting power." (*Spell*, by the way, has a similar history.) These terms

Altering Consciousness

In Chapter 4, we discussed premodern conceptions of self, pointing to understandings of identity they were inextricable from matters of the natural and the spiritual worlds. The "self" was not considered an independent object that floated through a pre-existing world; rather, self was complicit in the world, co-emergent with other events and forces.

An important element of this sense of self was a particular conception of time. In today's context, time is almost universally understood in terms of a steady progression along a straight line (hence "timeline") — a conception that has predominated since the invention of the mechanical clock. Earlier conceptions of time were somewhat more textured. In particular, "history" was not conceptualized in terms of a linear chronology of past events, but as a presence, a weight, a culmination of lives and events that were woven into the current moment. What happened in the past was thought to be collected together in the present, and this theme was surprisingly consistent across the stories, songs, dances, and rituals of various cultures.

It was only through literate practices that time could come to be understood in terms of the unrelenting ticking of a clock. This modernist conception is most often attributed to the works of René Descartes, Francis Bacon, and Isaac Newton and to scientific developments in the 17th Century. Its roots, however, are likely much deeper. Johann Gutenberg's invention of the printing press in the 15th Century, for instance, did a good deal to set the stage for a mechanized conception of time as it enabled the mass production of dated materials. As daily newspapers proliferated and accumulated, with their records of date-stamped events, it made more and more sense to think of time in strictly linear sequential terms.

Technologies for the mass production and distribution of writing also contributed to further and more dramatic transformations in the development and organization of human consciousness, in some ways amplifying the impact of the invention of alphabets and other symbol systems. In particular, even though the mechanically generated marks of the pages bore a striking resemblance to the handwritten marks of a manuscript culture, the words on a mass-produced document were more distanced from the

suggest an awareness of the transformative power of writing: The use of relatively stable symbols to represent transient experience was understood to affect those experiences.

In some ways, writing is still considered magical. This is particularly true of handwriting, largely because the presence of the writer is much more apparent. As handwriting experts have demonstrated, one's script can reveal such elements as the writer's mood, age, educational level, and an array of personality traits. In brief, one's complex history is in many ways woven into one's handwriting. Perhaps that is why a simple signature can transform a poster, a note, or a manuscript into an object of great value.

writer. They did not flow from a pen held by a hand, but were stamped by a machine. In this way, print technologies prompted a further objectification of language.

It should be noted that the seeds of these sensibilities — that is, of autonomous selves, objectified knowledge, and mechanized time — were already present in the written word, long before the invention of mass printing. Unlike oral communications, that tend to weave and wander through ideas, the written word compels a more word-to-word, line-to-line, page-to-page sort of movement. This implicit linearity of writing is almost certainly a key contributor to mechanized attitudes toward time.

A linear, sequential conception of time supports a sort of mechanization of other elements of the human world. The project of formal education, in particular, has embodied this sensibility in a number of ways. Curriculum documents, along with published resources to support those documents, have tended to represent schooling as series of discrete and linearized learning events through which one is expected to progress at a steady pace. The fact that human learning simply does not obey overly structured sequences is all but ignored within these curriculum formats.

Fictionalizing Acts

How do writing and reading influence writers and readers?

Whether the writer is composing personal narrative, historical account, technical exposition, or literary fiction, in every case she or he must engage in some act of imagination. To write is to imagine a whole set of relations: The writer formulates images to represent thinking; the writer structures narratives to account for these images; and the writer invents a reader who, it is believed, will interpret and respond to these linguistic representations.

Through these processes of representing ideas, the act of writing is not simply a matter of recording thoughts that have already occurred. Writing is much more than an afterthought or an event of consolidation. It is, rather, an act of thought and reformulation, one that contributes profoundly to one's interpretations of one's experiences. That is, every act of writing (and, for that matter, every act of reading) contributes to the formation of one's identity.

Fig. 5.7. There's a popular perception, generally manifest among persons who speak only one language, that translation is simply a matter of exchanging one set of words for a set of corresponding words in another language.

This belief betrays a lack of awareness of ways that word meanings occur in complex

Ne réveillez
pas le chat
qui dort!

webs of relationship and
association. As such, literal
translations can often be highly
problematic. They might ignore
the associations woven through
one or both languages — an
ignorance which could give rise
to very different meanings.

Difficulties with translations
foreground the role of interpretation in any event of language.

In other words, writing and reading are always acts of
fictionalizing — a realization that points to a departure
from popular understandings of the role of language. It is
often assumed that language is principally a system of representation. In this conception, what matters is not the
words, but the ideas that are put into words.

There is now an increased appreciation that words can
never capture the fullness of experience. That is, all efforts
to represent experience are partial. Whether scientific explanation, historical account, or ethnographic description,
all claims to truth must be understood as "fictionalizing
acts." This does not mean that linguistic representations
have little practical value or that they are always misrep-
resentations. Rather, the suggestion that all written representations are fictionalizing acts reminds us that they are,
necessarily, reflective of choices — conscious and nonconscious — made by the writer. They are as much statements
about the perceiver (including the personal and social conditions of perception) as they are about the phenomenon
perceived.

Such deliberate fictions as short stories, novels, and
movies are also included in this category. The same is true
of accounts that are aimed more at accurate representations, such as diaries, journals, and other personal writings. In fact, the point also applies to texts designated as
nonfiction. As with all written records, these documents
are rife with context- and era-specific assumptions and concerns. As powerfully evidenced by textbooks and encyclopedias from a century ago, all efforts at representation
are (or eventually come to be seen as) fictionalizing acts.

Such claims, of course, raise important questions about
the distinction between "truth" and "fiction." If all narratives are understood as fictionalizing acts, does that mean
that we should approach poetry and novels in the same
way that we approach memoirs and scientific reports? This
issue is further complicated by publications in which writers have invented characters to narrate events from their
own lives. Should such writings be considered factual or
fictional? Or, conversely, what of the case of a writer who
decides to invent events, but to present them as autobio-
graphical? What if an anthropologist visits a foreign culture and writes about it from her or his own ethnocentric
perspective? Can the ensuing account be considered a representation of that culture, or is it only a representation of

the anthropologist's experiences of interacting with that culture? And, whether the former or the latter, should these accounts be received as facts or fictions?

Literary theorists have long been dealing with such issues. Among them, there is a general agreement that every writing act is, in some way, an event of fictionalizing. What is at stake, then, is not whether something is truth or fiction, but how a text is presented to the reader. Over many generations, for instance, particular formatting strategies and expressive devices have been developed that, in effect, announce to the reader how the text should be engaged. For example, the way that the lines of a poem are organized on a page, or the unusual juxtapositions of images within a play or short story, or the manner in which a character is introduced in a novel all suggest to the experienced reader that the text should be engaged as a literary work. And that manner of engagement is not the same as the way one would approach, say, a history text.

What's the difference between these two modes of engagement? In brief, the historical (or scientific, or mathematical, or journalistic, etc.) text asks the reader to believe that what is being stated is an accurate account of some event or insight. The literary text, however, only asks the reader to pretend to believe what is being presented. The pretense creates very different interpretive conditions for the reader.

Why do these structural and experiential distinctions matter?

As discussed in Chapter 1, we are consciously aware of only a tiny fraction of the stimuli that impinge on our senses at any given moment. Moreover, our habits of perception are learned, and they are largely conditioned by social and cultural context. In other words, experience is always larger than attempts to interpret and represent it. Another way of making this point is to suggest that every attempt to represent experience is partial — where *partial* is understood both in terms of the fragmentary nature of perception and the cultural biases implicit in any event of noticing. Hence, there can never be a "full account," an "objective rendering," or a "literal representation" of an event or phenomenon.

This limitation is a problem for texts that claim to be factual. These sorts of writings are subject to such critical questions as, "Who is speaking?", "Whose truths are be-

Fig. 5.8. Analyses of eyewitness accounts of staged events — like a robbery — show that much of what is remembered is actually invented. Witnesses almost always insert details and include facts which they may not have noticed but

ing represented?", "Whose interests are being served?", and so on.

The case for the literary text is quite different. Although still limited by the writers' and the readers' culturally conditioned habits of perception, the literary fiction aims more at presenting occasions for alternative interpretive possibilities than at presenting already-interpreted accounts. The literary text is one that uses language playfully as it points to different ways that events can be experienced and understood. Authors use such literary devices as metaphor and irony to interrupt habits of perception and interpretation — in the process, perhaps enlarging the interpretive possibilities of the reader.

Once again, a key quality of the literary fiction is that it does not ask readers to believe, but to pretend to believe. Whereas the factual account is principally aimed at providing information, the literary work is more about providing access to experiences that are not otherwise possible. In effect, through one's participation in fictional events — that is, through these deliberate engagements of the imagination — one's sphere of experience can be expanded. And with widened experience, the doors are opened to new and different perceptual and interpretive possibilities.

This may be why religious texts, folk tales, mythologies, and other cultural narratives figure so prominently in all societies. These accounts are much more than tales. They are collecting places for wisdom, moral direction, and knowledge gleaned over the generations. They are powerful because they make it possible for the hearer or reader to imagine herself or himself in the narrative — allowing the narratives to become collected within the totality of the reader's remembered experiences. Fact-based accounts, which make it difficult to invoke the powers of the imagination, rarely have the same effect.

The creation of literary forms, then, is an important aspect in the ongoing evolutions of human cognition and subjectivity. It should thus not be surprising to note that modern and Western conceptions of identity or selfhood seem to have co-emerged with literate traditions, a point that was developed in Chapter 4.

By way of illustration, we might note that the emergence of the conception of personal identity as coherent, internal, and unchanging — which we linked to modern-

which they felt should have been in their memories. As well, particular convictions about events and appearances can often be implanted through careful suggestions or leading questions.

That is, there isn't much difference between imagined events and memories — except that, with imagined events, we're aware that we're inventing.

This is similar to the difference between the ways we approach nonfictional and fictional texts.

ist world views in the last chapter — coincided with the development of more introspective characters in the 19th Century novel. Whereas the characters in earlier narrative forms (including oral forms) were usually not described in great detail, characters in such 19th Century novels as Jane Austen's *Pride and Prejudice* and Emily Brontë's *Wuthering Heights* were presented in more psychologically intricate ways. As such novels grew in popularity, writers began to represent more explicitly the ways in which characters might interpret their own identities. Rather than simply asking the reader to join characters in events, novelists invited readers to participate with characters in introspective interpretations of those events.

Private Readings in Public

The invention of print technologies that made it possible for almost anyone to purchase and to own books was a major factor behind the emergence of the modern Western conception of and desire for personal privacy. With the increased accessibility and portability of books, they quickly became more naturalized parts of the modern citizen's life.

The possibilitiy of owning a book prompted a transformation in the nature of reading, from a mainly public event — where one was most often read to — to a mainly private one. Indeed, aligned with the culturally privileged conception of identity as autonomous and self-contained, silent and private reading has become a "basic skill" in Western societies.

Despite this prominence, it has only been over the last two hundred years that silent reading has emerged as a desirable practice. Literacy scholars suggest that silent reading arose alongside a conception of identity that foregrounded individuation, autonomy, personal control, and self-knowledge. Silent reading made it possible to engage in a very public discourse (i.e., with a popular text) without any public display of that engagement. (There's a certain irony, of course, to the fact that a medium which provides access to the thinking of other people can also serve to isolate the reader from contact with her or his immediate communities of experience.)

Along with silent reading came the possibility for rapid reading. Prior to mass production of books, handwritten manuscripts were often inattentive to such details as uniformity of font, evenness of spacing, standardization of spellings, and consistency of punctuation. Users of these manuscripts were thus compelled to read slowly and aloud. With the consistency of mechanically produced texts, however, the need to sound out each letter or word was eliminated. This consistency, in fact, made it possible for readers to begin to recognize the shapes of entire phrases. That ability, in turn, made it possible to "scan" texts.

Silent reading has become so important in our society that children who are not able to master this competency are not considered fluent readers. The consequent priority of silent reading in schools has supported teaching practices that may be giving short shrift to a key stage in learning to read: Beginning readers need oral models in order to develop fluency. That is, more competent readers need to read aloud to beginning readers, pointing to the words to "show" the learner the relationship of the oral performance to the printed text and to the unfolding narrative.

In the early parts of the 20th Century, with the emergences of the fields of sociology, anthropology, and semiotics, a more fluid, culturally contingent conception of identity was explored by leading novelists. Prominent contributions to this genre were Virginia Woolf's *Mrs. Dalloway* and James Joyce's *The Dubliners*.

More recently, novelists have begun to develop very different ways of representing their characters. In particular, there are many examples in current fiction that embody some of the sensibilities presented in Chapter 4 in regard to ecological postmodern conceptions of identity. Such novels as Michael Ondaatje's *The English Patient* or Anne Michaels's *Fugitive Pieces* have explored ways to represent and to play with such phenomena as the partiality of perception, the co-emergence of personal and collective identities, and complex paths of self-formation.

In each of these cases, the literary works were much more influential than the academic treatises that were written at the same time and that explored the same themes. Undoubtedly, a major reason for the more pronounced impact was a much broader readership. But a more important quality might have been the manner in which the literary text pulled readers into varied ways of thinking through the presentation of events that invoked their imaginations.

Fig. 5.9. In 1938, Orson Welles' *War of the Worlds*, a story about a Martian invasion of Earth, was broadcast on radio stations across the United States.

Though a fiction, it was presented in the style of a live news cast. That is, it was intended as a literary form, but had all the markers of a non-fiction.

This detail was announced at the start of the broadcast. Unfortunately, many listeners who missed the first few minutes took the program literally. Some even committed suicide rather than waiting helplessly for Martian domination.

Fortunately, most literary texts use explicit devices to announce to readers that they should not believe, but pretend to believe, what is written.

Complex Interpretive Forms

In Chapter 4, we discussed matters of human subjectivity, with a particular focus on how one's identity occurs through interpreted relations with objects and with other persons.

In literate culture, relationality and exchange of knowledge include practices of reading and writing. Within such contexts, one's sense of self is as much determined by one's interactions with print texts as with direct oral exchanges. Identity, then, becomes as much a product of one's intertextual relations as it is a product of one's interpersonal engagements.

In primarily oral cultures, persons are addressed directly by those who are communicating with them (whether in conversation or through story, poetry, song, dance, or other expressive forms). In literate cultures, in addition to the forms that are common to oral cultures, persons are addressed by the texts that they read.

Such texts often seem authorless, even to critical readers. This is especially true of texts written from the third person point of view, and it is a quality that is, in fact, quite deliberate. The removal of all evidence of authorship from "informational" texts has been (and continues to be) a purposeful project, driven by the desire for objective and accurate representations of reality. Writing from the third person, it is argued, is an effective strategy for sidestepping the biases that arise in more personalized accounts.

Practices of textual address are central to the social and epistemological structures of schooling. Even though students are organized into what appear to be social groupings, most of their schooling experiences are decidedly individualistic in nature, as those experiences tend to be developed around and by print texts. The conventional classroom stands in contrast to the pedagogical settings organized around oral knowledge, where the learning is structured around collective projects and shared work and that is under the direction of an expert. (Modern day examples of such pedagogical structures include the apprenticeship models used in a number of fields to prepare new members for their upcoming responsibilities.) In the conventional school setting, the focus is not on a collective project, nor is it on a subject matter. Rather, overwhelmingly, the goal of modern schooling is articulated in terms of the individual achieving his or her "full potential" — as though one's potentialities were predetermined, internal qualities, waiting to be realized. (See Chapters 3 and 4.) Oriented by this belief, the teacher is seen as the arbiter and primary interpreter of the text. Whether it is a text on history, mathematics, science, or literature, the goal is to have the individual learner master its contents to the extent possible.

Within this conception, the divisive and hierarchical relationships among texts, implied authors, teachers, students, and truth are the by-products of a mode of thinking in which individuality is valorized. In fact, it is fairly easy to generate a long series of dichotomies that are implicit in most events of schooling: individual vs. collective, internal vs. external, mind vs. body, teacher vs. learner, fact vs. fiction, written vs. oral, human vs. nature, and so on. In each case, the first term of the dyad is given privilege, priority, or authority over the second.

To read is to decode the symbols on a page. Instruction should therefore be **skills-based**, focused on the rules of grammar and the sounds of letters.

To be able to read is to be able to extract appropriate meaning from a text. Instruction should thus be global and **comprehension-based**.

SHAKY COMMON GROUND

The meaning is in the text; "reading" is a matter of gleaning that meaning through some process of translating print into oral language.

Fig. 5.10. Recent debates around reading instruction have been bogged down in disagreements over whether the emphasis should be on mechanics (e.g., training learners to associate letters with sounds) or on comprehension (i.e., ensuring that learners are able to make appropriate sense of stories).

Other subject areas are having similar debates. Mathematics teaching, for example, is prone to arguments over the importance of "basic skills" relative to "understanding."

Proponents of opposing views, however, tend to be working from almost identical perspectives on reading, seeing it in terms of the ability to glean meaning that is assumed to be embedded in the text.

A more complex account of reading — one which is aware that an event of reading pulls together past and present, writer and reader, self and other, fact and fiction — suggests a certain emptiness to popular debates.

The point that we're trying to make here is *not* that such dichotomous thinking is inherently bad. Clearly, the capacity to make distinctions — that is, to dichotomize — is critical to all perception and learning. The problem is not the making of distinctions, but a persistent forgetting that distinctions are rarely, if ever, absolute.

Within the contemporary school, language is seen mainly as a means of representing reality (rather than being understood as a technology for continuously interpreting experience). This narrow but popular conception is largely a consequence of the written word. The symbolic representation on the page projects a certain detachment or distance — from writer and reader alike. And that imagined gap supports the perception that language (and knowledge) is something tangible, something separate from the language user (and knower).

Such a conception would be simply untenable in a predominantly oral setting, where language is only present in acts of vocalization and thought and where knowledge only makes sense in terms of a capacity for action. Words and knowledge cannot be conceived as "things."

Hence, the oral citizen would be more aware of the transformative powers of language — attuned to the fact that, like every human action in the world, languaging impacts on the conditions of one's existence. That is, languaging is always an event of interpretation — recalling that "interpretation" refers to the connecting of one set of experiences to another.

In any case, with the somewhat flattened understanding of language that predominates in conventional culture, coupled to the centrality of print text in today's schools, we are left with an impoverished view of what it means to be literate. Currently, the hallmark of the effective reader is the ability to excavate the "truth" of the text. So conceived, reading is not so much about the subtleties of interpretation as it is about the mechanics of decoding. In the terms developed in previous chapters, reading tends to be seen in schools as a *complicated* process rather than a *complex* event.

Schools are not to be blamed for this conception. Current educational attitudes and practices are reflections of earlier movements in institutes of higher education. In particular, at the start of the 20th Century, there was a powerful movement among literary scholars that came together around the belief that literary texts could and should be closely read for their exact meanings. That is, according to this movement, literary texts should be considered in the same category as non-literary texts. Working from the premise that close analyses of text construction could yield accurate and consistent insights about the author's true intentions, these scholars labored to develop particular methods that were modeled according to those used by mathematicians and scientists of the time.

There was an important reason for the development of such "scientific" methods for literary analysis: Literary scholars were attempting to demonstrate that their field of study could be as rigorous as any other. If the study of literature was to have a place in universities, it had to measure up to the standards of the time with regard to analytic methods. And so, ironically, novels, poems, and other texts that were deliberately written to maximize interpretive possibilities for readers came to be read in ways that foreclosed on those possibilities.

Attitudes toward literary analysis have since changed among academics. For the most part, theories of "close reading" have been overtaken by "reader response theories" which suggest that the meanings arrived at through reading arise in the complex interplay of authorial intention, textual representation practices, readers' experiences, and contexts of reading. Even so, despite the transitions in institutions of higher education, it is not uncommon for students in public schools to be asked to explicate the author's "intentions" or to identify the "real meaning" of a literary text.

Fig. 5.11. One of the prominent goals of conventional reading instruction is the mastery of silent reading — a practice that has been argued to have

The problem here is not that learners are being asked to do close readings of a piece of writing. Clearly, there are places for comprehension questions, for analyses of story structure, for examinations of new vocabulary, and so on. What is at issue is, first, a narrow conception of what it means to read (i.e., to excavate meaning — or worse, simply to decode) and, second, a similarly narrow view of the social role of the literary text.

For the most part, practices of reading in public schools continue to be aligned with complicated (rather than complex) beliefs about the way that the world is organized, including the ways in which people learn about the world. These beliefs are focused on the acquisition or mastery of established knowledge and, as such, simply do not attend

contributed to the modern belief in the separability of mental and physical events.

It has thus come as a surprise to many that recent research into the practices of the most skilled readers has demonstrated that there is considerable bodily activity during acts of silent reading, including persistent subvocalizations. That is, one's silent readings are always accompanied by a sort of silent speaking.

In other words, the internalness or mentalness of silent reading is an illusion. Like all acts of knowing, silent reading is a bodily engagement.

to the ever-changing relational web in which we live. For example, if students are told what Shakespeare intended with a particular metaphor, in effect they are being asked to ignore the ways in which that metaphor might have played an important historical role in prompting changes in thinking. In contrast, if students are asked to explore possible webs of implication that might have arisen when Shakespeare introduced that metaphor, they are participating in a much more complex interpretation practice.

This more complex understanding of reading is now gaining broad acceptance — not only in literary and reading studies, but in all areas of academic inquiry, including mathematics and the sciences. With the emergent view that "reading" occurs in the complex interaction of texts, authors, readers, and contexts of reading (including past, present, and imagined contexts), scholars are beginning to think about experiences of reading and responding to texts as important interpretive commonplaces for the study of humanity.

Importantly, the word *text* is coming to be used in reference to all representations of experience, including music, dance, painting, and varied photographic and film media. Even more broadly, as discussed in Chapter 4 under the heading "The Postmodern," the complex relationships among humans and the various methods used to construct a subjectivity using forms of symbolic representation can, in themselves, be considered "textual" constructions. The ways in which humans chose to organize their sociality, along with the ways in which they make and wear clothing, mark their bodies, style their hair, and decorate their living spaces — all of these — become ways of creating a "textual" construction of identity that is continually subject to interpretation by oneself and by others.

Reading Bodies

The title of this section of the book, "Reading Bodies," is deliberately ambiguous. With it, we intended to highlight the interpretive responsibility of the reader and, alongside that, the complex character of reading.

Within a literate culture, personal and collective identities are caught up in ongoing practices of reading and interpretation. Such cultural interpretation practices as story writing and story telling are integral to the ways in which literate subjects learn about themselves, about others, and about their shared worlds.

What teachers and students believe about reading is influential to how they understand themselves, others, knowledge, and future possibilities. If reading is presented as a set of skills to be used to extract meaning from texts, the learner must be positioned as a non-participant, a more-or-less passive receiver of truths that have already been established. If, in contrast, reading is conceived as a complex interpretive event — one that pulls together past and present, writer and reader, self and other, fact and fiction — the learner comes to be viewed as an active and co-evolving participant in a dynamic world.

It is our contention that teachers must begin to understand the complex ways that literate practices help to organize sociality. The pervasive belief that words, in themselves, can capture the fullness of experience needs to be replaced by more complex appreciations of what language is and what language does.

Over the years, I (Dennis) have developed the habit of re-reading books, particularly works of literary fiction. Last month, for example, I re-read Madeleine L'Engle's classic children's book *A Wrinkle in Time* — a novel I had not read since I was a teenager. This re-reading experience was curiously strange and familiar. As I read details of plot, I was taken back in memory to moments of thinking that I had had 25 years earlier. Most surprising to me was the amount of detail that I did not recall at all. In fact, although there were moments of remembered contact, most of the reading experience felt new to me.

My deliberate re-reading practices were formally initiated a few years ago when I was involved in some research into the teaching of literature with a group of high school English teachers. As part of our shared research, we read and discussed Michael Ondaatje's award-winning novel *The English Patient*. Developed around the experience of four strangers who come together in an abandoned Italian convent at the end of World War II, this novel became symbolic of the way we, as a group of teachers who didn't really know one another prior to our shared work, came together to inquire into matters related to the teaching of literature.

As we read the novel the first time, we became very interested in two things: first, the ways in which reading of a common text can create interesting "gathering locations" for interpreting personal and collective experience; second, the way that one's re-reading of a text can function to generate deep critical understanding of one's autobiography. This latter point is demonstrated by a main character's habit of carrying a well worn and frequently read copy of *The Histories* by the ancient Greek historian, Herodotus. Although this book is formally known as an account of the war between the Greeks and the Persians, for the English patient it has become a "commonplace" for inserting and interpreting instances of his own experience. Within the book itself, he has added notes, drawn rough maps of his travels of the African desert, described love interests, asked questions, and inserted tokens and momentos from places he has visited. His copy of *The Histories* is more than twice its original thickness and, in important ways, it is now a very different kind of text than any other copy.

Reading about the English patient's involvement with *The Histories* prompted our research group to wonder about our own "hurried" reading practices. It also prompted us to become critical of the some of the classroom practices demanded by curriculum documents. Over the years, we were obliged to "cover" more topics by reading more and more literature. As part of our research into literature reading, we decided that we would slow down our own processes, taking time to re-read *The English Patient*. We also decided that we would continue our practice of "marking" our responses in our novels, leaving an ongoing "trace" of our thinking. Although we had not all agreed to do this on our first reading, as seasoned university students we had treated this novel as a textbook and had underlined and marked our books with notes in preparation for our planned discussions.

These first markings became extremely interesting during our second reading. Not only did they remind us of what we had been thinking at particular places in the book during our first reading, they demonstrated how first readings can often be faulty. Because *The English Patient's* plot is organized episodically, with past, present, and projected events alternating with one another, the first reading was a somewhat confusing one. In fact, the first reading of this novel is merely a preparation for the reader — an unveiling of the topography of the reading experience. Once this topography is perceived, a second reading helps strengthen understandings of the plot and, as a result, creates a more interpretively complex reading experience.

Most interesting for us were the discussions we had regarding the "space" between the first and second readings and the ways in which our in-text markings rendered materially present the evolutions in our perceptions, our interpretations, and our senses of ourselves as readers. By spending considerable time trying to develop a relationship with these characters and this plot, and by trying to resymbolize this relationship in writing and in discussions with other readers, we found that we had made significant changes to our understanding of the book, of each other, and of ourselves.

As we continued to discuss our re-readings of this book and our emerging theorizing of our teaching and learning practices, we realized that this novel was actually organizing our learning in important ways. The novel, we decided, was teaching. This statement needs to be qualified by also noting that, as students of literary engagement, we understood that the act of reading did not merely depend upon a text. Any meaning generated through reading depends upon a reader who brings her or his experiences and understanding to the text. The "reading," then, is not really contained in the text or in the reader but, rather, in the developing relationship between the two. These reading relationships are also situated in particular social contexts that affect the ways in which these reader/text relationships occur and develop. Reading a novel for school purposes (or research purposes!) is different from other forms of reading. However, if "teaching" is understood as a deliberately structured event that functions to organize the perceptions and experiences of students, then a novel written by an author can be considered a "teacher." Just as teachers choose material and present it in a particular manner, so do authors. Just as students choose to either engage with or dismiss these proposed structures and materials, so do readers.

As our research group began to understand our engagement with novels and with novelists as a form of pedagogy, we became even more interested in how this pedagogical structure — this novel — was teaching us about English teaching and about ourselves as English teachers. We were particularly interested in the idea of the "Commonplace Book" carried by the English patient and the way in which our copies of *The English Patient* were beginning to function similarly for us. Because we had, in our successive readings of the novel, underlined passages, jotted comments in the margins, inserted Post-it and other notes with comments on them, and written responses on the blank pages at the back of the novel, we found that traces of our thinking were embedded in the novel. Like the treasured photograph album, our copies of *The English Patient* had become transformed into deeply meaningful personal artifacts.

Soon after conducting this research I moved to Vancouver to take a position at Simon Fraser University. During my first year there I became involved in some research at an elementary school, working with a Grade 5/6 classroom teacher who was also interested in the complex ways literary experiences might organize thinking. Using Lois Lowry's award-winning novel *The Giver* as common class text, we decided that we would experiment with the idea of the "commonplace book." Using some research funds, we purchased soft-cover copies of the novel for the students. After passing them out I gave the students some directions that seemed very unusual to them:

"Does everyone have a copy of the novel? Put up your hand if you don't have one. Okay, good. Now, you'll notice that these are brand new books. No one else has ever read them. They are yours to keep. They don't belong to the school. They belong to you. The first thing that I want you to do is to print your name in the book. Also put in the name of the school so that, in case you lose it, whoever finds it can return it to the school. We will be reading this novel together, as a class. Most of it I will read aloud to you. Some pages I will assign for silent reading. What I'm going to say next may sound unusual to you: I want to encourage you to write in these books. Yes, I'm serious! As we're reading, I want you to do what I do with my novels: Underline things that are interesting to you; write in the margins; ask questions; make comments in the back. Have any of you ever done this before? (No hands are

raised.) Let me show you one of my novels."

I showed students my copy of *The English Patient*, pointing out all the markings on the pages, the Post-it notes, and the more extensive writing on the blank pages at the back of the book. I also pointed out the different colors of pen and pencil as well as the dates inscribed on the inside front cover denoting the number of times I've read the book.

"Over the past two years I've read this book six times! Each time I read the novel, I add more notes and more comments. Now, I'm wondering what you think about this? Do you think I've had the same *reading experience six times, or do you think I've had six different reading experiences?"*

Not surprisingly, the students did not really understand my question. I tried again.

"Okay, I want you to think about what happens when we read something. I'm going to write a sentence on the board and I want you to read it and picture in your mind what this sentence suggests to you."

On the blackboard I wrote, "The dog chased the ball down the road."

"Do you all have a picture of that in your head? Good. Now, I'd like you to write down answers to some questions I'm going to ask you about that sentence. First, what color is the dog? Is the dog large, medium, or small? Is the road gravel or pavement? Is the ball big or small? What color is the ball? Is the road in the country or in the city?"

After the students recorded their responses, we went around the room and shared answers. As predicted, the students had many different "pictures" in their mind. I asked them:

"We've now proven that we can all read the same words and have very different ideas about what those words represent. We could say that, even though we read the same words, a different 'meaning' develops for each of us. Now, how could we use this idea to explain what we mean when we say someone is 'reading'?"

The discussion that followed was as theoretically sophisticated and as interesting as any that I have had with adult readers. Although it was, at first, difficult for them to find words to express the complexity of reader/text interactions, by the end of the class period, all students appeared to understand that reading was not simply "decoding," but was the act of the reader developing a meaningful relationship with a text. "Reading" depended on readers who had had experiences as much as it depended on authors and publishers who were writing about experiences.

Teaching young children to theorize their reading experiences is vital to helping them understand some of the reader response activities that I have them do, particularly the practices of in-text marking. Without understanding that readers contribute as much to meaning making as authors, students often do not engage in the marking activity as fully as they might. Once they are able to represent an understanding of the way intertextuality functions to organize the meaning making process, they are much more enthusiastic about "marking" their responses in their novels.

The next day, we began our work with *The Giver*.

"I'm going to read Chapter One out loud this morning. As I'm reading, I'd like you to follow along in your books. If there's a word or phrase that you find interesting, underline or circle it. If there's something that you don't understand, put a question mark in the margins. If there's something that catches your attention that you'd like to comment on later, mark it with your pen or pencil, or put a small sticky note in the margin, just like I've done in my book (I hold up my copy of The Giver.*) After I've finished reading the chapter, I'm going to give you some time to add notes to your book, in the margin, or on the blank pages at the back of the book. Any questions?"*

The Giver is a science fiction novel about a futuristic society in which all of historical cultural memory is concealed from all citizens except for one, the "Receiver of Memories." Because it is understood by citizens that there are times when a knowledge of history is necessary to decision making, the Receiver functions as the main advisor for government. The plot of the story is developed around the apprenticeship of Jonas, the newly appointed "Receiver." As part of his learning process, Jonas receives memories in installments from the old Receiver (newly named "the Giver" by Jonas). As Jonas receives these memories, he comes to understand his and his family unit's current situations more clearly. He now knows, for example, that while his father is called "nurturer of babies" he is also responsible for the elimination of children deemed abnormal or otherwise unacceptable. He learns that the elderly meet a similar fate when they have lived out their function to the community. Through the transmission of memories of past wars and of sleigh rides, Jonas comes to experience the agony of pain and the delight of pleasure for the first times. At the same time, because one of the conditions of his new role as apprentice to the Giver is to refuse all medication, he does not receive the daily pill to deaden sexual desire. And so, in addition to learning about many of the hidden aspects of his culture, Jonas also begins to have what are called "stirrings" or sexual feelings for others.

As I read aloud the chapter that introduces the subject of "stirrings" I felt slightly uneasy, wondering how students would respond:

"In this chapter, the word 'stirrings' is used. Does everyone know what that means? Yes? No? Who'd like to volunteer an explanation? Donna?"

"I think that stirrings are like what we learned about in our health films — when people begin to change and start to like girls and boys. Is that stirrings?"

"Yes, that's it. Stirrings, in this book, is the same as what happens to all of us when we go through puberty. It's when people start feeling attracted, sexually, to other people."

Although I had thought that the discussion of "stirrings" would be the most challenging aspect of teaching this novel, I soon learned that it would only be one of the many moments of difficult public interpretation that would take place. As we read, I was continually challenged by students to help them understand issues that emerged from this book. On one occasion, an intense discussion of infanticide took place. On another occasion, the practice of making the youth of the community responsible for bathing the elderly at the senior citizen home was the focus. On yet another occasion, the required daily practice of "dream telling" within family units was the topic of conversation.

Like any experienced teacher, I found myself gaining new insights into this novel through public exploration with these students. I became particularly interested when, in response to a question about how communities were distinguished from one another in this society, one student developed a theory of "domes":

"I think that all the communities are separated from one another by large plastic domes. Like big upside down plastic bowls. That's why the planes have to fly low and that's why they had to flatten all the mountains and make all the land the same. I think that people get from one community to another through underground tunnels."

Because I had read each and every word of this novel several times, I was convinced that the word "domes" was never used. I asked the class if they could find any evidence in the novel to support Matthew's "dome theory." They could not. However, as Melissa pointed out,

"Just because domes isn't written about doesn't mean that they aren't there. I mean, what Matthew says makes sense, so I think that there probably are domes!"

I conceded that this could certainly be the case. Just because something is not represented does not mean that it does not exist. And so, even though there is no mention of domes in the novel, students in this class continued to use the concept of "doming" to conceptualize the way in which the communities depicted in the novel were organized. Domes began to organize much of their interpretations, including assisting them to develop an elaborate explanation of how unwanted babies were not really killed, but were only given a sedative, packed in a box, and sent through a "chute" to a truck that then used the underground passageways to deliver the babies to another community.

As I continued to work with these students and explore their reading of this novel, I was repeatedly reminded of the ways that print representations of experience always require interpretive work by readers. Although a great deal of information can be presented by the author, just as much must be "invented" by the reader. Coherence in reading experiences, in fact, depends upon these ongoing inventive interpretations. This is especially true when readers engage with literary fictions, since not only must the reader negotiate a "plot," he or she must learn to identify and understand characters who are living out this plot. In becoming immersed in these narrative forms, readers learn to expand the boundaries of their own experiences, including their experiences of self identity.

Once the first reading of this novel was completed, the students spent one month working with their classroom teacher on matters that were related to ideas and themes drawn from *The Giver*. They became particularly interested in the idea of "sameness" that was valued in the novel and they tried to understand why diversity needed to be valued. They studied matters related to eugenics and euthanasia and learned about different civil rights movements around the world. In all these studies, students were continually asked to think about the ways in which *The Giver* depicted these themes.

Because I was interested in continuing to develop the "Commonplace Book" idea, I returned after one month to re-read the novel with the children. Continuing my practice of orally reading most of the novel, we spent one week reading and discussing the book from beginning to end. I worried that the students might become bored, but this proved not to be the case.

As I concluded my reading of the first chapter, the children seemed agitated, almost bursting to speak all at once. Kaitlin spoke first about an event that had slipped by without comment in the first reading, the "release" of a pilot who had made a navigational error:

> "I now know what 'released' means! When I first read it I thought that when they said the pilot would be 'released' for flying too low that he would just lose his job! Now I know that it means that he will be killed! That's terrible! Why would someone be killed just for making a mistake?"

Jake was the first to connect "release" with the baby who, in earlier readings, was thought to have been sent to another community:

> *"It says in the book that the one twin was to be 'released' by Jonas's father. That must mean that he was killed too. I don't think that he was sent to another community to live."*

As we continued to read through the rest of the novel, the children became more and more interested in their first responses, as recorded in margin notes and on Post-it notes throughout their book. I encouraged them to use a different color pen or pencil to add new notes, to answer questions that they now have answers for, to record new impressions of characters, to offer new interpretations of events in the book. My questioning, after each reading, did not so much focus on the content of the book as it did on their interpretations of the "space" between the two readings. I was particularly interested in having students notice and explain how their perceptions had changed since the first reading. In our various discussions, I noticed, over and over, how what was studied "between" the two readings had strongly influenced their understanding of the novel. Students offered, for example, much more sophisticated and informed interpretations of issues related to the theme of "sameness." Irene, for example, thought of it in relation to a documentary film they viewed:

> *"When I first read this book, I thought that the idea of 'sameness' was pretty good. I mean, I didn't think that there was anything wrong with that idea. But when we saw the film about that place ... What was it? ... (I reminded her that the film was a documentary about the island of Mauritius.) ... I started to think that maybe sameness wasn't so good."*

Irene's comment prompted a large and wide-ranging discussion of "sameness" and how, even in a multi-cultural society like Canada, there were tendencies toward making things the same. Students began to notice how many of the girls, for example, wore their hair the same way. They noticed that most of the classrooms were arranged in the same way and that many of them read the same books for pleasure and had the same toys and games. In discussing the tendency for humans to "conform," students began to perceive, more deeply why "difference" was often resisted.

At the conclusion of our week of re-reading and interpreting, it was time for students to engage in the very difficult work of trying to resymbolize their knowledge and understanding into new forms. Drawing from the major thematics of the novel and the one month of study in between the two readings of it, students were asked to write expository essays that explored particular ethical problems: Should society accept the practice of euthanasia? Should all people have free access to all information? Should everyone be able to choose to have and raise their own children? Students were challenged to represent their thinking on these topics within the structures of a formal essay.

Because I knew that this would be difficult for these students, their teacher and I provided detailed and explicit instructions on how to begin to organize their thinking into this form. We first helped them to list what they had learned about the topic of their choice from the various sources provided. We encouraged them to use the notes in their novels, and notes from other materials they had been given. We held small and large group discussions, helping them to remember and to represent what had been learned from prior class discussions on these topics. We taught them how to organize their arguments with examples and illustrations. We encouraged them to engage in "timed writing" practices to help "work out" their thinking. We did not hurry the students. We knew that this period of interpretation and resymbolization would take some time. Rather than devoting long sessions to this work, we gave students short 30-minute focused work blocks each day for 2 weeks. Each of these began with some direct instruction that was intended to help them continue their work. On some days, the lessons were developed around specific advice about how to organize their information; on other days, there were lessons on how to focus their topic or how to write clear arguments.

By the end of two weeks, all students had produced short essays. In most cases, these essays expressed thinking and abilities that greatly exceeded what might be expected from Grade 5 and 6 students. Not only were students able to explain what they remembered from their study of *The Giver* and related materials, they were able to extrapolate from that learning and grapple with difficult ethical and moral questions.

Although the essays convinced me that the students had changed their perceptions and their understandings through this 6-week novel study, their attitudes toward their personal copies of *The Giver* suggested to me that they had also developed a more complex theory of reading. In a discussion with a group of four of the students, Gina mentioned, in passing, that her family would soon be moving:

> *"Because we're moving to Jamaica, my mum might not let me keep my copy of* The Giver. *I mean, she knows I've already read it twice, and because we have to cut down on things to take, she might make me ... well, throw it away!"*

By the way that Gina clutched her book, it didn't seem like she wanted to throw it away.

> *"You seem to be quite attached to your copy of* The Giver!*"*

"I can't throw it away. It's so, so ... lived in! I mean, it's stuffed with all my notes and all my writing in it. I'd like my mum to read this book and see everything that I've written in it and then I'd like her to write in it too so that I can see what she's thinking. I mean, if she gets to see what I'm thinking I want to know what she's thinking too. And then, maybe I'll keep the book and give it to my children and they can read it. And, and ... well, it will be like a history!"

As the students, their teacher, and I talked about their copies of *The Giver*, we began to understand more deeply how this novel had gathered together our personal and collective experiences. Not surprisingly, then, the children's marked up copies of this novel prompted a return to our initial discussion of reading. In examining the question of where "meaning" is located during and following acts of reading, the students all agreed that it is somewhere "between" the readers and the texts that are read. In coming to understand processes and practices of reading as complex acts of negotiating meaning with texts, with one another, and with one's own memories, these students were beginning to think about reading as an important interpretation practice. As a teacher, I was reminded yet again that all events of teaching contribute to the ways in which the students and the teacher construct and interpret their personal and collective histories.

Anyone who has learned a second language has experienced the complex and often subtle ways in which language shapes perception and understanding. The vocabularies and different lexical and grammatical structures of a new language compel the speaker or writer to find different ways of saying things. In the process, interpretations of past and present events come to be framed somewhat differently. Inevitably, the second language learner finds that she or he is unable to readily or accurately translate past experience from one language to another. That is, she or he usually comes to the realization that acts of translation are acts of transformation.

As in the first two parts of this chapter, in this section *language* is understood as any system of representation that can be folded back onto itself. It is this potential for self-reference and recursive elaboration that renders language such a complex and powerful form. Language is a liberating constraint: At the same time that it works to limit the possibilities for thought by preselecting associations and categories, it opens the floodgates to imaginative possibilities.

Teachers need to be critically aware of how language functions to organize and shape the learning structures that are created for students. At the same time, teachers must be mindful of how language creates worlds of experience for learners. The points in this chapter are all about being more mindful of the use of this powerful technology.

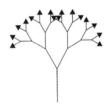

Point 1 • COMMUNICATING LIVES

In planning events of learning, teachers must remember that how reality is perceived and interpreted by the students depends on many things, among which are the specific uses of language in the classroom.

Until quite recently, it was commonplace for the masculine pronouns "he" and "his" and the noun "man" to be used in collective references to both males and females. Persons educated before and during the 1970s were likely told by teachers that using "man" was a neutral term that referred to all of humankind.

Feminist activists and theorists, however, disagreed, insisting that this usage represented a longstanding and pervasive sexism. Women, they argued, were not men — and the refusal to acknowledge this point in language constituted one form of subordination of females to males.

Coloring Skin

Harija was a student in Martin's "Critical Issues in Curriculum" class. Following a class on the subject of "racism in schools" she wrote the following in her weekly journal:

I'm very upset with what happened in class this week. As one of the very few women in the room of South Asian descent, I have felt conspicuous and vulnerable. Every time the phrase "person of color" is used, I feel like every eye in the class is on me. At first I thought that I was just being overly sensitive, but my beliefs were confirmed when, after class yesterday, one of my classmates asked me if I would be willing to help her with her project by talking about some of my experiences as "a person of color." I said that I didn't think that I wanted to do this, which seemed to annoy her. What I wanted to say was, "Hey! I'm not the only person of color in this room. White is a color! Pink skin is colored just like brown skin is colored!" I think that our class needs to examine the language it's using to describe people who are perceived as different. I have to say that I didn't feel so different from other people until we studied this in class.

When Martin read Harija's comments, he knew that he needed to help the class to understand the ways in which nuances of language can create particular ways of interpreting other persons' identities and experiences. He realized that, while his own reading of critical race theory had helped him to structure opportunities for his students to explore issues of race and ethnicity, it had in some ways made his students insensitive to the ways in which they represented the differences in their own contexts. After conferring with Harija, Martin developed an activity he hoped would help students to understand the way in which familiarity had deafened them to the racism embodied in language. Working from the assumption that their "realities" had to be interrupted in order to better perceive this covert racism, he decided that he would have his students work with paper and pastels rather than asking them to work with written language.

In the first part of the lesson Martin had a colleague provide introductions to using pastels and, particularly, to techniques of blending to achieve nuances of color. Students were then asked to use the pastels to mimic their own skin tones. Once they had found a suitable blend of colors, they were to fill in a six inch diameter circle that had been drawn on a white sheet of paper and to list the colors of the crayons used. Students were then asked to present their products.

In every case, students found that it was, in fact, quite difficult to determine an appropriate mixture of colors to reproduce skin tones. Most interesting, however, was how surprised students were to find that, in order to create Caucasian skin tones, they needed to use different quantities and shadings of a number of different colors.

Once the presentation was over, Martin asked students to answer, in a word or two, the question: "What color is my skin?" Again, students were asked to recite their responses. The answers ranged from "taupe" to "rosy brown" to "sandy" to "light beige." Not one student named their skin "white" or "black" — and mention of this fact created quite a stir. The students immediately became curious about why "identities" were generally organized into "white" or "black." Did black and white represent actual skin tones or were they historical markers of social and cultural difference? If one used the label *white* to describe skin that was obviously *not white* what did this say about how one understands the relationship between ethnicity, skin tone, and social position?

This activity and discussion helped Martin's students understand that it was really inappropriate to identify some people as being "of color" and other people "white." Further, it helped them to more fully appreciate the ways that longstanding traces of bigotry were woven through these common markers. As future teachers, they came to understand that, in order to become aware of how language functions to organize perception and experience, detailed examinations of the familiar relationships between the signifier (the word spoken) and the signified (the phenomenon represented) had to be made.

Today, most institutions insist that all public language (oral or written) be inclusive. In other words, the language used to represent humans and their experiences must be, as much as possible, representative of the subtle differences among individuals and groups of individuals.

While great theoretical strides have been made to understand the effects of language on the way in which gender is perceived, subtle linguistic discriminatory practices continue within contexts of learning, particularly with experiences and issues of race and ethnicity.

 Connecting Thoughts

A central — perhaps *the* central — theme of this text is that we must be attentive to those patterns of acting that we call *language*.

A useful exercise might be to assemble a list of the terms and phrases that are popularly associated with teachers and acts of teaching, with a critical eye toward the way such language derives from, assumes, and projects particular conceptions of what it means to teach.

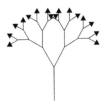

Point 2 • REMEMBERING LIVES

Memory continuously evolves with experience. Rather than assuming that learning is mostly a matter of accumulation, then, teachers have a responsibility to help students reconcile what is remembered to what is being learned.

Recent research has shown that the abilities to perceive patterns of organization and particularities of contexts are learned. The processes of learning to perceive some things and not others are continuous with ongoing experience, framed by physiological capacities, and conditioned by existing circumstances. This means that the worlds of perceiving entities (human and not human) differ.

Among the issues that are of greatest relevance for teachers are the complex ways that presently experienced perception is affected by memory and the ways that memory is changed by present perception. As suggested by the "shoe" activity that is described in Chapter 4B, "Creating Identities," the experiences one has with any object can be dramatically altered with new learning. To some degree, students' memories of their interactions with their own shoes were changed when they were juxtaposed with fictionalized narratives written by their classmates.

Such transformations are also demonstrated in the plot of *The Giver*, as developed in Chapter 5B. As Jonas receives memories from the Receiver, his understandings shift. As he learns to see color, feel snowflakes on his cheek, and experience pain, his world of present understanding changes. He begins to see his family and friends in new ways. Most significant for Jonas is how these new learnings affect memories of the past. When Jonas receives the memory of his father giving a lethal injection to a baby who was deemed imperfect, Jonas's feelings toward his father are revised.

The realization that memory, perception, and learning function as "loops" and not as linearly sequenced events prompts the assertion that all events of learning are events of synthesis and integration. Teaching a child the alphabet or a simple vocabulary provokes a significant shift in the way that the child understands her or his world of experience. Prior to developing literate sensibilities and competencies, the child experiences language as sounds associated with particular social events. Although she or he understands that there are particular sounds that represent certain objects and processes and feelings (e.g., mama, running, happy), he or she does not necessarily understand these as distinct words — or even, perhaps, distinct events. In deliberately teaching the child the symbolic, representative functions of written language, the child's perceptions of oral language change. With increased literate competence, the child begins to hear language as "connected words," learning to distinguish among different words and different purposes.

Literate competencies are most effectively learned when they are linked to the child's interests and past experiences. Learning to be literate is always an act of resymbolizing and reinterpreting past experience in relation to present and projected experiences. That means that no act of literacy teaching is neutral or benign. Teaching transforms worlds.

The theories of learning that have structured schooling for the past few decades, explicit and implicit alike, have tended to underacknowledge or dismiss this relationship among learning, memory, and identity. Instead, memory is understood as a "bank" or as a "data base" where increasing amounts of "capital" or "information" are deposited.

There is considerable resistance to this mindset among experienced teachers — as demonstrated, for example, in the widespread resistance to externally imposed exami-

---

Writing Difficulties

As an introductory activity in her teacher education class, Daya asked her students to work on a timed writing activity that began with the prompt: "Describe the floor of your mother's kitchen."

She chose this prompt because she thought it would be sufficiently "constraining" to focus students' attentions, yet greatly "liberating," since such a familiar place would likely be associated with many images and events.

A moment in the activity, one student, Anya, crumpled her paper and left the room. Daya was worried. What could have caused this sudden response? Anya eventually returned, her eyes betraying the fact that she had been crying. After class, Anya stayed to explain:

"I'm sorry to have left in such as a state, but that writing prompt reminded me of things that I didn't want to remember. I came to Canada from Poland ten years ago, against the wishes of my mother. It was a terrible time for me. Now my life is very good, but I haven't spoken to my mother since leaving Poland. I don't even know if she's alive. I just couldn't bear to write about the floor of my mother's kitchen!"

As Daya listened to Anya's story, she was reminded that curriculum is never neutral. What seemed like a benign writing prompt created very difficult moments for at least one of her students. What was she to do? Because Daya did not want to leave this event uninterpreted, she suggested the following to Anya:

"I'm sorry that the image I suggested was so difficult for you. And, I understand why you chose not to write. But it does seem that you're inter-

ested in learning more about your mother and the decisions you and she have made over the past few years. You might want to do some writing about that on your own — but not for me or for the class or for your mother. It would be writing that helps you to think about these matters. You can use your writing to help you organize your thinking; writing isn't just a summing up activity that you do after all the thinking has been done. If you'd like to do this, and need any help from me, I'd be happy to spend time working with you on it after class."

Anya still seemed anxious, but agreed that writing about past events might be a good idea. Over several weeks, she tried to write on a daily basis in her "Commonplace Book." Used as a location both to represent experiences and to interpret them, Anya's Commonplace Book helped her to reframe memories of Poland and her family in relation to things she had learned since coming to Canada.

Daya's experience with Anya reminded her that she needed to be mindful of the ways that her students were responding to the forms and the practices of learning that she chose for them. She especially needed to be respectful of students who chose either not to engage or to disengage from these structures. At the same time, Daya learned that sometimes difficult knowledge can become a generative and generous site for learning. However, these moments demanded an attentiveness and, when encountered, she had to be skilled enough to help her students create interpretive sites where the content of the curriculum could be interpreted in relation to students' memories.

nations and other related structures for schooling. Although it is certainly possible for students to memorize large quantities of represented knowledge and to reproduce that knowledge on final examinations, such learning tends to be "compartmentalized." Research has demonstrated that students are often unable to make use of this knowledge outside of schooling contexts.

This finding, of course, does not mean that final exams should not be given or that they are not useful. It does suggest, however, that the structure of the final examination must allow students to demonstrate the ways in which they are able to analyze and integrate required curriculum content with their own perceptions, experiences, and interpretations. Teachers who create forms of evaluation that ask for representation, application, and interpretation of curriculum content understand the complex ways that memory, present perception, and imagination continuously influence one another during all occasions of teaching and learning.

Understanding the complex reciprocal relationships among curriculum content, memory, and understanding has particular ethical implications for teachers. It suggests, for example, that when a student chooses to abandon a required novel, is not interested in learning more about particular events in history, or resists personal response to a curriculum prompt (as in, for example, a response journal), he or she may be resisting an involvement in a personal crisis of knowledge or perception. It is important for teachers to remember that resistances to learning are not always rebellions against authority or lacks of personal motivation. There are often occasions when students make conscious and nonconscious choices not to engage with (or to disengage from) curriculum materials and/or learning structures — for reasons that might never be clear, even to the learners themselves.

  Connecting Thoughts

Several instances of "difficult learning" — that is, of having to reconcile what is remembered with what is being learned — are presented in Chapter 5B, "Imagining Worlds." What were some of the things that the teacher did to structure these events?

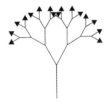

Point 3 • SHAPING LIVES

Teachers must help students to develop a critical understanding of the complex ways in which literacy processes, practices, and technologies both limit and enlarge human perception, consciousness, and cognition.

In recent years, considerable attention has been focused on questions of how computer and other electronic technologies are influencing human social interactions. The general opinion is that the use of computers in schools will radically transform the ways in which students learn and the ways that teachers structure classroom experiences. In fact, the use of emergent technologies to create interactive events of learning for students, in the absence of a live teacher, is one of the most active areas of innovation in many formal educational institutions.

There are as many critics as there are proponents of the use of electronic technologies in schooling settings. While the proponents insist that current technologies can offer more persons greater access to more information with fewer resources, critics worry about the lack of face-to-face, elbow-to-elbow human mentoring that is considered, by many, the hallmark of effective pedagogy. Whether computers are or are not used in classrooms, however, is almost a moot point in an era where computer technologies have been so extensively integrated into human social processes and practices. Current generations of school children tend to be well socialized into the current "computer culture" before attending school — and, in many instances, children are more fluent with electronic technologies than some of their teachers.

Rather than focusing on the this-or-that debate about whether or not computer and other electronic communication technologies should be used in formal school contexts, teachers might think about how any communication technology influences the developments of human perception, consciousness, cognition, and sociality. A good place to begin is to consider how already-familiar communicative technologies, such as print literacy, have already reorganized human perception and behavior. Although seldom described as a "technology," the practice of creating representations of words on paper is one that has, over the centuries, changed human thinking. As described in the first part of this chapter, most humans have become dependent on such representations of experience. The books that are written (including recipe books, manuals explaining the use of products, histories, and newspapers) are necessary tools for the maintenance of culture as it has now come to be organized.

Scholars and researchers who have studied the practices and effects of human interactions with print technologies have helped to highlight the complex ways in which consciousness is enlarged and differentiated through various practices and processes of reading. As suggested by the events described in Chapter 5B, "Imagining Worlds," for example, the engagements that readers have with texts announced as "literary fictions" are not identical to engagements with texts understood as "history" or "science." The stance that a reader adopts in relation to a text is strongly influenced by the forms these texts take, the purposes for reading, and the various overlapping conditions and contexts of reading.

The understanding that human perception and thinking is influenced — and even organized — by engagements with print technologies has been influential to researchers interested in cybernetics. (Cybernetics is a branch of science that is focused on the relationships between biological systems and human-made control systems in electronic and mechanical devices.) Rather than thinking of, for example, word processing and interactions on the Internet as processes that are simply "added" to already existing human practices, research emphases are now aimed at trying to understand the ways in which human attachments to these practices and processes fundamentally affect human perception, consciousness, and sociality. What happens, for example, when a child's early literacy experiences are structured around a word processor, rather than pencil-and-paper? Does typing words while sitting in front of a computer screen organize the writer's thinking in ways that differ from the use of pen and paper? In working with various technologies of representation (pens, pencils, word processors for writing, canvasses for painting, wood for sculpting, video cameras for filming, cameras for photographing, etc.), teachers should be attentive to that relationships among the human, the artifact, and the mode of representation that develop.

Processing Changes

Ten years after graduating from high school, June decided to attend university. Although she was committed to fulfilling her dream of becoming a high school history teacher, she was concerned that she did not have the necessary skills to embark on a university education. She was particularly worried about her knowledge of computers.

To prepare herself, June purchased a personal computer and took a few evening classes to familiarize herself with its uses. When September rolled around, she felt comfortable with basic word processing, e-mail, and Internet use.

Within 2 weeks, June was fully immersed in her program, studying history, English, and philosophy. Her lifetime habit of reading novels helped her to cope well with the demands. Problems began to emerge for her as mid-term papers were pending, however. Though she had no great difficulties reading the materials and keeping track of what she'd read, June had considerable trouble organizing her essays. Each day she would spend several hours in front of her computer, trying to represent her thinking. And, as each day passed, she became more frustrated. Deadlines loomed, and June began to worry that her university career would soon collapse around her.

In desperation, she arranged to see one of her professors who asked about the processes she had used to write her essays in high school:

"Did you use a computer word processor, or did you use pen and paper?"

"Oh, I always used pencil and paper. I always carried a hardcover notebook with a pencil attached on a string. I'd make notes while waiting for the bus or during a spare period. Usually, I planned all my writing in my notebooks. Now that I think about it, I wrote other things in those books — things that were personal. I still have all of them in a box in the basement!"

"So, you learned to write your essays using your notebooks. Did you write outlines? How did you do your rough drafts?"

"I never wrote outlines. They were always required. Whenever I had to hand one in with an essay, I'd write it after I was done. I never really knew what an essay would look like until I'd written it! I wrote all my rough drafts on pads of yellow paper. I always used my pencil and did lots of erasing and crossing out. Sometimes I cut out paragraphs and taped them to a wall. When I had to write the final draft, I would take the paragraphs down and tape them to new sheets of paper."*

"Why have you abandoned it that method?"

"Well, I'm using a computer now. I can do things like move paragraphs around, save multiple copies, edit on screen. It's supposed to save time ... but it hasn't yet."

As the conversation continued, it became clear to June that her earlier practices of composing and thinking with pencil and paper had organized her cognition in specific ways. The particular rituals and routines of her high school practices had become intimately connected to the ways that she organized her thinking. In abandoning these practices, June had, literally, "lost her mind."

She decided to try to write her mid-term papers using her old practice. It proved successful. The only change she made was to word process the final copies, during which she did some minor editing.

These changes marked the beginning of a transition to June's writing and thinking practices. The following semester, in addition to using her hardcover notebooks, June began typing quotes from books into a file entitled "booknotes." As weeks passed, she found herself adding personal and critical responses in parentheses. In her second year of university, June continued to keep a notebook, but elaborated her use of the computer to include a daily response file containing notes from books, critical reflections, and ideas for papers.

In her third year, June became more aware that she was using her computer "to think," rather than simply to record thinking. She found herself getting "lost" in the activities of entering quotes, responding to them, and typing her own ideas. Very often, once represented, these ideas were surprising to her.

Connecting Thoughts

One of the aims of the teaching episode around *The Giver*, described in Chapter 5B, "Imagining Worlds," was to help learners become more explicitly aware of the ways that acts of reading affected their lives. How was this done? In particular, how did the teachers structure experiences so that discussions of this topic complemented (rather than conflicted with) the requirements of the formal curriculum?

Point 4 • ORGANIZING LIVES

Teachers should help students understand the ways language becomes organized into categories that represent personal and cultural identities.

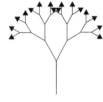

As children mature, they learn to distinguish their own developing identities from those of other persons in their family and social units. The transition from childhood to adulthood might thus be characterized as a process of differentiating oneself from others, although the degree to which this becomes manifest in daily practice varies widely across generations and cultures.

While there are biological markers that are interpreted as a movement into adulthood, there are also specific cultural rituals and practices that function to organize and structure the transition. This is particularly well described in *The Giver*, where processes of development are marked by ritualized annual events. In the "Ceremony of Naming," for example, all "acceptable" newborns are given names that have been selected by a naming committee. Following this are the Ceremonies of One, of Two, and so on, during which each child's development is marked with special gifts and new responsibilities. Nine-year-olds, for example, are provided with new two-wheel bicycles during the Ceremony of Nine. At the Ceremony of Ten, gender distinctions are made more obvious with new haircuts for girls and boys. The most significant of all, however, is the Ceremony of Twelve, the time when each child is assigned a life's work.

The specific rituals that comprise the Ceremony of Twelve distinguish it from the others. In an opening speech, the Chief Elder reminds all present that, while one spends the first 11 years of life learning to "fit in," the Ceremony of Twelve is a time when differences among individuals are noted. Significantly, these differences are used to determine each person's life work. Among the many possibilities, some girls are assigned the role of "birthmother" — which, though acknowledged as important, is not considered prestigious. Others are assigned to work as "nurturers of babies," since birthmothers do not care for their own infants.

It is significant that these occupational decisions are not made by the children themselves, nor by their caregivers or teachers. Instead, an elected committee from the community is charged with the responsibility of observing the children for a period of time prior to the Ceremony of Twelve, making note of each child's personal characteristics, attitudes, competencies, and aptitudes. Following the Ceremony of Twelve, the child is expected to assume a more adult-like attitude and is provided with an official letter that outlines her or his educational and training responsibilities. In the novel, some children are streamed into formal educational settings for academic study, while others are placed in apprenticeship situations.

The imposed practices of selection and differentiation, as developed in the novel, are supported by the social imperative to be precise with language. Children and adults alike are continually reminded that words have specific agreed-upon meanings. Alteration, substitution, and sloppy usage of existing vocabulary is strongly discouraged. In this society, words are considered exact representations of particular agreed-upon referents. Consensus of understanding and consistency of use are required.

Interestingly, within the "real" world of formal educational settings, there are many parallel practices to those that have been made explicit in *The Giver*. For example, although committees are not explicitly organized to make decisions about a child's future, the formal structures of schooling and curriculum are organized to affirm and reproduce mainstream social beliefs, values, and structures. The content, sequences, and outcomes of curricula continue to be determined by committees and mandated by governmental departments of education — practices that ensure that most publicly funded schooling will be centrally concerned with the production of particular sorts of citizens. While the profile of "ideal" citizens changes over generations, such conceptions are still largely organized and constrained by particular images and language that represent them. As a cultural practice, schooling participates in the production and sorting of "acceptable" and "other" identities.

Historical analyses of curriculum documents and supporting text materials demonstrate the ways in which categories of acceptable and not-acceptable have changed over time. Denigrating and pejorative language and images intended to describe and represent different cultural groups have slowly been eliminated from these materials. Changes in language use and popular image have often come about only after prolonged periods of social activism and public education by affected groups. Feminist activists, for example, were instrumental in not only helping the general population to understand how women's experience has been negatively affected by patriarchal structures and practices, they have worked successfully to point out how language has supported these inequities. The now-common practice of using gender-inclusive language in all public documents points to the success of this public education.

Another example of the changing of public perception about "acceptable" and "not acceptable" categories has been the appropriation of pejorative language by affected groups. In the 1960s and 1970s, for example, the word *Black* was claimed for use by African American and African Canadian communities in slogans such as "Black Power" and "Black is Beautiful." More recently, the gay, lesbian, bisexual, and transgendered communities have appropriated the word *queer* and used it, both academically and socially, to describe and represent non-heterosexual identities. Today "queer theory" has become a widespread interdisciplinary study that includes the study of all sexual identities and identifications.

Reclamations of such words as *Black* and *queer* represent deliberate efforts to transform popular meanings and uses of particular terms — that is, to undermine the practices of discrimination and stereotyping that go along with certain habits of identification. While such practices are not always immediately altered, over time perceptions and interpretations can be powerfully affected through contact with this new use of language.

Categorizing Differences

During a graduate class discussion focused on how social practices of representation produce stereotypical minority identities, Ruth comments:

"You know what really bugs me? People who don't know me think that I spend my days weaving dream catchers in my teepee. Well, I am of First Nations descent, and there are some things that my family and I do that are not the same as what other people do. But, you know, I live in a 3-bedroom house in the suburbs, I haul my kids to hockey practice and swimming lessons in my Ford Explorer, and sometimes we stop on the way to eat at McDonald's. I mean, sure, I have a particular heritage that I value and try to learn about, but I'm just as much a product of modern Canadian society as anything!"

Ruth's comments prompt Jim to offer his perspective:

"I've made no secret of the fact that I'm gay. But I usually don't mention anything to people that I don't know very well. Why not? Well, when I say that I'm 'gay,' most people immediately say, 'Gee, you don't look gay!' Or, 'You don't act gay!' Now, what does that mean? Am I supposed to take that as a compliment? Or does it mean that, not only am I not straight, but I don't even know how to be properly gay? I think it's important for everyone to understand that people's experiences of sexual identification are really quite broad and can't be confined to the narrow set of characteristics suggested by words like 'gay' or 'lesbian.' That's why I'm always reluctant to say that I'm gay. It means that I am immediately known by my 'category.'"

As the class continues to explore these issues, it becomes clear that not one member of the class feels comfortable with her or his "assigned" identity category. Mark explains:

"Since coming back to univer-

sity, I've been in classes that have a deliberate 'feminist' agenda. And I've learned a lot by reading histories of feminisms. But I have to say that it really bothers me when it's assumed that because I'm a man that I'm sexist. Just like it's hard to live in the categories that Ruth and Jim describe, it's difficult to be a white guy these days!"

June further complicates the discussion:

"You think that you've got it rough! I'm a third generation Canadian but, because I have brown skin, people usually immediately assume that I'm an immigrant. I can't tell you how many times I've been asked if I speak English! I'll bet that doesn't happen to many of you."

Since all participants in the class are teachers and teacher educators, they decide to create lists of words that help represent the complexity of their experienced personal and cultural identities. As they do so, they come to understand that, while they resist the linguistic markers of identity categories that have been created for them by history, they also identify with them. Jim explains:

"Though I don't want to be stereotyped as 'gay,' I also want it to be known that I'm not straight either. And, I feel some commitment to the history of the gay activism. The fact that I can actually talk about my sexuality in this forum is one of the important products of that work. So, I both resist and embrace the word 'gay.'"

As the seminar concludes, the participants agree that it is important to be critically aware of how language helps to organize and structure identity categories. It is also important to be aware of the histories of these linguistic constructions and the many ways in which they have been used. As teachers, all seminar participants agreed that it was important for them to help their students to understand these ideas.

Connecting Thoughts

The structures of public schooling have greatly contributed to conceptions of "development," along with such categories as "childhood," "adolescence," and "adulthood." What are some of the markers that used in schools to distinguish among of to define these categories?

Point 5 • PRACTICING LIVES

Learning always extends beyond the planned structures and times of pedagogy. Teachers should thus help students learn methods and techniques for ongoing interpretation and resymbolization.

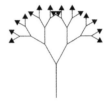

As Jonas, the main character in *The Giver*, continues to accumulate the memories from the old Receiver, he finds himself more and more concerned about current conditions in his community. In particular, he is worried about the infant child Gabriel who, he has deduced, is about to be "released." Contrary to everything he has learned as a young child, Jonas uses his new knowledge to make a fundamental decision: He must take Gabriel outside of the community. He must transgress familiar geographical and social boundaries and journey to unknown places, hoping to find refuge elsewhere. As he travels, he must remember what he learned from his father about infant care and what he has learned about the greater world from the memories transmitted by the old Receiver. In interpreting a relationship between previously lived experiences and "transmitted" knowledge, Jonas engages in the most difficult and most important aspects of learning: interpretation and resymbolization. The juxtaposition of different forms of knowledge with contexts that demand decision-making compels Jonas to extrapolate from what he has learned, to interpret these learnings, and to make decisions.

Experienced teachers understand that learners may not immediately be able to interpret and resymbolize new understandings within the contexts of planned pedagogy. Because human consciousness is small, it is unlikely that the full effects of learning can be immediately known. To some degree, this understanding of learning is embedded into common sense: When confronted with a new situation or a problem, a learner may suggest that he or she needs to "sleep on it" or "mull it over for a few days." Persons engaged in the production of creative works often interrupt their deliberate production practices with "diversions" such as housework, exercise, or meditation. The most significant insights often bubble to the surface of conscious when one's focus is on another matter entirely — when boarding a bus, or doing the dishes, or dreaming.

Recent research clearly shows that learning can neither be "contained" in one part of the brain, nor isolated to one particular set of activities or perceptions. Since "knowing" and "knowledge" are global events, dispersed across and involving all parts of the brain, every event of learning is influential to the learner's entire experience. For Jonas, learning to notice color in a previously black and white world is not merely an added feature to his store of knowledge. It does not merely enhance what he already knows. Instead, learning to notice color changes the way he feels about everything.

However, precisely what is learned through an experience is rarely, if ever, immediately evident to the learner or to the teacher. When there are immediate and discernible effects, teaching is deeply satisfying. But the most profound learning often occurs long after the time of deliberate pedagogy. Because new learnings — new memories — are always developing, the effects of teaching are often experienced for a lifetime.

● **Connecting Thoughts**

How can we evaluate teaching?

The most common response to this sort of question has been to make lists of competencies and behaviors — with virtually no attention paid to the enduring effects of the teacher's contributions to one's thinking.

A useful exercise might be to examine the sorts of structures that have been put into place to evaluate your professional practices — and, perhaps in conjunction with some colleagues, to think about and propose some changes that might reflect a deeper appreciation of what it means to teach in a complex world.

Living Teaching

As Kate prepares to leave her university residence after graduating with her teaching degree, she thinks about her high school French teacher, Mrs. Collins. She has a particularly vivid memory of a "bull ring" story:

"Yesterday someone asked me why I don't wear a wedding band. I'll bet some of you wonder why, too. I'm going to tell you! To me, a wedding band is like the ring in a bull's nose. You know, in some countries, they pierce the bull's nose and insert a ring that's used to lead the bull around. Before I was married I decided I was not going to be led around like a bull on a ring. So, no ring for me! I love my husband, but he understood that when we got married I would be an independent person. I am not Mrs. John Collins. I am Margaret Collins. There's a big difference between the two."

Kate went on to study French in university and, after completing her first degree, lived for several years in France. Now she looks forward to teaching high school French. As she remembers Mrs. Collins, she realizes that her love of French is closely associated with her affection and admiration for Mrs. Collins. Not only did she help Kate and other students to understand French, she helped them to understand why knowing French mattered:

"My mother was French and she always spoke to us in French. I remember learning all her French songs and the old Quebec farm recipes that she learned from her mother. That's really how we should be learning French. By cooking together."

Now, 10 years later, Kate thinks about Mrs. Collins, her teachings, and her love of French Canadian language and culture. It seems that for Mrs. Collins, teaching was more than an aspect of her life. For Mrs. Collins, teaching was woven through the entire fabric of her experience. Mrs. Collins did not just teach, she lived a teaching life.

Remembering Mrs. Collins and the strong impact she continues to have on her thinking helps Kate understand her own role as a teacher. Not only does she teach the French language, she teaches her students to be interested in the French language. She realizes that she must be interested in the French language and the effects it has on her as a French language speaker. She must not only care for her students, she must care for what she is teaching. Most important, however, she understands that she must accept that most of what the students learn she can never know. Learning spills outside the official times and places of pedagogy. This, she thinks, is the most amazing and wonderful thing about teaching.

Reading Possibilities

User's Guide

This isn't a bibliography — at least, not in the sense of a comprehensive listing of the sources that have influenced this writing. We have deliberately chosen to avoid such a structure, for two main reasons:

First, any such listing would be hopelessly partial — not only in terms of the inevitable omissions of key texts, but with regard to the manner in which such structures compel us to ignore the conversations, debates, chance associations, seminars, conference presentations, news reports, and the myriad of other occasions that were as pivotal to the writing as any of the books listed below. We wanted to avoid any pretense of completeness and to openly acknowledge that the reference list, like the book itself, does not (and can not) tell the whole story.

Second, a more thorough listing of the texts that have directly and indirectly influenced this writing would be unruly. An alphabetized inventory can say little about how and why any particular entry came to be mentioned, especially given the fact that this book has few direct in-text references. A standard sort of listing would be, for the most part, unhelpful.

As we prepared this list of reading possibilities, then, we settled on a structure that we believe is both an admission of our partialities and a useful tool for those who might wish to delve more deeply into some of the topics explored in this book. Our strategy in this project was to think of a reference list not in terms of an end point to writing, but as a starting place for reading — that is, not as a self-contained form, but as a fractal generator of sorts. (See pp. 16, 70–71, & 72.)

Like the branching branches of a fractal tree, we regard each entry below as a source of further references ... which are themselves sources of more references ... and so on. Our main task in compiling this list, then, was to structure effective means for interested readers to enter the flow of possibilities. We've attempted to do that by arranging the entries by topic and arranging the topics according to the chapters where they are developed.

1. Learning and Teaching Frames

Consciousness

Cairns-Smith, A. Graham. *Evolving the mind: On the nature of matter and the origin of consciousness.* Cambridge, UK: Cambridge University Press, 1996.

Dennett, Daniel. *Consciousness explained.* Boston: Little, Brown and Company, 1991.

McCrone, John. *Going inside: A tour round a single moment of consciousness.* London: Faber and Faber, 1999.

Norretranders, Tor. *The user illusion: Cutting consciousness down to size.* Trans. J. Sydenham. New York: Viking, 1998.

Polanyi, Michael. *Personal knowledge.* Chicago: University of Chicago Press, 1962.

Thompson, William Irwin. *Coming into being: Artifacts and texts in the evolution of consciousness*. New York: St. Martin's Press, 1996.

Perception

Ackerman, Diane. *A natural history of the senses*. New York: Vintage, 1990.

Bateson, Gregory. *Mind and nature: A necessary unity*. New York: E.P. Dutton, 1979.

Dewey, John. *Experience and education*. Chicago: The University of Chicago Press, 1963 [1938].

Frye, Northrop. *The educated imagination*. Toronto: Stoddart, 1963.

Geertz, Clifford. *Local knowledge: Further essays in interpretive anthropology*. New York: HarperCollins, 1983.

Merleau-Ponty, Maurice. *Phenomenology of perception*. London: Routledge and Kegan Paul, 1962.

Merleau-Ponty, Maurice. *The primacy of perception*. Evanston, IL: Northwestern University Press, 1964.

Ong, Walter. *Orality and literacy: The technologizing of the word*. New York: Routledge, 1982.

Pinker, Steven. *How the mind works*. New York: W.W. Norton, 1997.

Sacks, Oliver. *Seeing voices: A journey into the world of the deaf*. New York: HarperPerennial, 1989.

Sacks, Oliver. *An anthropologist on Mars: Seven paradoxical tales*. New York: Alfred A. Knopf, 1995.

Stewart, Ian & Jack Cohen. *Figments of reality: The evolution of the curious mind*. Cambridge, UK: Cambridge University Press, 1997.

Varela, Francisco, Evan Thompson, & Eleanor Rosch. *The embodied mind: Cognitive science and human experience*. Cambridge, MA: The MIT Press, 1991.

Fractal Geometry (See also "Complexity Theory," under Chapter 2.)

Barnsley, Michael. *Fractals everywhere* (2nd edition). New York: Morgan Kaufmann Publishers, 1993.

Gleick, James. *Chaos: Making a new science*. New York: Penguin, 1987.

Mandelbrot, Benoit. *Fractal geometry in nature*. New York: W.H. Freeman, 1988

Peitgen, Heinz-Otto, Dietmar Saupe, H. Jurgens, & L. Yunker. *Chaos and fractals: New frontiers of science*. New York: Springer Verlag, 1992.

Pickover, Clifford A. *Chaos in wonderland: Visual adventures in a fractal world*. New York: St. Martin's Press, 1995.

Information

Bateson, Gregory. *Steps to an ecology of mind*. New York: Ballantine, 1972.

Borgmann, Albert. *Holding on to reality: The nature of information at the turn of the millenium*. Chicago: The University of Chicago Press, 1999.

Zurek, W.H., editor. *Complexity, entropy and the physics of information*. Redwood City, CA: Addison-Wesley, 1990.

Artificial Intelligence (See Chapter 3 listings.)

Discussions of Formal Education

Bruner, Jerome. *The culture of education*. Cambridge, MA: Harvard University Press, 1996.

Eisner, Elliot W. *The enlightened eye: Qualitative inquiry and the enhancement of educational practice*. Upper Saddle River, NJ: Merrill, 1998.

Greene, Maxine. *Releasing the imagination: Essays on education, the arts, and social change*. San Francisco: Jossey-Bass, 1995.

Willinsky, John. *Learning to divide the world: Education and the empire's end*. Minneapolis, MN: University of Minnesota Press, 1998.

Teaching Resources

Hess, Karin K. *Enhancing writing through imagery*. Toronto, ON: Trillium Press, 1987.

Ondaatje, Michael. *The collected works of Billy the Kid*. New York: Norton, 1974.

Van Allsburg, Chris. *The mysteries of Harris Burdick*. Boston, MA: Houghton Mifflin, 1984.

2. Learning and Teaching Structures

Complexity Theory

Briggs, John & F. David Peat. *Seven lessons of chaos: Timeless wisdom from the science of change*. New York: HarperCollins, 1999.

Capra, Fritjof. *The web of life: A new scientific understanding of living systems*. New York: Anchor Books, 1996.

Casti, John L. *Complexification: Explaining a paradoxical world through the science of surprise*. New York: HarperCollins, 1994.

Cohen, Jack & Ian Stewart. *The collapse of chaos: Discovering simplicity in a complex world*. New York: Penguin Books, 1994.

Lovelock, James E. *The ages of Gaia: A biography of our living earth*. New York: W.W. Norton, 1988.

Prigogine, Ilya. *The end of certainty: Time, chaos, and the new laws of nature*. New York: The Free Press, 1997.

Waldrop, M. Mitchell. *Complexity: The emerging science at the edge of order and chaos*. New York: Simon & Schuster, 1992.

Complicated Learning Theories

Ausubel, D.P. *Educational psychology: A cognitive view*. New York: Rinehart & Winston, 1968.

Skinner, B.F. *Beyond freedom and dignity*. New York: Knopf, 1971.

Watson, John B. *Behaviorism*. New York: Norton, 1924.

Complex Learning Theories

Constructivism

Inhelder, Barbel & Jean Piaget. *The growth of logical thinking from childhood to adolescence*. New York: BasicBooks, 1958.

Johnson, Mark. *The body in the mind: The bodily basis of meaning, imagination, and reason*. Chicago: University of Chicago Press, 1987.

Piaget, Jean & Barbel Inhelder. *The psychology of the child*. New York: Basic Books, 1969.

von Glasersfeld, Ernst. *Radical constructivism: A way of knowing and doing*. London: Falmer, 1995.

Social Constructionism

Lave, Jean & Etienne Wenger. *Situated learning: Legitimate peripheral participation*. Cambridge, UK: Cambridge University Press, 1991.

Vygotsky, Lev S. *Thought and language*. Cambridge, MA: The MIT Press, 1962.

Vygotsky, Lev S. *Mind in society: The development of higher order psychological processes*. Cambridge, MA: Harvard University Press, 1978.

Wertsch, James V. *Voices of the mind: A sociocultural approach to mediated action*. Cambridge, MA: Harvard University Press, 1991.

Cultural and Critical Discourses

Apple, Michael W. *Official knowledge: Democratic education in a conservative age*. New York: Routledge, 1993.

Bruner, Jerome. *The culture of education*. Cambridge, MA: Harvard University Press, 1986.

Olson, David R. & Nancy Torrence, editors. *Modes of thought: Explorations in culture and cognition*. New York: Cambridge University Press, 1996.

Spivey, Nancy N. *The constructivist metaphor: Reading, writing, and the making of meaning*. San Diego, CA: Academic Press, 1997.

Walkerdine, Valerie. *The mastery of reason: Cognitive development and the production of rationality*. New York: Routledge, 1988.

Ecological Discourses

Abram, David. *The spell of the sensuous: Perception and language in a more than human world*. New York: Pantheon Books, 1996.

Bowers, C.A. *Education, cultural myths, and the ecological crisis*. Albany, NY: State University of New York Press, 1993.

Doll, Jr., William. *A post-modern perspective on curriculum*. New York: Teachers College Press, 1993.

Maturana, Humberto & Francisco Varela. *The tree of knowledge: The biological roots of human understanding.* Boston: Shambhala, 1987.

Thelan, E. & L.B. Smith. *A dynamic systems approach to the development of cognition and action.* Cambridge, MA: The MIT Press, 1994.

Varela, Francisco, Evan Thompson, & Eleanor Rosch. *The embodied mind: Cognitive science and human experience.* Cambridge, MA: The MIT Press, 1991.

Evolutionary Dynamics

Brockman, John, editor. *The third culture: Beyond the scientific revolution.* New York: Simon & Schuster, 1995.

Lewin, Roger. *The origin of modern humans.* New York: Scientific American Library, 1993.

Varela, Francisco, Evan Thompson, & Eleanor Rosch. *The embodied mind: Cognitive science and human experience.* Cambridge, MA: The MIT Press, 1991.

Neuroscience (on Memory and Thought)

Calvin, William H. *How brains think: Evolving intelligence, then and now.* New York: Basic Books, 1996.

Damasio, Antonio R. *Descartes' error: Emotion, reason, and the human brain.* New York: G.P. Putman's Sons, 1994.

Johnson, Mark H. *Developmental cognitive neuroscience: An introduction.* Oxford, UK: Blackwell Publishers, 1997.

Kotulak, Ronald. *Inside the brain: Revolutionary discoveries of how the mind works.* New York: Andrews and McMeel, 1996.

Thompson, R.F. *The brain: A neuroscience primer.* New York: W.H. Freeman, 1993.

Stories mentioned in Chapter 2B ("Working Stories")

Short stories by Audrey Thomas, Claire Harris, and David Arnason are included in: Bowering, George & Linda Hutcheon, editors. *Likely stories: A postmodern sampler.* Toronto, ON: Coach House Press, 1992.

Browne, Anthony. *Gorilla.* London: Walker Books, 1983.

Lively, Penelope. *Moon tiger.* London: A. Deutsch, 1987.

Urquhart, Jane. *Storm glass.* Erin, ON: The Porcupine's Quill, 1987.

Teaching Resources

Behn, Robin & Chase Twichell, editors. *The practice of poetry.* New York: HarperPerennial, 1992.

Dillard, Annie. *The writing life.* New York: Quality Paperback Book Club, 1989.

Gardner, John. *The art of fiction: Notes on craft for young writers.* New York: A. Knopf, 1984.

Goldberg, Natalie. *Writing down the bones: Freeing the writer within.* New York: Quality Paperback Book Club, 1986.

Kowit, Steve. *In the palm of your hand: The poet's portable workshop*. Gardiner, ME: Tilbury House, 1995.

Lee, Dennis. *Body music*. Toronto, ON: Anansi, 1998.

Shields, Carol. "Arriving late; Starting over." In *How stories mean* (pp. 244–251), edited by John Metcalf & J.R. Struthers. Don Mills, ON: General Publishing, 1993.

3. Learning and Teaching Occasions

Normality, Abnormality, and Measurement

Mainstream Perspectives

American Psychiatric Association. *Diagnostic and statistical manual of mental disorders*. New York: APA, 1998.

Andrews, Jac & Judy Lupart. *The inclusive classroom: Educating exceptional children*. Scarborough, ON: Nelson, 1993.

Sternberg, Robert J. & Janet E. Davidson, editors. *Conceptions of giftedness*. New York: Cambridge University Press, 1986.

Stigler, Stephen M. *The history of statistics: The measurement of uncertainty before 1900*. Cambridge, MA: Harvard University Press, 1986.

More critical Perspectives

Cohen, David. *Your drug may be your problem*. New York: Perseus Books, 1999.

Gould, Stephen J. *The mismeasure of man*. New York: W.W. Norton, 1981.

Rorty, Richard. *Contingency, irony, and solidarity*. New York: Cambridge University Press, 1991.

Walker III, Sydney. *The hyperactivity hoax*. New York: St. Martin's Press, 1998.

Creativity

Csikszentmihalyi, Mihaly. *Creativity: Flow and the psychology of discovery and invention*. New York: HarperCollins, 1997.

Dewey, John. *Art as experience*. New York: Perigee Books, 1934.

Dowling, John E. *Creating mind: How the brain works*. New York: W.W. Norton, 1998.

Grudin, Robert. *The grace of great things: Creativity and innovation*. New York: Ticknor & Fields, 1990.

Warnock, Mary. *Imagination and time*. Oxford, UK: Blackwell, 1994.

Winterson, Jeanette. *Art objects*. Toronto: Knopf, 1995.

Intelligence

Deacon, Terrance W. *The symbolic species: The co-evolution of language and the brain*. New York: W.W. Norton, 1997.

Egan, Kieran. *The educated mind: How cognitive tools shape our understanding*. Chicago: The University of Chicago Press, 1997.

Gardner, Howard. *Multiple intelligences: The theory in practice*. New York: BasicBooks, 1993.

Khalfa, Jean, editor. *What is intelligence?* Cambridge, UK: Cambridge University Press, 1994.

Seligman, Daniel. *The IQ debate in America*. New York: Birch Lane Press, 1992.

Piaget, Jean. *The origin of intelligence in the child*. London: Routledge and Kegan Paul, 1953.

Piaget, Jean. *Adaptation and intelligence*. Chicago: University of Chicago Press, 1980.

Richardson, Ken. *The making of intelligence*. London: Weidenfeld & Nicolson, 1999.

Sternberg, Robert J. *Metaphors of mind: Conceptions of the nature of intelligence*. Cambridge, UK: Cambridge Univeristy Press, 1990.

Artificial Intelligence

Brooks, Rodney & P. Maes, editors. *Artificial life 4*. Cambridge, MA: The MIT Press, 1994.

Clark, Andy. *Being there: Putting brain, body, and world together again*. Cambridge, MA: The MIT Press, 1996.

Norretranders, Tor. *The user illusion: Cutting consciousness down to size*. Trans. J. Sydenham. New York: Viking, 1998.

Hofstadter, Douglas. *Gödel, Escher, Bach — An eternal golden braid*. Harmondsworth, UK: Penguin, 1980.

Weizenbaum, Joseph. *Computer power and human reason: From judgment to calculation*. New York: W.H. Freeman, 1976.

Nature/Nurture

Calvin, William H. *The cerebral code: Thinking a thought in the mosaics of the mind*. Cambridge, MA: MIT Press, 1996.

Harris, Judith Rich. *The nurture assumption: Why children turn out the way they do*. New York: Touchstone, 1998.

Stewart, Ian. *Life's other secret: The new mathematics of the living world*. New York: John Wiley & Sons, 1998.

Developmentalism

Bloom, Benjamin S., editor. *Taxonomy of educational objectives. Handbook 1: Cognitive domain*. New York: David McKay, 1956.

Erikson, Erik. *Identity: Youth and crisis*. New York: Norton, 1968.

Kohlberg, Lawrence. *The psychology of moral development*. New York: Harper & Row, 1984.

Inhelder, Barbel & Jean Piaget. *The growth of logical thinking from childhood to adolescence*. New York: Basic Books, 1958.

Teaching Resources

Davis, Brent. *Teaching mathematics: Toward a sound alternative*. New York: Garland, 1996.

Drummond, Mary Jane. *Learning to see: Assessment through observation*. Markham, ON: Pembroke, 1994.

Kieren, Thomas E., Brent Davis, & Ralph T. Mason. "Fraction flags: Learning from children to help children learn." *Mathematics Teaching in the Middle School*, vol. 2, no. 1 (January 1996): 14–19.

4. Learning and Teaching Forms

Narrative and Identity

Bruner, Jerome. *Acts of meaning*. Cambridge, MA: Harvard University Press, 1990.

Conway, Jill Ker. *When memory speaks: Reflections on autobiography*. New York: Knopf, 1998.

DeSalvo, Louise. *Vertigo: A memoir*. New York: Dutton, 1996.

DeSalvo, Louise. *Breathless: An asthma journal*. Boston: Beacon, 1997.

Epstein, Julia. *Altered conditions: Disease, medicine, and storytelling*. New York: Routedge, 1995.

Graham, Robert J. *Reading and writing the self: Autobiography in education and the curriculum*. New York: Teachers College Press, 1991.

Griffin, Susan. *A chorus of stones: The private life of war*. New York: Anchor Books, 1992.

Kerby, Anthony Paul. *Narrative and the self*. Bloomington, IN: Indiana University Press, 1991.

Probyn, Elspeth. *Outside belongings*. New York: Routledge, 1996.

Postmodernism and Identity

Butler, Judith. *Bodies that matter: On the discursive limits of "sex."* New York: Routledge, 1993.

Danto, Arthur C. *The body/body problem: Selected essays*. Berkeley, CA: University of California Press, 1999.

Foucault, Michel. *The history of sexuality: An introduction*. New York: Vintage, 1990.

Freire, Paulo. *Pedagogy of the oppressed*. New York: Seaview, 1971.

Johnson, Mark. *The body in the mind: The bodily basis of meaning, imagination, and reason*. Chicago: The University of Chicago Press, 1993.

Kearney, Richard & Mara Rainwater, editors. *The continental philosophy reader*. New York: Routledge, 1996.

Lyotard, Jean-François. *The postmodern condition: A report on knowledge*. Minneapolis, MN: University of Minnesota Press, 1989.

Silverman, Hugh J. *Textualities: Between hermeneutics and deconstruction*. New York: Routledge, 1994.

Taylor, Charles. *The malaise of modernity*. Concord, ON: Anansi, 1991.

Taylor, Charles. *Sources of the self: The making of the modern identity*. Cambridge, MA: Harvard University Press, 1989.

Ecological Postmodernism and Identity

Abram, David. *The spell of the sensuous: Perception and language in a more-than-human world*. New York: Pantheon Books, 1996.

Barton, David. *Literacy: An introduction to the ecology of written language*. Oxford, UK: Blackwell, 1994.

Berman, Morris. *The reenchantment of the world*. Ithaca, NY: Cornell University Press, 1984.

Bookchin, Murray. *The philosophy of social ecology: Essays on dialectical naturalism*. New York: Black Rose Books, 1990.

Bowers, C.A. *Education, cultural myths, and the ecological crisis: Toward deep changes*. Albany, NY: State University of New York Press, 1993.

Bowers, C.A. & David J. Flinders. *Responsive teaching: An ecological approach to classroom patterns of language, culture, and thought*. New York: Teachers College Press, 1990.

Capra, Fritjof. *The web of life: A new scientific understanding of living systems*. New York: Anchor Books, 1996.

Lakoff, George & Mark Johnson. *Philosophy in the flesh: The embodied mind and its challenge to Western thought*. New York: Basic Books, 1999.

Merleau-Ponty, Maurice. *Phenomenology of perception*. London: Routledge and Kegan Paul, 1962.

Norris, Kathleen. *Dakota: A spiritual geography*. Boston: Houghton Mifflin, 1993.

Orr, David W. *Ecological literacy: Education and the trasition to a postmodern world*. Albany, NY: State University of New York Press, 1992.

Orr, David W. *Earth in mind: On education, environment, and the human prospect*. Washington, DC: Island Press, 1994.

Rorty, Richard. *Philosophy and social hope*. New York: Penguin, 1999.

Rose, Gillian. *Feminism and geography: The limits of geographical knowledge*. Minneapolis, MN: University of Minnesota Press, 1993.

Thompson, William Irwin. *Imaginary landscape: Making worlds of myth and science*. New York: St. Martin's Press, 1989.

Thompson, William Irwin. *Coming into being: Artifacts and texts in the evolution of consciousness*. New York: St. Martin's Press, 1996.

Varela, Francisco, Evan Thompson, & Eleanor Rosch. *The embodied mind: Cognitive science and human experience*. Cambridge, MA: The MIT Press, 1991.

Technology

Borgmann, Albert. *Crossing the postmodern divide*. Chicago: The University of Chicago Press, 1992.

Franklin, Ursula. *The real world of technology*. Toronto: Anansi, 1990.

Haraway, Donna J. *Simians, cyborgs, and women: The reinvention of nature*. New York: Routledge, 1991.

Heidegger, Martin. *The question concerning technology and other essays*. New York: Harper Torchbooks, 1977.

Martin, Luther H., Huck Gutman, & Patrick H. Hutton, editors. *Technologies of the self: A seminar with Michel Foucault*. Amherst, MA: University of Massachusetts Press, 1988.

Olson, David R. *The world on paper: The conceptual and cognitive implications of writing and reading*. New York: Cambridge University Press, 1994.

Ong, Walter. *Orality and literacy: The technologizing of the word*. New York: Routledge, 1982.

Discussions of Formal Education

Britzman, Deborah P. *Practice makes practice: A critical study of learning to teach*. Albany, NY: State University of New York Press, 1991.

Dewey, John. *The child and the curriculum*. Chicago: The University of Chicago Press, 1956 [1902].

Doll, Jr., William. *A post-modern perspective on curriculum*. New York: Teachers College Press, 1993.

Ellsworth, Elizabeth. *Teaching positions: Difference, pedagogy, and the power of address*. New York: Teachers College Press, 1997.

Grumet, Madeleine R. *Bitter milk: Women and teaching*. Amherst, MA: University of Massachusetts Press, 1988.

Pinar, William F., William M. Reynolds, Patrick Slattery, & Peter M. Taubman. *Understanding curriculum: An introduction to the study of historical discourses and contemporary curriculum discourses*. New York: Peter Lang, 1995.

Usher, Robin & Richard Edwards. *Postmodernism and education*. New York: Routledge, 1994.

Wells, Gordon. *The meaning makers: Children learning language and using language to learn*. Portsmouth, NH: Heinemann, 1986.

Stories and Novels mentioned in Chapter 4

Fox, Mem. *William Gordon McDonald Partridge*. New York: Kane/Miller, 1985.

Michaels, Anne. *Fugitive pieces*. New York: Alfred A. Knopf, 1997.

Yolen, Jane. *The devil's arithmetic*. New York: Viking Press, 1988.

5. Learning and Teaching Lives

Literacy and Pedagogy

Berthoff, Ann E. *The making of meaning: Metaphors, models and maxims for writing teachers*. Portsmouth, NH: Heinemann, 1981.

Berthoff, Ann E. *The sense of learning*. Portsmouth, NH: Heinemann, 1981.

Dooley, Deborah Ann. *Plain and ordinary things: Reading women in the writing class-room*. Albany, NY: State University of New York Press.

Finders, Margaret J. *Just girls: Hidden literacies and life in junior high*. New York: Teachers College Press, 1997.

Mayher, John S. *Uncommon sense: Theoretical practice in language education*. Portsmouth, NH: Heinemann, 1990.

Willinsky, John. *The new literacy: Redefining reading and writing in the schools*. New York: Routledge, 1990.

Reader-Response Theory

Appleyard, J.A. *Becoming a reader: The experience of fiction from childhood to adulthood*. New York: Cambridge University Press, 1990.

Beach, Richard. *A teacher's introduction to reader-response theories*. Urbana, IL: National Council of Teachers of English, 1992.

Bleich, David. *Subjective criticism*. Baltimore: The John Hopkins University Press, 1978.

Eco, Umberto. *Six walks in the fictional woods*. Cambridge, MA: Harvard University Press, 1994.

Holland, Norman N. *The dynamics of literary response*. New York: Columbia University Press, 1968.

Iser, Wolfgang. *The act of reading: A theory of aesthetic response*. Baltimore: The John Hopkins University Press, 1978.

Iser, Wolfgang. *The fictive and the imaginary: Charting literary anthropology*. Baltimore: The John Hopkins University Press, 1993.

Luce-Kapler, Rebecca. "As if women writing." In *Journal of Literacy Research*, vol. 31, no. 3 (September 1999): 267–291.

Mackey, Margaret. *The case of Peter Rabbit: Changing conditions of literature for children*. New York: Garland, 1998.

Rabinowitz, Peter J. *Before reading: Narrative conventions and the politics of interpretation*. Ithaca, NY: Cornell University Press, 1987.

Rosenblatt, Louise M. *The reader, the text, the poem: The transactional theory of the literary work*. Carbondale, IL: Southern Illinois University Press, 1978.

Sumara, Dennis. *Private readings in public: Schooling the literary imagination*. New York: Peter Lang, 1996.

Literary Experience

Bakhtin, Mikhail. *The dialogic imagination*. Austin, TX: University of Texas Press, 1981.

Bruner, Jerome. *Actual minds, possible worlds*. Cambridge, MA: Harvard University Press, 1986.

Derrida, Jacques. *Acts of literature*. New York: Routledge, 1992.

Lorde, Audre. *Sister outsider: Essays and speeches*. Trumansberg, NY: Crossing Press, 1984.

Meek, Margaret. *On being literate*. London: The Bodley Head, 1991.

Morrison, Toni. *Playing in the dark: Whiteness and the literary imagination.* New York: Vintage Books, 1993.

Turner, Mark. *The literary mind.* New York: Oxford University Press, 1996.

Electronic Technologies and Literacy

Birkerts, Sven. *The Gutenberg elegies: The fate of reading in an electronic age.* New York: Fawcett Columbine, 1994.

Cherny, Lynn & Elizabeth Reba Weise, editors. *Wired women: Gender and new realities in cyberspace.* Seattle, WA: Seal Press, 1996.

Heim, Michael. *Electric language: A philosophical study of word processing.* New Haven, CT: Yale University Press, 1987.

Landow, George P. *Hypertext: The convergence of contemporary critical theory and technology.* Baltimore: The John Hopkins University Press, 1992.

Murray, Janet H. *Hamlet on the holodeck: The future of narrative in cyberspace.* New York: The Free Press, 1997.

Discussions of Formal Education

Ashton-Warner, Sylvia. *Teacher.* New York: Touchstone, 1963.

Barrow, Robin. *Giving teaching back to teachers: A critical introduction to curriculum theory.* Totowa, NJ: Barnes & Noble, 1984.

Clandinin, D. Jean & F. Michael Connelly. *Narrative inquiry: Experience and story in qualitative research.* San Francisco: Jossey-Bass, 2000.

Delpit, Lisa. *Other people's children: Cultural conflict in the classroom.* New York: The New Press, 1995.

Miller, Janet L. *Creating spaces and finding voices: Teachers collaborating for empowerment.* New York: State University of New York Press.

Mintz, Ethan & John T. Yun, editors. *The complex world of teaching: Perspectives from theory and practice.* Cambridge, MA: Harvard Educational Review, 1999.

O'Reilley, Mary Rose. *The peaceable classroom.* Portsmouth, NH: Heinemann, 1993.

van Manen, Max. *The tact of teaching: The meaning of pedagogical thoughtfulness.* London, ON: The Althouse Press, 1991.

Novels mentioned in Chapter 5

L'Engle, Madeleine. *A wrinkle in time.* New York: Dell Publishing, 1962.

Lowry, Lois. *The Giver.* New York: Bantam Doubleday, 1993.

Ondaatje, Michael. *The English patient.* Toronto: McClelland & Stewart, 1992.

Index